Democracy's
Stepchildren

A Study of
Need and Belief

Elizabeth Léonie Simpson

DEMOCRACY'S STEPCHILDREN

Jossey-Bass Inc., Publishers
615 Montgomery Street • San Francisco • 1971

DEMOCRACY'S STEPCHILDREN
A Study of Need and Belief
          Elizabeth Léonie Simpson

Copyright © 1971 by Jossey-Bass, Inc., Publishers

Copyright under Pan American and Universal Copyright
Conventions. All rights reserved. No part of this
book may be reproduced in any form—except for brief
quotation (not to exceed 1,000 words) in a review or
scholarly work—without permission in writing from
the publishers. Address all inquiries to:

Jossey-Bass, Inc., Publishers
615 Montgomery Street
San Francisco, California 94111

Library of Congress Catalog Card Number 73-146735

International Standard Book Number ISBN 0-87589-089-X

Manufactured in the United States of America
          Composed and printed by York Composition Company, Inc.
          Bound by Chas. H. Bohn & Co., Inc.
          Jacket design by Daniel N. Talpers, Yellow Springs, Ohio

FIRST EDITION

Code 7108

THE JOSSEY-BASS
BEHAVIORAL SCIENCE SERIES

General Editors

WILLIAM E. HENRY
University of Chicago

NEVITT SANFORD
Wright Institute, Berkeley

For
Anne Roe

Preface

It has been said that a book is never finished, only abandoned. Before this one is laid aside as a single chapter in a continuing work on socialization, I would especially like to thank Paul F. Brandwein, Harrison Gough, Jeanne Knutson, and John U. Michaelis. During the time of the genesis and development of the work, all of them helped to make clear, as Aristotle wrote, essence among accidents or, in more modern terms, signals among noise. My gratitude goes, too, to the University of California, Berkeley, Graduate School, and the Anthropology Curriculum Study Project (Theodore W. Parsons, director) for research aid; to Stanley Naparst, statistical consultant, and to Joy Hussey, typist and interested reader, for support of another nature; to the principals, teachers, and students of Tramontane, Bayamo, and Debouchement; and, above all, to my children—Martha, Garth, and Bethany—enduring ground in an ecstatic world.

My book is ordered in a developmental sequence. The first chapter presents the problem and reviews literature in psychology, sociology, and political science which suggests a connection between basic human needs and the attitudes, values, motivation, and behavior of human beings, whatever their position in society. The second chapter discusses the biosocial origins of needs and analyzes conceptual differences in the theories of Sigmund Freud, Karen Horney, Erich Fromm, and Abraham Maslow. Chapters Three through Five explore the hierarchical needs which Maslow hypothesizes and relate them to the theory and data of other scientists and theoreticians. In Chapter Three, deprivation on a fundamental, existential level—physiological and security needs—is defined and analyzed. Chapters Four and Five move on to the higher, healthier reaches of the deficiency hierarchy: the needs for belongingness, social esteem, and self-esteem.

At this point, the description of motivating needs and the superordinate values which are their outgrowth is concluded, but personality operates as a whole; its conative aspects cannot be considered apart from cognitive and affective modes of functioning. Chapter Six is an attempt to explore these interrelationships. In Chapter Seven, through political philosophy and history, I inquire into the nature of the person in whom these interactions may be termed democratic and into his antithesis, the authoritarian. Methodology and results of the field study measuring the democratic syndrome and its correlates in the high school subjects are described in Chapter Eight, and the relationship between these empirically demonstrated needs and values is summarized in Chapter Nine.

Chapters Ten through Thirteen relate the earlier historical synthesis and empirical findings to the American educational situation today. In Chapter Ten, the reciprocal interchange between the psychological organization of the individual and the structure of his society is examined in reference to the democratic society. Chapters Eleven and Twelve deal with process and content within the educational institution. In the former, the problem of activating responsiveness in the child is considered, and the attitudinal and structural dimensions of possible school change are examined; in the latter, substantive knowledge and methodology for the establishment of strategies of information-processing—including role-playing and actuality practice—are discussed. The chapter ends by emphasizing an environmental goal of productiveness and the transfer of capability from the self to the social context. In the concluding portion of the book, Chapter Thirteen, theories of value learning are reviewed and applied to the development of democratic value systems. Socialization agents—parents, peers, schools—are discussed, and my conclusions, as well as their implications, are summarized.

The Index of Psychological Deprivation, in its entirety, the history of its development, brief descriptions of the other measures here used, a few sample protocols from projective questions, and the summary statistical tables are included in the appendices.

Human nature being what it is, I will not now tell the reader my findings or the serious implications which I drew from them. The problem, its meaning, and its possible amelioration lie ahead in the pages of my book. I invite the reader to examine the evidence and criticize the cure.

Los Angeles
January 1971

ELIZABETH LÉONIE SIMPSON

Contents

7.   *What is a Democrat*   79

8.   *Who is a Democrat*   97

9.   *Psychic Needs and Democratic Values*   118

10. *Personality and Society*   135

11. *Structures of Intimacy*   143

12. *Opportunity of Environment*   166

13. *Democratic Socialization*   176

A.   *Description of Measures*   188

B.   *Samples from Projective Protocols*   195

C.   *Summary Tables*   198

     Bibliography   211

     Index   233

Democracy's Stepchildren

A Study of Need and Belief

Background to the Study

It has been said that biological facts have nothing to do with human values, with what ought to be. The answer to that assertion is: if it can be shown that there exist certain biological facts, biological functions of the organism, which are constant and which if treated in one way, lead to malfunctioning of the organism, to sickness, and to disoperative behavior, and treated in another way, lead to well-being, mental health (the ability to love and the ability to work), and to cooperative behavior, then it could be stated that the biological functions of the organism determine the nature of the values of the world in which it must live, for the words should and must are here equivalent if the organism is to survive creatively as such.

M. F. Ashley Montagu
The Direction of Human Development

1

This book is the product of an ill-contained and annoying suspicion that the schools, suffering from an ideological itch left over from the nineteenth century, may be doing their tasks out of order. For some years now, it has been clear that the American educational system is not the bastion of democracy it is labeled in the national ideology. Values and the cultural myths of equality and opportunity are memorized, and the mundane problems of a representative system are analyzed. Elections and voting are even walked through. Everywhere the power of the flag and the President's picture shelter the school symbolically, and the stigmata of democracy are ritualistically displayed. Yet the political and social structure of our schools is not democratic, and many graduates of these socializing institutions are emerging class-conscious and difference-conscious, with an abiding lack of faith in the capability of their fellows to govern either themselves or the country.

These young people are learning the words, but where is the evidence that they know what they mean, feel what they mean, value them, live them out? Where is awareness that belief in the majority is an affirmation of belief in the individual and his capacity to function, autonomously, as a discrete unit among the multicellular constituency of that majority? Where is awareness that it is the shape of relationships between men, and between men and their own powers, which defines the true business of democracy? If instruction in democratic values is being given (and it is), why is it being assimilated in such a highly differential way? All of these questions raised a larger one: What prior experiences may be essential to the accommodation of democratic training?

From a study of the literature, a theoretical relationship between psychological deprivation and attitudes, beliefs, and values, grounded in a limited but highly suggestive number of empirical studies, began to emerge. The basic postulate for a simple theory of value and two correlates followed: Existential belief systems, that is, values, are the product of biogenetic needs acted on by the social environment. Therefore, prediction of value orientations should be possible from the knowledge of need states. Therefore, diagnosis of needs and subsequent gratification should make responsiveness to direct socialization possible. The wild problem was being tamed by

2

definition: Is there an association between prior experience, expressed as needs, and democratic values which may be found empirically? If so, what is its shape? The answers lay outside the library.

In a field investigation in three communities, 412 high school
students in western and southern United States were studied. These
subgroups, forming a three-increment sociological continuum of race
and social class, constitute the sample. Tramontane High School,
set in the warm lands east of the California coastal mountains, has
an upper middle-class, white population; Debouchement, at the
other pole of the continuum, is a working class, black enclave in
southern Georgia. Somewhere in between, characterized by a range
of race and social class, lie the students of Bayamo, a California bay
city. Using projective questions, direct questions of ideological belief, and scales utilized in previous psychological research, as well as
an index of psychological deprivation based on the need gratification theory of Abraham Maslow, we studied the basic needs and
social and political values of the subjects.

Tramontane High School

Tramontane High School is part of a unified district serving
five sociologically similar communities which have grown up in the
warm lands just east of the western coastal range.[1] All are "bed-
room" towns with almost no industry, whose population, until
recently, has been nearly completely white. These are WASP communities, nearly homogeneous in race, class, education, and occupation. Their members average 13.4 grades of schooling and earn
their wages largely as executives, managers, and self-employees or
at upper-level clerical jobs. As parents, they have high aspirations
for their children, including good grades and college attendance,
and they are willing to support quality education by voting a high
tax rate, participating in school activities, conferring with teachers,
and paying for school equipment or programs not regularly bud-
geted by the school district. From 1965 to 1970, in an analysis of
over 2,000 responses, a recent follow-up study found that 83 per
cent of Tramontane's students had indicated a four-year college as
their goal and that 81 per cent had graduated from, or were con-

[1] Informant: John Sanford. Winter 1969–1970.

tinuing to attend, one. Every year the school has two or three National Merit scholars and up to twenty finalists.

Although most classes at Tramontane are run traditionally, with about equal amounts of time given to lecture and to guided discussion, there are exceptions to this pattern. The American history and American government courses are taught almost entirely by the lecture method by teams of two or three teachers. At the time of the study, the American history course had a lecture section only two days a week, while American government for juniors was conducted entirely in lectures to large groups of 142 to 165 students. All courses are planned by and under the control of the teacher, and little or no administrative guidance is offered or sought except in cases where a testing program may interfere with the total school schedule.

During the three months preceding the study, a significant change took place in the responsibility which students accepted for the curriculum. Although their activities could hardly be described as militant, students began to sit in on the curriculum meetings of each department and offer suggestions concerning their interests. In the past, student involvement in outside political issues had not been particularly deep either, although a group of about 150 to 200 students had become very concerned about the war in Southeast Asia, ecological problems, and other national issues. Even this concern was being expressed in traditional ways, through an active World Affairs Club.

Day-to-day conflict is of the traditional adolescent-adult variety; the students reflect strongly a shared pattern of socialization to conventional middle-class values. Cooperativeness and a lack of generalized hostility were reflected in the high percentage of complete and useable inventories (77.3 per cent) in spite of absences on one or the other of the two testing days.

The sample (n = 232) was drawn from senior social science classes ranging in age from sixteen to eighteen years. (Almost 88 per cent were seventeen years old.) Slightly more males than females were included (53 per cent and 47 per cent). Ninety-six per cent were white, a racial distribution which accurately reflects the homogeneity of the larger community. Ninety-eight per cent speak only English at home in households where the father is still undisputed boss (93.5 per cent). The head of the household in 70 per cent of the cases is an executive or a professional who has graduated from college or gone further in school. While few mothers have had graduate training, almost 75 per cent have had some college education.

These subjects come from small families—almost 60 per cent have fewer than three siblings. About 62 per cent have not moved during the past five years. About 60 per cent believe themselves among those with the highest incomes in the community, and the percentage swings sharply upward when they rank themselves against economic status within the nation at large: 82.3 per cent perceive themselves among the top half in the country.

Participation in high school groups is high: 83.96 per cent of the subjects have belonged to some school group. About 30 per cent have held offices in at least one school or community group.

Bayamo High School

Bayamo has only one main high school.[2] East Campus is attended by deviant students at opposite ends of the spectrum: returned dropouts, as well as the gifted and highly organized who are capable of a good deal of self-direction in their studies. West Campus is for the ninth grade. Drawn from a bordering industrial city as well as from Bayamo, from the hills as well as from the flatlands which stretch from their slopes to the great bay below, the school's population spans the races and the social classes. The children of professionals go to Bayamo High School, as well as those of the cleaning folk who ride the buses to care for the houses in the hills. About 41 per cent of the student body is black; about 9 per cent is oriental or Spanish-American. In the elementary schools, about 20 per cent of the faculty is black; in the high schools probably not more than 6 per cent.

In the high school a Black Student Union is active; an Asian Student Union has been formed but suffers from disinterest and apathy. Since Bayamo has always been a one-high-school town, that high school has always been integrated, although integration by busing did not begin for the elementary schools until 1969. These

[2] Principal informant; Jeff Tudisco. Spring 1969.

facts, coupled with a local social environment which, perhaps because of the presence of a university, condones deviation from conventional middle-class behavioral and dress norms, have made the
school an appropriate target for student dissatisfaction based on developing racial consciousness. They also made it predictable that
channels would exist, or be quickly found, for the amicable settling
of differences. Such has proven to be the case.

During the year this study was made, radical changes took
place in the institutional structure, not without controversy, but
with a minimum of friction. The tracking system was abolished for
the social studies program, and the school board was committed to
its removal in other areas. Open tracks, with assignment by demand, and cluster grouping were among the programs planned for
the fall. African literature, Afro-American economics, black journal-
ism, Afro-American history, African civilization, African dance,
and Swahili were all part of a new Black Studies program staffed
largely by blacks. Black counselors were added to the faculty. Even
the character of the school lunches changed; once a week, "soul
food" (hominy grits, chitterlings, greens) was served, in spite of the
fact that many black youngsters were eating it for the first time and
disliking it.

At the time the study was made, the active dissidents had
reason for satisfaction. On the institutional level their demands were
being met. As in the past, those students who personally found the
going roughest either had dropped out or were trying again at East
Campus. However, hostility, apathy, and alienation had by no
means disappeared from the school. A situation, private or public,
which probes personality variables, even under the most pacific
or static social conditions, probably always presents a threat to
the insecure. The hateful, the anxious, the indifferent, and the estranged, understandably, do their best to avoid or destroy the painful moment. They select themselves out. For this reason, it appears
unlikely that the subjects here recorded represent the true range of
psychological needs. Some were lost by illness on the first or second
day of testing; some were lost because a test day was the day before
a holiday; some were lost because they deliberately defaced or otherwise rendered unusable their schedules. Two hundred and thirty

students were ordinarily assigned to these classes; 49 per cent of them filled out completely usable inventories.

Where subjects were lost through illness or hostility, the sample remaining (n = 114) undoubtedly cants toward the satisfaction end of the need continuum rather than the deprivation end. However, if deficiencies appear even under such circumstances, when the low extremes are self-selected out, their presence within the population may indeed be real.

Within the overall environment already described, the cases studied were drawn from United States history and sociology classes. Their ages ranged from fourteen to seventeen years with the majority either fifteen (67.27 per cent) or sixteen (22.73 per cent) years old. There were more females in the sample than males (53.64 per cent and 45.45 per cent), and, although the majority were white (56.36 per cent), blacks (25.45 per cent) and orientals (11.82 per cent) were substantially represented. Note that blacks were underrepresented and orientals overrepresented with respect to the total population.

Over 11 per cent of the subjects speak some language other than Spanish (2.73 per cent) and English at home, where, in almost one-quarter of the families, the head of the household is the mother. In this sample, almost a third of the household heads are professionals or executives; only 10 per cent are manual laborers with 22 per cent upper white-collar workers and the remainder scattered between lower white-collar workers and self-employed merchants. Many students have educated parents: over half their fathers have graduated from college; 20 per cent have done at least some graduate work. Fifty per cent of the mothers are college graduates, and 16 per cent have had some graduate training.

The majority of families are small (57 per cent have fewer than three siblings), but a substantial number (42 per cent) have from three to more than five siblings. Most of these children have lived in the same residence for at least five years, although more than 13 per cent of them have moved over three times during that interval. In the community where they live now, most of them (almost 62 per cent) see themselves as having among the highest or next to highest incomes of anyone in their town. Perceptions

about their income status in the nation as a whole move downward
(the second quartile equals 39 per cent; the third quartile equals
49 per cent), but over 5 per cent still believe that their families
have incomes among the highest in the United States.

More of these young people participate in community groups
than in school groups, just as more participate in more different
types of activities within the larger environment than at school.
Scores on attitudes toward school may give an important clue. On
questions dealing with the interest of administrators and teachers
in the students and fairness specifically directed toward the subject,
over 83 per cent of the subjects indicated a positive attitude toward
Bayamo High School. At the same time, however, more than 22
per cent believed that most people would be better off without any
schooling, and almost a third perceived their teachers as prejudiced.
In a sample including over 37 per cent nonwhites, it may reasonably
be expected that groups organized and led by prejudiced teachers
would be rejected in favor of participation within the community
or no participation at all.

Projective questions asked these respondents tapped two related areas: needs for a good life and present anxieties. (See Appendix B for sample protocols.) Their answers supported other
data suggesting that these subjects are not, in general, physiologically deprived; survival needs are not among their basic anxieties
and they tend to take them for granted in a good life.

Debouchement High School

On a rectangular piece of parched earth roughly a city block
by two and a half, Debouchement High School, as well as the lower
grades, is housed in single-story brick structures joined by covered
walkways.[3] A new high school–elementary wing holds classrooms,
labs, libraries, and offices, but it is a measure of social concern that
in the main high school building even on winter days there is often
no heat because the failing system is out of repair. Broken windows,

[3] Principal informant: Richard Smith. Much of the sample data
reported here was collected in spring 1969 as part of an on-going study by
Theodore Parsons and Richard Smith.

cracked walls, high ceilings, and an inadequate heating system there make the gym a cold, drab place.

The school population is black, both faculty and students, with the exception of five white staff members. Of working class background, the students are the products of broken homes and disadvantaged on many levels. (Parents' occupational mean prestige rank was 53.78 for Debouchement in comparison with national mean occupational prestige rank of 69.8 computed from tables of NORC data—Bendix and Lipset, 1966, p. 411.) Like the failure of the administration to provide adequate heat, the restriction of the free lunch program may be seen as a measure of social deprivation, neglect, and low status of children who may not have this basic need adequately supplied at home. How clearly the students recognize their social position is shown in the high need for social esteem reported here as well as in interview protocols. These latter reveal the determination to seek gratification through a variety of means, some of which involve denial mechanisms: academic achievement, northern migration, adaptation to welfare life, or adjustment within the community of family and friends.

As participants in an ongoing investigation into the social world of the Negro teenager, these subjects were studied in four major psychosocial areas: the self, their social world, their educational and vocational world, and their home and family. The measures chosen were the Mooney Problems Checklist, the Bell Adjustment Inventory, and the Gordon Survey of Interpersonal Values. Findings from the study are briefly summarized here:

Home and family: Unlike the findings of other studies of comparable samples, as measured by the Bell Inventory, the mother is not the dominant figure in the home.

School and vocation: According to data collected using the Mooney Checklist, there is a significant lack of interaction between teachers and students, an anxiety-producing situation.

Social milieu: According to the Gordon instrument, these subjects do not find social fame as such important to them. They are not dependent upon others for self-esteem but on themselves— a finding which is supported strongly by high self-esteem scores in the present research. Career ideals are altruistic, but, although, according to the Bell Inventory scores, the sample showed extreme extroversion, there is real reluctance to assume leadership. (The investigators suggest that extreme extroversion may be culturally patterned in this situation and that altruistic ideals may be the outcome of the civil rights movement.)

The self: Without being characterized by psychosomatic patterns, these students show considerable anxiety regarding both their morals and their future. The self-concept is not good; they see themselves as inferior and prone to commit moral offenses (an attitude which was supported by school and vocational data). Data on the self indicate that altruistic ideals are counteracted by an avoidance of involvement or permanent dependency. Others are to be taken care of if need be.

(Demographic characteristics of the three subsamples may be obtained by writing the author.)

CHAPTER I

Origin of Values

The business of a theory of values is to find and to elucidate those values which are expressed by the way men act and live in their age. These deep and unspoken values in action are no less human than the precepts of sages.

Jacob Bronowski
New Knowledge in Human Values

Social scientists have long recognized that the development and application of value systems by the individual depend upon more than the socialization process alone. Like other aspects of personality, they depend also on the cultural environment in which socialization takes place, on the predisposition of the individual to internalize cultural values, based on his previous personal history and his innate characteristics, and on the situations in which the individual is asked to act. The research reported here is concerned primarily with the second of these determinants: What, we are asking, are the factors which may predispose individuals to incorporate certain social values into their value systems or to fail to do so? Since the given and the learned, the genetic and the acquired, are inextricably intertwined, the definition of the needful and valuing individual at any time of study is a biosocial matter. (Not all social scientists agree. Like some sociologists, anthropologist Jules Henry [1956, p. 97] describes the origins of values without the biological constituent: "A value to all intents and purposes will not exist unless there is an institutional device through which it can be expressed." Furthermore, "since social experiences are involved in the generation of all these needs, psychogenic needs evolve out of the social field in which a person lives, they are not inborn. Thus, psychogenic needs develop out of interpersonal relations, not the other way around. Once the need is developed, of course, it then enters with its own dynamics into interpersonal relations and conditions them" [p. 106].)

Here we are asking only the results of past experience: What is the individual today, what motivates him, how does he believe and feel and act now as a result of his biologically established needs and of his continuing interaction with the social environment which not only defines those needs but provides him with the capability of supplying them? Our inquiry is into the nature of personality, the result of the "invasion of the human organism by the social environment" (Smith, Bruner, and White, 1956, p. 31). We are asking, then, what are the superordinate values, the prepotent conative needs, which support and govern a particular view of life, the world, and one's own place within it, and we are predicting that the extent to which the individual has achieved gratification of these basic needs is associated with the social and political values he holds and utilizes in day-to-day thought, feeling, and behavior. We are suggesting that essential among the antecedents of democratic values is the psychological determinant of need gratification, that the fulfillment of physiological, security, belongingness, and esteem needs—as hypothesized by Abraham Maslow (1954)—is integral and prerequisite to democratic socialization.

Much past work has been devoted to the relationship between democratic political values, personality, and interpersonal behavior. Nonpolitical human relations have been seen as a prime source for understanding political relations, and, indeed, human interaction within specific cultural groups may be said to generate the social values of which economic and political values are only a part. In *Escape From Freedom* (1941), Erich Fromm developed a conception of social character which "internalizes external necessities and thus harnesses human energy for the task of a given economic and social system" (p. 311). Families, he believes, act as transmitters of the type of personality required by the social system.

In 1965, Roberta Sigel stated that the stability and continuance of political systems depend on the political socialization of their members. In her view, incidental community and family learning are probably more important than deliberate education, for the socialization of values which are not in themselves political affects political values. Graham Wallas, Harold Lasswell, James Davies, Alex Inkeles, and James Almond and Sidney Verba have also linked socially determined psychological deprivation to the acceptance of certain political values and consequent behavior. Lasswell, probably the most devoted proponent of the theory that psychological attributes underlie political attitudes and behavior, has built an equation around the relationship: $p \{ d \{ r = P$, where p is equal to private motives derived from needs, d means displace onto public objects, r is the rationalization of these motives in terms of the public interest, $\{$ is equal to transformed into, and P is political man (McConaughy, 1961, p. 45). "Private insecurities will be displaced upon . . . symbols of public objects" (Lasswell, 1935, p. 85). Davies (1965), writing of the family's role in political socialization, posits a strong relationship between the satisfaction of physical, social, self-esteem, and self-actualization needs and political behavior. Upon the degree and kind of physical and social nurturance depend the degree and kind of politization of the adult.

From their explorations into the political cultures of the United States, Great Britain, Germany, Italy, and Mexico, Almond and Verba (1963) developed the concept of the "civic culture" in which "the working classes could enter into politics and . . . find the language in which to couch their demands and the means to make them effective" (p. 6). The civic culture is "neither traditional nor modern but partaking of both; a pluralistic culture based on communication and persuasion, a culture of consensus and diversity, a culture that permitted change but modulated it" (p. 6). The most striking characteristic of its mixed quality is the manner in which the participant role is added to the passive role of subject. The civic culture grows from patterns of activity toward nonpolitical authority in the family, at school, and at the work place. The roles that the individual plays at these places may be considered training for the performance of political roles, since he is likely to generalize his expectations from one to the other. The impact of participation in decision-making is cumulative; other social factors, particularly education on the secondary level or above, may substitute for their effects, and participation on the three levels of family, school, and job appears to have a rank order of importance in producing the vital sense of "subjective competence" in influencing government.

Ungratified psychological and social needs, then, appear to affect the political values of the individual. These political values have their isomorphic counterpart in social values, values which also depend on the satisfaction of basic psychological needs such as security and love. The work of Harry Harlow, Joel Aronoff, R. Spitz, and Daniel Miller and Max Hutt bears out this relationship. In his study of the appeal of communism, Herbert Krugman (1952) stressed the anxiety and lack of self-esteem which characterized middle-class party members who were not at all distressed by the authoritarian structure of the Communist party. Warren Bennis and Philip Slater (1968) also believe that the development of democratic attitudes in nonpolitical situations contributes to political democracy. They conclude that American egalitarianism has its most important manifestation in the family, not in the Constitution, and because authoritarianism is generated or inhibited in the family, destruction of family authoritarianism impedes the political, as well as the familial, variety (p. 17). An interesting corollary to this theory is that the flow of influence from family or other institutions to government is not necessarily unidirectional. According to Almond and Verba (1963, p. 270), norms of political democracy are "often used as arguments in favor of further democratization of school and employment relationships." See W. Stahl (1961) for a discussion on the appropriateness of democratic schools in politically democratic West Germany.

Support for Bennis and Slater's position is found in a study of the values of activists and their families (Derber and Flacks, 1967). The activists came from upper-middle-class families who were strongly oriented to humanistic values and whose child-rearing practices were democratic. The parents were described as deviating from conventional middle-class norms derived from the Protestant Ethic, extremely nonauthoritarian in political orientation, and with strong intellectual, creative, and aesthetic commitments. The investigators suggest that variant families may create predispositions toward radical social action whose actualization depends on activating situtions which may or may not be encountered by their children.

The link between social and political values was further demonstrated in another study of college students in which faith in human nature proved highly predictive of political views, attitudes toward freedom of speech, and readiness to justify calling the state's repressive power into action (Goldsen, Rosenberg, Williams, and Suchman, 1960). To those who believe the people are not to be trusted, the function of government is to control.[1] In a related study of high school participation in extracurricular activities, Ziblatt (1965) concluded that it was not direct participation in itself which resulted in the building of positive attitudes toward political activity, but the development of "social trust," an underlying attitude which

[1] Thomas Jefferson wrote this relevant statement to his French friend Dupont de Nemours: "We both consider the people as our children. . . . But you love them as infants whom you are afraid to trust without nurses, and I as adults whom I freely leave to self-government" (quoted in Padover, 1939, p. 6).

seems to incorporate both Morris Rosenberg's concept of faith in people (1965) and Julian Rotter's concept of generalized expectancies that the environment is controllable (1968, 1966).

Basic social trust—the positive beliefs upon which political orientation of a democratic nature rests—is built in early life experience. T. W. Adorno, Else Frenkel-Brunswik, Daniel J. Levinson, and Nevitt Sanford (1950) describe the authoritarian, potentially fascistic personality in their study as typified by anxiety, a threat-orientation to the world, and a cold and unresponsive home environment as a child. Although he may not be directly taught fascist values, the child learns them from the social environment which surrounds him. Through the processes of reinforcement, identification, and modeling, he internalizes his parents' behavior in the home and develops his own psychological relationship to authority and power. As he matures and goes to college, he begins to demonstrate the authoritarianism which has become an emotional and intellectual part of his infrastructure. (Although in its heuristic scope this study provided fertile ground for further theory and research, its methodology has been severely criticized. See, for example, H. H. Hyman and P. B. Sheatsley, " 'The Authoritarian Personality': A Methodological Critique," in *Studies in the Scope and Method of "The Authoritarian Personality,"* ed. by R. Christie and M. Jahoda [Glencoe, Ill.: Free Press, 1954], pp. 50–122.) Work on the fascistic personality was extended and modified by Milton Rokeach (1960) to include authoritarianism of the left and to delimit aspects of the cognitive functioning of persons as characterized by open or closed belief systems.

Clearly, openness to experience, acceptance of others, and faith in one's ability to manage one's own life are negatively associated with psychic deficiencies. One of the purposes of this study was to explore such relationships and also those between failure of need gratification and the development of anomie, expressed as the belief that the environment cannot be controlled. The latter relationship has been suggested by the work of Leo Srole (1956) and Melvin Seeman (1959). Srole, for example, finds in subjective anomie (feelings of helplessness or alienation) such components as belief in the unpredictability of the social order and the meaninglessness of life, lack of trust in others, and a general belief that social conditions are becoming worse. The sense of personal powerlessness and its reverse—the generalized sense of efficacy or the belief that the individual's "own behavior, skills, or internal dispositions determine what reinforcements he receives"—have been identified as personality variables which are the psychological equivalent of the sociological concept of alienation in the sense of powerlessness (Rotter, 1966, p. 4). As Almond and Verba have pointed out, the individual who believes himself trapped by the mysterious and all-powerful forces of a world neither of his making nor under his control is little likely to value or to participate in self-government.

How can we justify the inclusion of socioeconomic factors in a study of beliefs? What is the relationship between social class and the development of specific social values? Sociologists and anthropologists alike have suggested that active participation in any group, large or small, provides certain shared experiences and needs which predispose its members in a common direction. Interpretation, meaning, feeling, and goals are learned in interaction with the members of the groups to which each person belongs. M. Brewster Smith, Jerome Bruner, and Robert White (1956) point out the importance of the individual's definition of the situation and its origin in this shaping process. Like other social groups, then, class is not merely a description of place in the socioeconomic hierarchy; it is also a descriptive label for a set of cultural patterns, that is, regular, patterned situations and responses. The label is a conceptual tool for the isolation of certain expectancies about the group and within it, and as such, it may help to explain the origins of social values.

We must, however, add two important qualifications to the use of social class as a concept. First, position on the class hierarchy is not fixed. The individual or his parents in the process of raising him may move from one class to another and be subject to new socializing forces and different need satisfactions. Second, income, education, and other indices commonly used to delineate social class in a psychological study have meaning only insofar as they indicate a certain level of capacity to fulfill the basic needs of the individual and, in so doing, to shape his view of the world.

Objective social conditions, quite apart from individual experience, would lead us to expect members of the lower classes to

suffer a greater amount of psychological deprivation and so to hold
beliefs and values designed to protect, rather than to enhance, life.
In a comparative study of authoritarianism in Japanese and American high schools, for example, A. M. Niyekawa (1960) found
greater authoritarianism among students in Japan. Among these,
subjects from lower class and rural backgrounds scored higher, independent of family authoritarianism. From his study of more than
six hundred New Haven schoolchildren in the fourth to the eighth
grades, Fred Greenstein (1965) concluded that upper status children, that is, those with white-collar occupational backgrounds, ex-
ceeded children with blue-collar occupational backgrounds in both
capacity and motivation for political participation. The child of low
socioeconomic status was also more deferential toward leaders than
the high status child, a symptom, along with lack of self-confidence
and a sense of personal inadequacy, of deeply imbedded psychological impediments to democratic values and behavior which are exacerbated by situational factors shaping the child's belief in his ability to control his environment. Although participation in voting and
elections may be expected to vary as either an expressed or enacted
value within the general population (Saenger, 1953), Greenstein
found verbal agreement on these modal American values in his dif-
fering socioeconomic groups.

Through a series of economic indices, Seymour Martin Lipset (1959a, b, c) established cross-culturally a positive correlation
between wealth, urbanization, and industrialization and the development of democratic social values and behavior. "Average wealth,
degree of industrialization and urbanization, and level of education
is much higher for more democratic countries" (1959c, p. 75). Education as a social requisite to democracy ranks high. *"The most
important single factor differentiating those giving democratic responses from others has been education.* The higher one's education,
the more likely one is to believe in democratic values and support
democratic practices. All the relevant studies indicate that education
is far more significant than income or occupation" (1959c, p. 79).

The poor, whose economic values concerning welfare, wages,
graduated taxes, and unions are highly democratic, are social authoritarians on such issues as civil liberties and internationalism, a
circumstance which, Lipset notes, poses a "tragic dilemma" for in-

tellectuals who believe that the proletariat must necessarily be a force for liberty, racial equality, and social progress (1959c). Although Lipset is careful to point out that authoritarianism of any class is modified by organizational commitments to democracy and by individual cross-pressures, and that it is highly relative from culture to culture, his findings support a point of view which political theorists since Aristotle have stressed—the importance of the middle class, with its comparative freedom from economic and social wants and concomitant psychic deprivation, in the maintenance of democratic values. (There are some dissenters from the view that individuals of low socioeconomic status are less democratic. Lewis Lipsitz [1965], for example, reports that, with education controlled, the middle-class subjects whom he surveyed in the 1950s were not consistently less authoritarian than working-class subjects. When the comparison was restricted to subjects of high school education, he found less authoritarianism in the working class. Since the cultural environment exerts pressures to continue schooling beyond high school, these middle-class subjects must have compelling reasons for not doing so, reasons which may be grounded in the unfulfilled needs which also underlie their authoritarianism.)

Robert E. Lane (1961), writing convincingly of the "fear of equality," cites material from his interviews with working-class men to show the values which inequality has for them. Where emphasis is on equal opportunity, he says, rationalization is needed for lack of success. There is less strain on the self-esteem of low-status individuals, therefore, to believe themselves in their natural and proper place in the social order, and as long as some opportunity, if not equal opportunity, is available, their relative status is still satisfactory. Lane also points out that it is the professional classes with different organization of interests and different training who defend equality and freedom.

The subjects whom James Martin and Frank Westie (1959) studied were preselected on the basis of tolerance or prejudice not on the basis of social class. Although the modal income was the same for both groups, the tolerant sample showed a significantly higher mean occupational and educational status. More ethnic intolerance was associated with lower occupational status and little education. Angus Campbell, Gerald Gurin, and Warren Miller

(1956) also found low socioeconomic status, as defined by income, education, and low occupational status, correlated with a low sense of political effectiveness. Consistent with these findings, in 1955 Samuel Stouffer found that respondents low in socioeconomic status were less liberal on questions of civil liberties and that persons of low education were more intolerant about civil rights.

In the Srole (1956) study cited above, anomie appears to a much greater degree among persons of lower socioeconomic status. Edward C. McDill (1961) and Alan H. Roberts and Rokeach (1956) replicated Srole's investigation and obtained the same results. Rotter (1968) reports the consistent indication that subjects low in socioeconomic status are more likely to believe that nothing they or anyone else can do makes any difference in what happens. At the same time, however, he suggests that this finding is open to alternate explanations. This type of anomie—the belief that luck, not the individual, controls the environment—may be a realistic response to existing limitations of opportunity or, since a correlation exists between the degree of externality which the mother has and the views of her high school children, it may be learned. (Some investigators go even further and relate anti-social values, or an anomic lack of norms, to neither personal needs nor social class. Marcia Guttentag [1968], for example, concludes from her study of juvenile delinquency that community reinforcement of family values [that is, stable norms] and intergenerational stability, not improved socioeconomic conditions, are needed to prevent delinquency. This questionable point of view follows a line of thinking which places the burden of socialization on direct values teaching.)

From his studies in Taiwan, Malaysia, and Turkey, as well as among the working and middle classes in the United States, Lawrence Kohlberg (1968) suggests that the level of development of moral thought is tied to literacy, industrialization, and social class. Preliterate villagers rarely attained the highest level of individual principles, and lower-class children were consistently behind middle-class children in moral and ethical development. Richard Centers' work (1948), based on the relationship between need gratification and personal values, has direct relevance to the present study. In a unique inquiry into the etiology of job choices, he studied a thousand white male adults from a representative national sample. They were classified by job groups and asked to give three choices of the kind of job they would like best. The results were analyzed, together with the reasons given for the choices made. These included opportunity for leadership, interesting experiences, esteem, power, security, self-expression, profit, fame, social service, and independence. Business, professional, and white-collar groups expressed preference for self-expression and interesting experiences, while manual workers showed a preference for security. The upper strata preferred occupations which entailed large components of esteem and leadership. For Centers (1948), social class is an intervening variable between lack of need gratification and values in their motivational, or conative, form. He writes:

Persons in the lower socioeconomic levels manifest a safety or security need much more frequently than do people in higher socioeconomic positions, we might assume, because these latter have already in considerable numbers satisfied this need, whereas the former have not. With the security need satisfied, other and higher needs take its place, and so we find people in the upper occupational strata manifesting desires for self-expression, esteem, leadership, and interesting experience more often than we find such manifestations among the lower occupational groups.

As may be seen from this brief review, a substantial body of theoretical and empirical literature has been built up which suggests a connection between basic human needs and the attitudes, values, motivation, and behavior of human beings, whatever their position in society. The problem, then, was to see whether it would be possible to find relationships between these needs and democratic values in the field, in subjects of high school age and varying race and social class. But first, three fundamental questions must be asked: What are man's basic needs? How do these directive needs affect cognitive and affective functioning? Considered in terms of basic needs and the beliefs which are their outgrowth, what does being a democrat mean?

CHAPTER II

~~~~~~~~~~~~~~~~~~~~~~~~

Meaning of Need

~~~~~~~~~~~~~~~~~~~~~~~~

All the ideals in the world won't feed us Although they give our crimes a certain air.
W. H. Auden
Letters from Iceland

Three kinds of needs plague and delight, guide and drive man in his divaricating passage through life: those which are common to all and have their origins in human physiology, those which are acquired within specific cultural contexts and are generally possessed only by the members of a specific group, and those which are specific to the individual and arise through the expanding complexity of the developmental process and personal experience. Without the uniquely human and biological capacity which underlies learning and development, the last two kinds of socially induced needs would not exist. Learned or innate, social or genetic, needs have their origins in the physiology of the organism, the evolution of the species, and the ontology of the individual—in short, in the biologically determined nature of humans which is acted on by the social environment. Perhaps it is most accurate to say that all needs of human beings are ultimately organismically based, in spite of the fact that various workers have found it useful to emphasize either social or genetic factors. Psychologists have studied needs from the point of view of sickness and of health, and various theories of normality—in the sense of a medical criterion of health, rather than a criterion based on the statistical average—have developed. Let us briefly review some conceptual differences among need theorists—the first, a view of needs based almost completely upon instinct and the biological inheritance of the individual, and the two following, which emphasize the importance of the social environment: Freud, Horney, and Fromm.

Like Hobbes, Sigmund Freud viewed normal human nature as biologically determined competition and hostility, both irreconcilable and mutual. The major premise of his work is that man is a sexual and instinctual beast (the Id) who is kept in check only by the mediating controls (the Ego) of the conscience (the Superego) which society imposes through the psychic mechanism of anxiety which forces identification with parents as society's representatives. The Id, operating on the pleasure principle, demands instant and total gratification of needs and wants and is restrained only by the Ego which, functioning on the reality principle, is informed of the nature of the environment and develops the operational responses necessary for the satisfaction of basic needs without conflict with society. Society itself was considered by Freud to be primarily the product of repressed or sublimated biological drives and not the result of complex social processes. The more completely these drives are suppressed, the higher the stage of development a culture attains. Neuroses are the price which humanity pays for the capacity to build civilization (Freud, 1930).

To Freud, sexuality and aggression are the basic human motives and needs, the result of chemical and physiological forces which are determined by constitutional factors, that is, by heredity and by early childhood experiences which act upon it. Present needs are conditioned by the past; nothing new develops, for the new is merely a changed form of the old. Repetition is inevitable since, in this mechanistic evolutionistic view of human motivation, instinctual drives are paramount and environmental influences merely shape them (Freud, 1938).

In comparison with Freud's strongly biological orientation, Karen Horney emphasizes life conditions as molding the character of man and disturbances in human relationships as the crucial factors in the genesis of neurosis. Central to her theory of neurotic personality is the concept of basic anxiety which arises from culturally derived role conflicts. An anxious individual, in an insecure and potentially hostile world, needs above all to allay his fears of isolation and helplessness. To do this, as a child he develops one or a mixture of three general modes of behavior which Horney calls "neurotic trends": moving toward people (accepting), moving away from people (rejecting), and moving against people (hostility). The first of these may be manifest in the need for affection and approval, in the need for a dominant partner to assume one's responsibilities, or in the need to restrict one's life within such narrow borders that no demands are made by or on it. Rejecting people may take the form of insistence on self-sufficiency, independence, and perfectionism. Hostility is demonstrated by the need for power, the need to exploit others, and the need for social recognition, personal admiration, or personal achievement.

According to Horney, these needs are not innate in man. They are neuroses and are unsuccessful attempts to resolve anxiety engendered by an unreliable and conflicting cultural environment.

The conflicts experienced by the neurotic are experienced by all, for the difference between the normal and the neurotic is quantitative only; the neurotic simply knows these culturally determined difficulties in an accentuated form. Emphasizing the environmental roots of anxiety, Horney calls the neurotic the "stepchild of our culture."

Erich Fromm, like Horney, attributes the major traits of human personality to conditions of life. While he does not deny that the needs he describes are biologically based, his emphasis is on social causation. He ascribes strictly physiological needs (such as hunger, thirst, sex) to man's animal nature; other needs are somehow meta-organismic. There are, he says, "no corresponding *physiological* substrata to the needs for relatedness, transcendence, etc. The substratum is not a physical one, but the total human personality in its interaction with the world, nature, and man; *it is the human practice of life as it results from the conditions of human existence*" (1955, p. 69). In contrast to Freud and Horney, with their emphasis on negative instincts or neurotic adaptation, Fromm describes the basic needs of man in terms of health. There are indispensable satisfactions which man must have if he is to have a life in which he can work, reason, and love, a life which is unalienated from nature and his fellow man and which is productive. These needs are relatedness (the need for productive love between humans with its implication of mutual care, responsibility, respect and understanding); transcendence (the need to create as well as to be the creature of others' creation); rootedness (a need expressed not as chauvinistic devotion to one group, but as brotherliness to mankind as a whole); identity (the need to be an individual and aware of being one); and a frame of orientation and devotion (the need for a belief system relating the self to the world, an orientation which contains elements of sensing and feeling, as well as intellectual elements, the affective as well as the cognitive).

Satisfaction of these needs permits a productive orientation which is what man was meant to hold and which allows him to use his prowess and realize his potentialities. When this occurs, the personality of the individual is characterized by mature genitality (without the emphasis of Freudian libido theory), creativity, spontaneity, care, responsibility, respect, and knowledge. While the needs which he describes are present in all men, Fromm believes that they are everywhere incompletely satisfied. Their gratification will remain only an ideal as long as societies are designed to shape man to their needs rather than to shape themselves to provide man with his needs. Fromm's deepest interest is in what Freud calls "the pathology of civilized communities" and in social change which will permit the development of man's productivity.

Perhaps, as Frederick McDonald (1959) has said, there are as many lists of needs as there are psychologists tempted to formulate one. (See, for example, Arthur Combs [1962], Henry A. Cronbach [1963], Ralph Linton [1945], and Lee J. Murray [1938].) At any rate, there are many, and the brief discussion which has preceded this comment only demonstrates the character of these classifications and provides the basis for the selection of the theoretical substructure which has been chosen for the study. What needs are chosen varies with the chooser, his definition of human nature, and the centrality, in his view, of certain human characteristics. We have tried here to defer to biology, to adhere conceptually to a model neither culture-bound nor so detailed that it could not describe generally, and with some power, the motivating forces of human beings everywhere, forces which (as we will discuss in the next chapter) provide man with his superordinate values. These criteria seem to have been met in the theory of motivation developed by the psychologist Abraham Maslow, a formulation which bridges the schism between the biological determinism espoused by Freud and the largely cultural determinism of Fromm's view. Holistic in its consideration of the complete individual as part of his total environment—in the tradition of Max Wertheimer, Kurt Goldstein, and gestalt psychology—the theory is also dynamic, as those of Freud and Alfred Adler were, in treating human behavior as motivated or driven by emotional forces which are influenced by changing developmental and environmental factors.

Like Freud, Horney, and Fromm, Maslow sees thwarted needs as the basis of much human misery and neurosis. While avoiding the strong terms of discredited instinct theory, he yet roots human nature in physiology by describing specifically human "instinctoid" drives which are activated to secure gratification of needs. Maslow's theory is both positive in its view of essential nature and

concerned with that nature at its healthiest, when it is fully functioning, as a goal possible to attain under certain conditions. From
his clinical studies of healthy people ("normals") he has isolated
a number of instinctoid, organismically based needs which, in his
view, form a hierarchy of increasing mental health: physiological
needs, security needs, belongingness needs, esteem needs, and finally,
self-actualizing needs which appear at the level of psychological
health, the stage at which the person is freed from inferior motivation and enabled to actualize his own potential as a unique individual.[1] (Beyond self-actualization but synergic and interrelated
with basic needs, another hierarchy operates: the need to know,
the need to understand, and the need for beauty. Because these
needs apparently act as primary motivators in adults only after the
achievement of psychological health, they are not included on Maslow's basic list. As we will discuss later, these higher needs may
appear in conjunction with lower ones and operating as assistance
in gratification at those levels. The need to know and understand,
for example, functions as part of the control dimension necessary
for the attainment of self-esteem. See also Robert White's [1963]
concept of competence motivation.)

These basic needs are identifiable as fundamental to human
nature because lack of gratification produces "deficiency sicknesses"
in the same sense that lack of certain minerals or vitamins may
cause the body to become ill. Open and spontaneous expression of
them occurs in very early ("precultural") life. Unlike neurotic needs
which cannot be satisfied, it is possible to satisfy them and, in fact,
suitable availability of a gratifier throughout life acts as a "prophylactic control" which prevents pathology. At all levels, they are species-wide, cross-cultural, and instinctoid, although decreasingly so
at each higher level of the hierarchy, so that the higher the position
of the need, the weaker and more suppressible it is. Few people—
according to Maslow, about 1 per cent of the total population—are
motivated to satisfy the growth needs such as self-actualization
which appear when the lower, deficiency needs are gratified, and,
indeed, there is a strong qualitative difference between these two
sets of needs. Pursuit and gratification of higher needs produces

[1] Health as the highest value and self-actualization as the fulfillment
of human potential were first described in the work of Kurt Goldstein.

not only a healthier and stronger individual, but also desirable social and civic consequences (1948a)'.

The basic needs form a pyramid with its broad base representing prepotent needs which must be supplied before the next higher need can become activated. Gratification is the simplest means for rendering certain needs unimportant and shifting motivation to a higher level. Lack of satisfaction, conversely, results in fixation of primary motivation at a particular level. This is true notwithstanding the fact that the individual may also be motivated situationally by a variety of derivative needs or by other needs in the hierarchy. No one, in short, is striving to fulfill only one goal all the time, nor is the need with major priority the only one which directs action. Behavior is multi-motivated, although on a more fundamental level, according to Maslow, most individuals are likely to be motivated and their orientation directed by one need.

Perhaps the only deficiencies which can never be permanently satisfied are loneliness and lack of sex. But all man's needs are recurrent, although if well-gratified in the past, they may be foregone as goal-objects over a long period of time. The origin of basic needs may be biological, but the shape of their definition, as well as the source of their gratification, is social. Since the satisfaction of needs at each level permits the individual to function at the next higher level of motivation, the quantity and quality of these cultural influences considerably affect the operational stage of instinctoid man.

A difference in emphasis between Fromm and Maslow concerns the social attainment of need gratification and consequent mental health. Fromm believes that the nature of modern society must be changed to make the social environment responsive to man's deepest needs. Maslow's focus is much less on changing basically depriving conditions and more on the effects of the pursuit of higher need gratifications for both individuals and society once the lower needs have been met. In his later writings, Maslow makes the assumption that throughout the American culture the basic needs are supplied. As a society, we are "relieved of the scrabbling for a living," and so self-actualization is "partially or wholly" possible for us when it is not for other societies (Combs, 1962)'. This is a class-bound assumption which some of Maslow's disciples have distorted into a universal goal of self-actualizing behavior, an impossibility according to the theory whose definition of lower needs they are ignoring. In no society are these needs satisfied for every member, and self-actualization is not achieved metaphysically—it is explicitly based on the satisfaction of fundamental needs. No one can will himself healthy. We understand this fact today after thousands of years of what Horney calls the moral, as opposed to the medical, model of mental illness. As we will discuss when we consider the implications of our findings, fulfillment of potential occurs under circumstances above and beyond basic gratifications; it does not follow inevitably from them, any more than it is possible for anyone at any need level to transcend his needs and become a self-actualizer. This would be a contradiction in the theory which describes the stage at which self-actualization is motivating as the level of mental health.

Three correlates of Maslow's theory should be briefly discussed before we examine the basic needs in depth: First, needs may be permanently extinguished or impaired by atrophy if they are not satisfied. For example, a man who has been the victim of chronic unemployment may, even in times of prosperity, want nothing more than food and shelter. A person starved for love during the first months of life may grow up psychopathically unable to give or receive affection. Second, needs may also be devalued if they are well-gratified. A prosperous second-generation professional man who has never known hunger or insecurity may find it impossible to believe that he could ever want a job just to have a job. Third, Not all deprivation represents a threat to the security of the individual. If needs have been gratified in the past, the person may be able to withstand deprivation without finding it traumatic or an attack on his personal security.

To summarize, there are three basic propositions to Maslow's theory of human needs (1948b): First, the motivational life of the individual has organization or structure which is sometimes almost unitary. Second, there exists a hierarchy of needs of lesser or greater priority or potency. The "chief dynamic principle animating this organization is the emergence of less potent needs upon gratification of the more potent ones." Third, cognitive and aesthetic needs form another hierarchy whose relationship to emotional

needs is "not clear." Because he believes that the healthy self-actualizer is man as he is intended to be, using his capacities to the ut-
most, Maslow has called his theory one of "human diminution"
rather than of psychic illness. Let us consider the lacks which most
diminish man, their theoretical structure, and the empirical evidence for their existence, form, and dynamics.

CHAPTER III

Existence

I *worry about my future destiny; the destiny of the world; pollution, wars, cars, overpopulation, whether I should have children to contribute to overpopulation and whether my children will survive the future. I am afraid of criminals and of being attacked.*

Upper middle-class white teenager

Food, drink, love, sleep, health, shelter—these are the prepotent human needs. Survival itself depends on their at least partial satisfaction. More than any of the other needs, when these have not been gratified, the world is likely to be defined by them, and anything else, including freedom and respect, is likely to be considered irrelevant and unimportant. Deprived consistently of self-esteem, friends, material possessions, and these most fundamental needs, under most circumstances a man would probably seek first to satisfy the latter. Although physiological catastrophes on a grand scale—flood, famine, and earthquake—are less and less common, at least in modern Western societies, quiet disasters of lack, like e. e. cummings' "silent terrors of the snow," occur in the ordinary course of events to prevent gratification and to affect man's goals, values, and desires in very basic ways.

A number of studies, as well as common observation, support Maslow's position that these needs are fundamental. To observe the effects of the deprivation of maternal contact, for instance, Spitz (1949)' compared institutionalized children who were raised by their mothers with those who were not. Over a third of those not raised by their mothers died within two years. The survivors were barely less unlucky: during the same period of time their personality characteristics polarized between hyperexcitability and apathy. Other investigators have found that, without cuddling, fondling, and loving, infants in institutions with good physical care tend to develop a condition known medically as *marasmus* (Greek for "wasting away")'. They lose weight, fret, whimper listlessly, and sometimes even die (Ribble, 1943; Provence and Lipton, 1962; Burlingham and Freud, 1962)'. In a study of social deprivation of macaque monkeys, Harlow and Harlow (1965)' and Harlow (1958)' found that baby monkeys have a vital need for social contact. Adequately fed from a bottle but left alone in a wire cage, they were dead within five days; food alone was not enough. In other experiments when baby monkeys were given a choice between cloth "mothers" without bottles and wire "mothers" with them, the monkeys frequently chose cloth. Fear, induced through the mechanism of a wind-up toy, sent them scurrying to the cloth, not the wire,

32

"mother." Harlow's findings seem to indicate that these babies, and possibly their human counterparts, have a need on the survival level to touch, to be stroked, and to be comforted by contact.

Hunger of various types may affect what man is and does. Ancel Keys (1952) and Russell Wilder (1952), for example, in separate studies found that severe malnutrition or restriction of an essential vitamin such as thiamine can induce personality disorders. Stunted growth, depigmentation, emotional apathy, and intellectual retardation have been associated with protein deficiency in Africa (Brock and Autret, 1952). When they were deprived later as adults, rats who had been irregularly deprived of food in infancy tended to hoard more than those who had not been deprived until maturity (Hunt, 1941). Affective arousal is more intense in infancy than later, and early deprivation, in Maslow's theory, causes an over-reaction later. Without suggesting species equivalence, the rat studies seem to indicate that early gratification for the human child might also produce the capacity to cope with later deprivation.

Deprivation also takes its toll on the cognitive processes. David McClelland and John Atkinson (1948), for instance, found direct effects on perception associated with hunger. Hungry persons were more likely to be aware of food-related objects. Extent and quality of need appear to shape cognitive structures—the belief systems which individuals develop regarding their world—and the degree of openness by which such systems are characterized. If this is so, we would expect the perception of stimuli to be related to need. "The eye," it seems, "is never quite innocent but comes to its task sensitized" by the past history of the total organism (Homans, 1950, p. 13).

In an experiment designed to test whether the perceptions of children were affected by their values and their needs, Jerome Bruner and Cecile Goodman (1947) asked subjects to judge the size of coins with the same dimensions as gray cardboard discs. In general, they found that the children saw the socially valued objects as larger. More important from the view of our interest in physiological needs, poor children from the Boston slums—to whom the money was highly significant as a means of gratification—overestimated the size of the coins considerably more than did rich subjects.

(See also Jerome Bruner and Leo Postman [1948] on the social influences on perception.)

A man who is deprived on the physiological level "may fairly be said to live by bread alone" (Maslow, 1954, p. 83). Under these conditions, writes Muzafer Sherif (1936), *"the restless state of deprivation becomes the dominating factor.* The aspects we notice in the stimulus field are those which are connected in some way with the frustrated need, and which will ultimately lead to its satisfaction" (p. 192). "The times of great deprivation or denial of the satisfaction of needs for the masses of people are the unstable and critical times" (p. 193). The latter are times which neither social nor political restraints will prevent. "People cannot eat and drink norms" (p. 202), and in a desperate society or social stratum, actions which provide the wherewithal to eat and drink will usually come first. It is also possible that, especially in an affluent society, individuals may feel physiologically deprived when they are far from a life and death state. Lack of a fifty thousand dollar shelter, filet mignon for food, or mink skins for warmth may seem depriving where the common belief is that everyone has these things. Or they may also be desired for reasons little associated with a physiological base, for, as Maslow points out, any of the physiological needs and the consummatory behavior associated with them serve as channels for all sorts of other needs as well. A person who feels hungry may be looking for love; a person who drinks water may partially satisfy the hunger need (1954, p. 81).

Psychologically sound reasoning lay behind the indignant furor which followed Black Panther breakfasts for ghetto children who have been deprived of some of their basic needs. Gratification may be a powerful means for affecting belief and the reinforcements of the supplying agent are effective in persuasion. In Red China, the same awareness of the relationship between values and basic satisfactions led to a recent campaign against revolutionaries who were accepting dinner invitations from "class enemies."[1] But

---

[1] From a dispatch from Peking in the *San Francisco Chronicle,* March 5, 1970, quoting an article in the journal *Red Flag:* "Are eating and drinking really trifles? No, absolutely not. There is class struggle, waged with chopsticks." "By eating and drinking together with the class enemy, you

what happens when there is bread, when man's belly is chronically full? A want that is satisfied is no longer a want. Although it may emerge again if it is thwarted in the future, in the current dynamics of the individual it becomes unimportant. According to Maslow, the gratified individual will then turn to the satisfaction of those related needs which are next most vital to him: his safety needs.

Like physiological needs, the need for safety[2] may serve as the principal organizer of behavior and thought. Lacking security, the individual, in all his actions, is dominated by fear and avoidance. In the child, this fear may be as simple and fundamental as apprehension about the loss of physical support while being carried. It may concern the absence of parents, the assurance of their love, or the limits of the protection which they provide which may be set by their inability or the refusal of the mother and father themselves to interfere with the behavior of the child or to defend the borders of his environment. The parents, and the adequacy of the shelter they build, are the source of security. To the child, "The parent seems omnipotent because he has the power to withhold the substance of life—food" (Bettelheim, 1960, p. 296). (Bruno Bettelheim goes on to say that, under Hitler, the state had exactly the same power. "Living in such a society, all citizens were as dependent as children for the substance of life—the parent can inhibit his child's freedom of movement, the mass society can do the same to its recalcitrant citizens." As it destroys individual autonomy, the mass state makes it necessary to internalize new values and standards which destroy the ones which successful parental power over the child has built [pp. 296–297].)

The person who has early found his world to be unsafe and unpredictable may be ruled all his life by the primary principle of self-protection. He may seek this protection by a neurotic drive for independence and individualism or by abandoning his human autonomy either to the collective leadership of societal norms or to

---

have been sitting on the same bench with him. As time goes on you will collude with the enemy, speak for him, and do things for him" (Webster, 1970).

[2] Davies (1965) has suggested that all psychological deprivation is tied to the search for security. Therefore, he eliminates this deficiency from Maslow's list of needs.

the authority of strong causes, individuals, or gods. "Most people, when they must choose between integration on a low human level and intolerable inner strain, will probably take the first and forego the second to regain peace," a peace which Bettelheim (1960, pp. 298–299) compares to death rather than human existence. Like the teachers whom Harmon Zeigler (1967) studied, they abandon their right to functional autonomy for the sake of safety. In such a moral economy, decisions are made by cost accounting. "The greater the perception of probable sanctions, the less proper the behavior is perceived to be. . . . Teachers' perceptions of propriety are clearly pragmatic, not products of abstract choice or searching of conscience" (p. 101).[3]

In a stable society, peace and prosperity and the possibility they hold for security may act as a prophylaxis against anxiety. In a time of crisis, war, depression, natural disaster, or widespread open hostility within the society create the threat that this essential psychic protection may be curtailed; whatever psychic shelter exists is more of a lean-to set on a windy beach than a fortress. Fears of dependency, separation, and annihilation become widespread and, under conditions of social trauma, individual deprivations become cultural. In any society, the economic underdog is likely to lead an apprehensive and fearful life, a life without predictability and without sense of control. To protect himself, he adopts beliefs and actions which seem to insure at least his physiological needs and, not always effectively, to exclude change, foreigners, the unknown, and the unfamiliar. "The poorer strata everywhere are more liberal or leftist on economic issues; they favor more welfare state measures, higher wages, graduated income taxes, support of trade unions, and

---

[3] The neurotic demand for protection by absolute power is well illustrated by this anecdote: Following the publication of *Humanae Vitae*, the Pope's encyclical condemning birth control, a group of Washington, D.C., priests announced publicly that it was not to be taken literally or bindingly. Shortly thereafter, Patrick Cardinal O'Boyle was given a standing ovation in his cathedral after an emotional sermon denouncing the dissenters. "He satisfied the crowd's hunger for authority in a day when radicals trample it everywhere. . . . It was a great moment, before the altar of God, seeing a man of power use his might to strike back. As an elderly lady remarked to me on leaving the church. 'That's just the way God would have handled it, sonny' " (McCarthy, 1968, p. 23).

so forth. But when liberalism is defined in noneconomic terms—
as support of civil liberties, internationalism, etc.—the correlation
is reversed. The more well-to-do are more liberal, the poorer are
more intolerant" (Lipset, 1959b, p. 92).

Economic insecurity may be manifest in many forms. Sav-
ings, life insurance, health insurance, social security, as well as the
desire for a job with tenure and a good retirement plan, are all
expressions of the drive toward predictability and control. But where
early family life and a peaceful and plentiful social environment
ordinarily protect each individual, the need for safety may become
largely sated or at least moderated. Where it is not, the individual
may worry greatly about his capacity to provide his basic physiological needs. Thwarted and insecure, in an attempt to limit and
control the dimensions of a frightening environment, the dependency needs of the economically insecure may be disguised beneath
an aggressive assertion of autonomy—"I don't need nobody to take
care of me"—which is the cultural norm. As Walter Miller (1958)
has shown, lower-class persons tend to seek out restrictive environments such as the armed forces, disciplinary schools, and prisons.
While protesting the rules, they act in ways which are calculated to
bring themselves back under them and into the safety which those
rules represent.

An insecure person of any social position may look on group
work, political participation, or team efforts on any level less as a
chance to share and utilize different skills than as a method of re-
lieving himself from personal responsibility by sharing it, or pro-
tecting himself by attachment to a group which does have power,
prestige, accomplishments. Within his total culture, his constant
search for control and protective strength may have important social
and political consequences. Political strength feeds on the needs of
the insecure. Urban machine politics, for example, mushroomed
through the gratification of security needs of newly arrived immi-
grants. "I think that there's got to be in every ward somebody that
any bloke can come to—no matter what he's done—and get help.
Help, you understand; none of your law and justice, but help"
(Martin Lomasny, Boston ward leader, to muckraker Lincoln Stef-
fens). It is not unreasonable to infer that prolonged social crisis,
with its widespread personal insecurity, could mean the death of

democracy. As Quincy Wright (1951, p. 201)˙ has written in his classic work on war, "The legal claims of the state come to be conceived as inherent in the value system and way of life of the people." The essence of democracy, as of science, is to accept solutions tentatively, with the possibility of their review always in mind.

In the United States, where many strong cultural values compete with each other, social power rests in the hands not of one group but of many—the wealthy, the socially prominent, the popular or skilled, and religious, military, and political leaders. It is easy to understand how threatening this democratic diffusion of power must be to the insecure individual who desperately wants some power concentration with which he can identify.[4] The right-winger's fearfulness manifests itself as insistence that the nation was founded as a republic, not a democracy, and as denial of the one man, one vote principle in order to provide himself with a political elite with which to identify.

To the other disabilities of the insecure are added problems of perception and cognition. On whom can he count? Who will trust him and like him? Who is a stranger, an enemy? The insecure person does not perceive others as outgoing, warm, or accepting.[5] The anxiety he feels is a protective response to threat, a marshalling of forces for flight from death at the same time that it is a death experience—an end to exploration, imagination, and self-extension. It is a denial response to experiences of separateness, of frightening individuality, and of the unreliability of his contingent world. He lives with the finality of the unretrievable—death, pain, and parting—and is left, with St. Paul, to the cold acknowledgment of his inner state: "I die daily." He may end in a final accommodation to unbearable tension, in denial or repression of reality and in an attempt to become his own world. Personal defeat and eventual acquiescence may lead to protective impairment of the child's faculties, suspension of environmental transactions, and retreat into fixed ways of knowing.

[4] For a further description of this state of mind and a powerful plea for continuing this diffusion of power, see Geoffrey Gorer (1966, Chap. 6).
[5] Bossom and Maslow (1957) asked 105 subjects to rate standard photographs. The twenty-two most secure judges, as determined by scores on the Maslow S-I Test, rated them warm more often than the twenty-two least secure.

Under crisis conditions, habituation to chronic anxiety may be its only relief. The unbearable outer environment is turned off by insensitivity and defensive avoidance and the results reverberate within the cognitive structure of the individual. In his account of the Japanese atomic bomb victims, Robert Lifton (1967) describes this psychic closing off which is the process of denial and, at the time of stress, has a highly adaptive function for survivors. "A way of maintaining life when confronted with unmanageable death anxiety, it threatens always to snuff out the vitality being preserved (1967, p. 510), and may become both psychic numbing and psychosomatic entrapment—in its extreme form, a fatalistic surrender to the environment. Bettelheim (1960) tells of the *Musselmann* of the Nazi concentration camps who became walking corpses in the totality of their will-less withdrawal inward. Under the Nazi regime, doctors who performed the inhuman experiments on human beings demanded of them survived psychologically by focusing on pride in their professional skills and deleting from consciousness the meaning or the purpose of their acts. "In a more indirect manner patterns of psychic numbing have surrounded the overall creation, testing, and military use (actual or planned) of nuclear weapons: a combination of technical-professional focus and perceived ideological imperative which excludes emotional perceptions of what these weapons do" (Lifton, 1967, pp. 508–9). Psychic numbing surely accounted, in large part, for the Pentagon's idiot pleasure in announcing a weapon, the laser, which destroyed only people and left what was valuable (buildings) intact. The slaughter at My Lai serves as another example of this schism between perception and feeling.

Intellectual growth and mastery proceed from conflict, from the necessity of reaching out to try and then appraising the attempts. As Rudolph Ekstein (1969, p. 162) has written, openness to conflict is "essential to the task, and, in many ways, is the task." But what happens if the individual's psychic economy cannot afford these conflicts? Learning, which depends on such responsiveness to the environment, is impeded; motivation is radically altered. The whole range of behavior is likely to be narrowed and limited to those familiar actions which have been successful in the past, and exploration and trial on any level are abandoned as too threatening.

In all three spheres—through affect which is flattened or anesthe-titized, closed cognition, and the restriction of motivation—the individual may become a functional cripple.

Because the person with ungratified safety needs can be sure of nothing, he must be sure of everything. He wants his facts to be completely, immutably, true, and he is likely to adopt some way of knowing—through religion or philosophy or misunderstood science—which permits him a convincing sense of intellectual security. His lack of safety displays itself in cognitive closure and the restriction of perception, for he maintains his belief system unmodifiable by rigidly excluding new information and experience. Insecurity may not only restrict the possible reception of stimuli in the environment, it may also act as a force for regression. In Jean Piaget's clinical studies of Swiss children, he has found that the developing child, moving from the level of concrete cognitive operations toward a capacity for formal or abstract reasoning, may find insecurity a major stumbling block to progress. "Every new acquisition of more advanced objective behavior initially involves only surface behavior. When threatened, the child automatically returns to his previous intuitive and egocentric mode of thinking and reasoning" (Maier, 1965, p. 130)'.

A person who feels unsafe may develop an exaggerated fear of death or loss from death. For self-protection, he uses regimen as a brace of steel to shore up a structureless, dissolvent, variable world. Irregularity, strangeness, unpredictability and spontaneity produce in him a *lebensneid*—fear of life—which accurately reflects his inability to harness his own life forces and structure his internal universe. Imagination is threatening, as are change, all unplanned and casual actions, privacy and social withdrawal and separation of any sort.[6]

[6] Lasswell, in his 1965 introduction to *World Politics and Personal Insecurity* (1935), predicted a shift from "class struggle to skill struggle" and a "war of extermination against introverted types" in both the United States and the Soviet Union—a war based on the "apprehension aroused by privacy and seclusiveness." He also described the emergence of a new ideological orientation in which "preciseness" is becoming a value. Mechanical devices (such as automobiles and computers) are becoming eligible targets for incorporation into the self-system, and the self is becoming more and more commendable as it approximates a machine. To the insecure, precision is a structural value.

To a man deprived of a basic sense of safety, the future is as fearful a place as the bottom of the sea—abysmal, airless, dark, and filled with unknown terrors. His days are filled with threat and his nights with anxiety. Uncertainty for him is always the expectation of danger and hatred, never of pleasure, joy, or kindness. The victim of such deprivation lives on the ragged edge of catastrophe, his mind, feelings, and behavior tense and mobilized like a standing army into a constant defense against potential disaster. "He is usually responding as if to an emergency" (Maslow, 1954, p. 88), for, within such an orientation, reality is shaped by the possible occurrence of every kind of unfortunate contingency. A qualitative break occurs between physiological and safety needs in human beings and those which emerge upon their gratification, for "whatever words we use, there is a character difference between the man who feels safe and the one who lives his life out as if he were a spy in enemy territory" (Maslow, 1948b, p. 408). What is it that motivates the man who is secure?

CHAPTER IV

~~~~~~

Community

~~~~~~

On cesse de s'aimer si
quelqu'un ne nous aime.
                Madame de Staël

The need for love on the physiological level is fundamentally different from the need to belong which emerges when the individual is secure. The lower need, for example, is essentially passive. The child is not required to love back, to touch, to initiate, or provoke. Nor may he deliberately generate or control the love he needs in any way. It happens or does not—a source of creature comfort, of contact and stimulation, of one human body with another, in the essential touching and stroking which signal mammal life, dependency, and caring. At the higher level, the need to belong is based on the sense of unity, membership, and identification which derives from the expression of self against a nexus of common meanings. Security is derived from the ability of the individual to predict; to belong to a human group is to be able to make mutual predictions with the added dimension of mutual, reciprocal satisfaction.

Since the beginning of humanness, the species seems to have carried with it a biologically based drive toward entelechy or the placement of the idiosyncratic within some larger whole (Angyal, 1965).

Human behavior cannot be understood solely as a manifestation of the trend toward autonomy. Seen from another angle, human life reveals a basic pattern very different from self-assertiveness, from striving for freedom and mastery. A person behaves as if he were seeking a place for himself in a larger unit of which he strives to become a part. In the first orientation he is struggling for centrality in his world, trying to mold and organize objects and events, to bring them under his own control. In the second orientation he seems rather to strive to surrender himself and to become an organic part of something that he conceives as greater than himself. Processes concerned with procreation are evidence that even at the physiological-biological level the individual is integrated into superindividual units. At the cultural level, the person's conception of the larger unit to which he belongs, or to which he strives to belong, varies according to his cultural background and personal orientation. The superordinate whole may be represented for him by a social unit—family, clan, nation—by an ideology, or a meaning-

fully ordered universe. The objective question of such superindividual wholes is a metaphysical question with which the empirical scientist need not be concerned. For the student of personality, the important fact is that the trend toward homonomy, the wish to be in harmony with the unit one regards as extending beyond his individual self, is a powerful motivating source of behavior.

The need to belong seems to be almost as old as humanity itself. Thousands of years ago Homer wrote of "the tribeless, lawless, heartless one" who had no ties and belonged nowhere, who wandered the world beyond fellowship, trapped in the desperate regions beyond community and kin. Where is my *home?* cried Nietzsche. "For it do I ask and seek, and have sought, but have not found it. O eternal everywhere, O eternal nowhere, O eternal in vain" (quoted in Lippmann, 1929, p. 7). Long before Colin Wilson's "outsider" and the stranger Meursault of whom Albert Camus wrote so movingly, the alienated and outcast walked the face of the earth diminished in the inclusive humanness which is born of interaction and acceptance. Through history, such people have been literally estranged, not by the central categories of the shared, finite yet infinitely lonely human condition, but by rejection, rejection which, even when perceived as voluntary, has yet been done by those who were rightfully their people out from the place which was rightfully theirs.[1]

Seen in this way, as the desire to find a unit source for mu-

[1] Fromm believes that psychic alienation and estrangement are the product of present social conditions and will disappear when societies are built which supply man's deepest needs. In his rebuttal, Schaar (1961, p. 317) finds every man inevitably lonely "almost to the extent that he is an authentic and integral person." He diminishes Fromm's concept of alienation into a "category of sociology rather than of metaphysics." Sociologists since Marx have also considered alienation a descriptive term for a sociological state without necessarily separating it conceptually from the existential psychic state. In his definition of alienation as "the refusal of commitment to, or identification with, a group which claims sovereignty but which by one means or another inhibits the development and maintenance of a satisfying identity," Wallace (1968, p. 86), too, stresses the social foundations of alienation. In his view, whether the evils attributed to a society by the alienated are those which actually produced the state of alienation is not certain; the triggering factors may be simply the obvious vulnerabilities in an identity struggle between opposing segments of a society.

tual prediction and reciprocal satisfaction, belonging is not the self-abandonment it is perceived to be by the insecure (and as such desired as a psychic anchor)` but rather a self-discovery. It is the location of the self in, and the extending of self by means of, membership. Its opposite—the lack of a place to belong where others know too that one does—is accompanied by fear of the loss of usefulness and function and doubts about the roles (of husband, worker, citizen)` which adults must assume in society. According to Lane (1962, pp. 179–181)`, this homelessness is the root of political alienation. The "homeless man seeks a penetrating intimacy in human relations, which he may not be able to find." He "constantly finds himself as the outsider, the stranger trying to enter or find a 'we group' to join" (pp. 185–186)`.

Social or political homelessness may degenerate quickly into a threat to existence itself, for belonging is the sine qua non of human effectiveness. A man without the protection of the group has only the stripped-down defenses of the loner. He has lost, as Hannah Arendt (1958)` has documented, the rights of man, for these rights adhere to the individual only insofar as he is a member and the group, in defining its boundaries, grants him the privileges and protection which it affords all its constituency. Natural rights, rights apart from the covenants of men, do not exist. They are, as Jeremy Bentham graphically wrote, "nonsense on stilts." In practical demonstration, no historical inalienable rights exist. The minority treaties guaranteed by the League of Nations, for example, clarified what had previously been implicit—that only nationals could be citizens and enjoy the full protection of legal institutions. Group interest held priority over the law, and, where shares were not held in that interest, laws were inapplicable to the individual situation. The new totalitarian Europe emerging during the late thirties and forties drove prosperous and educated citizens, as well as the poor, to cross national borders without passport, money, or nationality to become unidentifiable beggars. Such forced migrations and loss of homes have hardly been unprecedented in history; what has been unprecedented in the twentieth century is the impossibility for enormous groups of people of finding a new home. The need for belonging has been elevated to a permanent, existential problem.

There are now over ten million displaced persons, victims

of World War II. Repatriation, when the refugee did not want to return to the country of origin, and naturalization, which affected the precarious social position of earlier naturalized citizens of the same origin, have both failed. The logical solution has been found in the internment camp which substitutes for a nonexistent homeland. Thus, loss of acceptance by a national group results in the annihilation of humanity, role, and rights, and ultimately deteriorates into loss of the right to life itself.[2] "The prolongation of their lives is due to charity and not to right, for no law exists which could force the nations to feed them; their freedom of movement, if they have it at all, gives them no right to residence which even the jailed criminal enjoys as a matter of course; and their freedom of opinion is a fool's freedom, for nothing they think matters anyhow" (Arendt, 1958, p. 296). For these people, loss of home has become identical with expulsion from humanity, for, John Henry notwithstanding, a man who is nothing but a man has lost the attributes which make it possible for others to regard him as a fellow man. The paradox lies in the fact that, at the same time he is becoming more individual, he is also becoming more generalized or abstracted into the universal species mold and losing that humanity. Deprived of its expression within a specific shared world, his uniqueness loses its significance.

Manifest affection is often part of the positive gratification pattern of the need to belong, although it is not necessarily so. Tenderness has been taboo in our society, although even the very tough gangs which Walter Miller (1958) describes allow expressions of solidarity and strongly affectionate feelings if they are disguised as verbal or physical aggression. Unlike the lower need for contact, the love which gratifies the need to belong is not merely received; it has also an active, reciprocal nature, and it assumes a measure of control and some efficacy in shaping its course. It involves giving as well as getting, although not always in obvious displays, and results, as

[2] Arendt (1958, p. 286) includes a compelling account of the way that a man deprived of the essential national membership may find entry into another recognized social category—that of the criminal. By doing so, he regains some of the rights denied a law-abiding but stateless person, for to be a law-breaker, or even a slave, is to have a distinctive character, a definition, and a place in society.

Harry Stack Sullivan (1953) has pointed out, in mutual gratification through the nurturing process.

Early deprivation of this love may result in permanent inability either to give or to receive it. In his chilling account of the *hibakusha* of atomic-bombed Hiroshima, Lifton (1967) describes the effect of parental loss on these tainted survivors. Loss of one's mother resulted in a basic deprivation of essential nurturance and created a profound mistrust of subsequent relationships, which might also be terminated. When both parents were killed, the children became permanently vulnerable, faced with "a lifelong struggle against total incapacitation." As an adult, the prototype of the atomic bomb orphan was a profoundly disaffected individual, "working irregularly at low status jobs, moving about frequently and having no permanent address, diffusely anxious and in poor health . . . on the fringe of society . . . sometimes in difficulty with the law" (p. 259). Deprivation left the survivors with a sense of abandonment and vulnerability toward further victimization by bad luck or being looked down on by those without the death-in-life stigma of being affected by the blast. Their interpersonal relationships were permanently impaired.

Nor is man alone in being stunted by early belongingness deficiencies. Harlow and his associates (1966) found abnormalities in the sexual role of female monkeys who had been deprived of mothering and peer association in infancy. They resisted impregnation and, when infants were finally born, rejected them even to the extent of injuring or killing them. The unfulfilled needs of the adults shaped their orientation toward their offspring. Although there was some variability among mothers, abuse was more common toward the first-born child than toward later progeny—a finding which suggests that the deprived monkeys recouped some of their deficiencies through the act of belongingness involved even in unwanted infant-raising.

How vital acceptance and concern are for socialization and the development of mature ethical values may be seen in Sheldon and Eleanor Glueck's work (1959). After many years of carefully controlled comparisons between delinquent and nondelinquent youth, they concluded that juvenile delinquency is 90 per cent predictable where five "highly decisive factors," all related to belongingness needs, are unfavorable in family life. Where, first, the father's discipline is harsh, erratic, and unsympathetic; second, the mother's supervision is indifferent or unconcerned; third, the mother's affection is cold, indifferent, or hostile; fourth, the father's affection is lacking; and fifth, family cohesiveness is lacking so that the group is unintegrated and empty of companionship, children become delinquent. Where these five factors were favorable, the Gluecks found virtually no serious delinquency.

From his comparative study of dropouts and high school graduates, Lucius Cervantes (1965) developed a dropout prediction table based on school, family, and peer relationships. Failure, lack of participation, a sense of not belonging at school added to problems at home, and few close friends who are not approved by parents and are not school-oriented produce a weak self-image, little ability to defer gratification, and much resentment toward authority. Dropouts, as S. M. Miller (Schreiber, 1967) reminds us, are the "displaced persons of the affluent society." Under social pressure, they may return to school, but as exiles only, in many cases to again become expellees and refugees from an unchanged situation. Most important to the destruction of this pattern are adolescent face-to-face memberships. "If the teen-ager has a primary relationship favorable to his remaining in school, all disadvantages are fairly readily overcome" (Cervantes, 1965, p. 199).

Like the fearful lower-class persons who have abandoned their autonomy where it is most loudly claimed, the aggressive boys whom Albert Bandura and R. H. Walters (1959) studied were forced to inhibit their dependency relations. Parent-child relationships were characterized by lack of warmth and affection and, in every case, the fathers showed little acceptance or esteem for their sons and were more punitive than the fathers of nonaggressive boys. Although value standards were upheld within the household, they were not internalized since, for these deprived boys, family life provided no rewards for identification with their fathers.

Upon the specific content of conscience depends the child's ability to live happily in a given society. This vital social and emotional learning occurs through motivation, performance, and reinforcement—through trial and error, direct tuition, and role practice which he is most likely to undertake if his dependency motivation is strong and he identifies with the main caretaker as a means of satisfying his needs. "An important motive leading to role practice is the child's desire to reproduce pleasant experiences" or "worry about whether or not he has his parent's affection and approval" (Sears, Maccoby, and Levin, 1957, p. 388). The child will learn to do whatever he must do to obtain the love he needs, and withdrawal of love given is powerful motivation to develop a conscience, that is, to learn the values of the withholder. But what happens to the child who is not receiving love? What is not given cannot be withdrawn, and if acceptance and recognition are not rendered the child, his unsatisfied needs will continue. His role-playing may be an endless search for identification or an authority which is external to himself to replace the missing internal one.

Damaged family relationships are also associated with loss of political values. Where problems existed between fathers and sons, Lane (1959), for example, found limited political information, authoritarianism, a need to stifle antiauthority feelings expressed as inability to criticize legitimate political figures, and a pessimistic view of social improvements. In the United States much public dismay was shown over the twenty-one soldiers who defected to China after they had been taken prisoner in Korea. Assumed to be traitors to the values they had learned as Americans, eighteen of these young men turned out to be non-Americans. They had not found their place within society in the way in which every child must—from the inside out, from membership and acceptance in home and school. None had close family ties nor had they taken part in school activities or sports during school (Pasley, 1955). Just how hard is it to abandon a group to which you have never truly belonged?

Maslow believes that the needs he describes are species-wide and anthropological studies seem to bear out this supposition. Gregory Bateson and Margaret Mead (1942), for example, have made a study of Balinese character which concluded that, by Western standards, these people are far from loving as adults. As children they are rejected and slapped for demanding attention and they do not like it—they cry and, in many other ways, show that they want the love which is denied them. In Israel, the ego-strong, well-adjusted children of the kibbutzim find their belongingness abundantly supplied within societies which are structurally, but not functionally, family-less. To them, the whole kibbutz is the family and their peers are the shared occupants of an intimacy which begins at birth and may end only at the grave. So deep and intense is the feeling invested in these communal relationships and meanings that, during the Six Days' War with Egypt, fighters from the kibbutzim were unable to abandon their comrades under any conditions and, consequently, were very poor soldiers, in the sense that they often were injured or killed unnecessarily (Bettelheim, 1969, p. 264).[3]

Warm, loving, caring families seem to best produce the positive influences which are essential to social and intellectual growth, but even a bad family seems to be better than none. In his study of infants and institutional care, William Goldfarb (1944) found that lack of family interaction produced emotional and intellectual impoverishment. His experimental group moved from institutions to foster homes at a mean age of three years and three months; the control group had its entire experience after the age of fourteen months with families. From a comparison of the two groups, Goldfarb concluded that "children who have experienced institutional deprivation during infancy are clearly differentiated from those whose total rearing has been in families." They are "less mature, less controlled, less differentiated, more impoverished . . . more passive and apathetic, less ambitious, less capable of adjustment related to conscious intention or goal" (p. 445).

"Inference," wrote Bruner (1959, p. 95), "depends upon the establishment of rules and models." "Not only does early [sensory] deprivation rob the organism of the opportunity of constructing models of the environment, it also prevents the development of efficient strategies for evaluating information, for finding out what leads to what and with what likelihood" (p. 95). Where social contacts and the texture of interaction with families are maintained,

---

[3] Although, in Maslow's theory, gratification releases motivation at a higher level and this presumably reduces further need and search for gratification on the lower one, it seems likely that any of man's basic needs may be overgratified in the same sense that a chemical solution may be supersaturated. To the dead Israelis, the extent of their communality hardly proved to have survival value. Under almost any conditions, a group which truly incorporates the self may guarantee the survival of the group, but it equally assures the destruction of the individual.

the "cognitively debilitating effects of reduced stimulation are nota-
bly reduced" (p. 94). At least for the development of cognition,
then, interaction alone, as well as accompanied by affection, seems
to have positive value. The gratification of belongingness needs
seems also to be related to the achievement of certain types of moral
judgment. Kohlberg (1966), studying the movement of children
from one type of moral judgment to another at a higher level of
development, found that children with peer group participation
("integrates") advanced more rapidly than isolates of matched socioeconomic status and IQ (p. 16).

R. G. Taylor (1964) found in "overachievement" a com-
pensatory, pseudo-love fulfillment which substituted identification
with the school for love missing at home. "Underachievers," in another deficiency response, reduce their anxiety about their status
through their peer group affiliations. In fact, low achievers in general depend heavily on the support of their immediate peers, although they are not well accepted by the broader group (McGuire
and others, 1961). In the sense that they do not conform to the
group at large, they are independent. However, it is also true that
they do not serve as models for those in the larger group any more
than those in the larger group serve as models for them. Independence which is based in a nonconforming group and true autonomy,
however, are not the same thing; in persons of high or low self-
esteem, its manifestations may have very different meanings, as we
shall see.

About us everywhere lie disintegration and re-formation.
The shape of human interaction is being altered, apparently for all
time. Yet out of the emerging structure of mass industrial life has
come no functional substitute for human communication on a personal, intimate, and primary level. Shall we become what Emile
Durkheim (1902, p. 463) has called "a society made up of a bound-
less dustheap of unrelated individuals," and the social sciences the
ideographic recording of human entropy? Or, from the dissipating
ashes of the small town and the extended family will new structures
of intimacy arise, close and tightly woven, with a dynamic warp
and woof from neither kin nor the fictional boundaries of the polity?

As George Homans (1950) has pointed out, small groups—
interest groups, kin and clan, economic and ethnic groups—have

survived the massive destructive forces which have destroyed empires, religions, cultures, and civilizations. The only historical continuity of men in society has been through the small groups they have established to serve their most fundamental human needs. "All grander sociologies must be true to the sociology of the group" (p. 21), for only at this level have societies invariably been able to cohere. Inclusion in such groups means the taking for granted which permits extended activities instead of a constant and fearful reassessment of the environment. If human life as we know it in its highest form is to stand, some of the intimate features which characterize the small group must be preserved in some form, for its boundaries serve not only to present the nature of their membership to outsiders, but also to provide that crucial labeling, the identification of themselves to those who belong.

CHAPTER V

Self

The sense of not being needed, not being able to support oneself, not fully belonging, being relatively but not absolutely deprived, and not being able to undertake socially significant action may be more damaging to identity than any amount of hunger, violence, or verbal assault. On these grounds, indeed, one would expect that it would be the young, carefully raised, adequately fed, and well-educated of any group who would be most likely to be alienated from its Establishment.

Anthony F. C. Wallace
"The Psychic Unity of Human Groups"

The development of human personality, as Gordon Allport (1968, p. 182) has written, is a matter of "slow growth" and "non-dramatic facts." By experiencing himself as the subject of his powers, the same to himself and others over time, the individual gains an enduring sense of self. What the specific ingredients of that self are may vary from culture to culture, but everywhere the process of unifying them into a coherent whole is the same, and everywhere the definition which is achieved is a composite of evaluative and normative elements as well as the objective observation of the actual. At all ages, the individual needs a stable and firmly based self-description. Evaluation, as Charles Osgood, George Suci, and Percy Tannenbaum (1957) have pointed out, is pervasive, and regarding himself, the individual is forced to take his measure not only against his highly personal ego-ideal, but against the common rule provided by his society. By and large, that rule is built out of his capability to fulfill a role, or series of overlapping roles, adequately. If he succeeds, he achieves respect from others and self-respect for himself.[1]

Is he "good?" Is he "bad?" At what and to whom? Besides knowing what he is, the individual needs to know whether that being is valuable, whether he is capable, competent, able to be what it is "good" to be and to do what it is "good" to do. Beyond the prominent features of his own subjective experience, he needs to know what he is and where he stands in the eyes of others, the members of his society or group who share his standards of excellence. "The city clerk and the razor gang, the tax collector and Azeff the great *agent provocateur,* the girl on the beach and Murder, Incorporated—their inarticulate mouths all utter one cry. And their cry is one with the wish of the churchwarden and the toff

[1] Loss of his role, and its concomitant status and respect, through rapid cultural change or old age and retirement may bring deep despair. The title *senior citizen* adopted in the United States is probably an attempt to relieve some of this distress, but is a highly limited one since it describes a nonfunctional role, not a positive status. Among other cultural adaptations for the preservation of self-esteem in old age, Gorer (1966, Chap. 15) suggests the denotation of old age as a culturally approved time of license and training for compulsory leisure—as a time for new functions and the culturally sponsored provision for learning them.

and the squire's lady. They want a place in the world. They want to be among friends. And they want to stand and be recognized" (Bronowski, 1955, p. 59). The need for self-esteem has, then, two subsidiary sets: First, the "desire for reputation or prestige, status, dominance, recognition, attention, importance, or appreciation"; and second, the need for a feeling of "mastery and competence, confidence in the face of the world, and for independence and freedom" (Maslow, 1954, p. 90). The satisfaction of the former is directly derived from interaction with others. The latter, with its inclusion of feelings of competence and independence, is intimately related to the satisfaction of deficiency needs and the growth of the need to actualize one's potential.

The ability to do anything at all is probably based on this composite need whose gratification builds the sense of capability, strength, and adequacy, for low esteem is associated with low participation and low interest. The low-esteem individual has no psychic space left, for he is trapped in "overwhelming absorption in his own psychological problems" (Rosenberg, 1965, p. 211). Like the protagonist in Eugene O'Neill's play *The Hairy Ape,* he despises himself as an untouchable. Weakness, helplessness, and feelings of inferiority are the outcome of deprivation at this level. Basic discouragement, belief in luck, and acceptance of a passive role seep into every undertaking, victimize the actor, and prevent accomplishment. "The judgments, being internal, cannot be evaded and hence serve as constant reminders of inferiority" (Coopersmith, 1967, p. 69). The person with low or uncertain self-esteem is more persuadable than one whose feelings about himself are more positive. Because his behavior is not mediated and integrated by a unified self-concept, it is directly linked to environmental circumstances so that he tends to passively conform to the influence of the prevailing field or context. In contrast, a person who knows the assured value of his self exhibits a high degree of stimulus control. His cognitive processes are characterized by selective consideration of relevant social elements within his environment—a process which in its exaggerated form leads to the association between high self-esteem and dogmatism (Ziller and others, 1969).

For this unfortunate individual, negative self-appraisals are indicative of limited defensive abilities which are associated with fearfulness and the expectation of failure, an interior prophecy which becomes self-fulfilling. In his study of the adolescent self-image, Morris Rosenberg (1965, p. 225) found twice as many ego-phobes (persons with extremely low self-esteem) as egophiles (their opposite) who did not expect to do the kind of work they wanted to do, an expectation which their low self-estimates will help them to actualize.

All men are what others perceive them to be, and this is all the more true when shared values are attached to those perceptions common to a society.

We change things by the capacities which we have that other people do not have. Such capacity is what makes us effective. The immediate attitude is one which carries with it a sense of superiority, of maintaining one's self. The superiority is not the end in view. It is a means for the preservation of the self. We have to distinguish ourselves from other people, and this is accomplished by doing something which other people cannot do or cannot do as well [Mead, 1934, p. 208].

When the governors of a society spend less for vital services such as schooling, housing, and health, on its poor and the disadvantaged minorities, the worth of these members has been debased and they are likely to know it (Sexton, 1961). Such knowledge may begin very young. Bernice Neugarten (1946) reported that by the fifth or sixth grade children in a typical midwestern town had already developed a set of negative images about lower-class children, images with which those children agreed. In his New York State study, Rosenberg (1965) found an association between class and the self-images of adolescent boys. High scores on his measure were obtained by 36 per cent of the lower-class boys, 47 per cent of middle-class boys, and 55 per cent upper-class boys. Since Neugarten's and Rosenberg's samples were not from social extremes (such as rural southern blacks or northern urban slum dwellers), it seems quite likely that, as Inkeles (1968, p. 116) has written, "the socialization process early impresses on young people an image of themselves in accord with their position in the status hierarchy and that that image is regularly reinforced at each step in the life cycle."

People belong to groups and develop relationships with other humans because of their deep needs for companionship and contact, but also because these affiliations, these intimate interactions, define to them what they are. So dependent are they on the stability of this definition and on its generally positive nature, that, at the developmental stage of moral reasoning below the principal level, the individual cannot "separate himself from the social order, even when he recognizes covenanted injustices" (Haan, Smith, and Block, 1969, p. 29). His reasoning is based on what others have decided is the right. Since his image of self is derived from those others, he has no autonomous way of deciding what is right or wrong. At the lower level of conventional role and conformity morality, he behaves himself for the sake of maintaining good relations with others and keeping their approval. On a somewhat higher level, he believes that justice and rights belong to the rule enforcers and obeyers and that morality must be maintained by authority. If he can, he will avoid political or social activity which might produce conflict to jeopardize his position and the secure nexus of relationships around him.[2] "Status honor"—in Weber's term—is central to his life.

Just as individuals seek to be like others, at least in certain important ways, in order to be accepted into membership, so do they try to gain certain types of affiliations and relationships in order to assure themselves of memberships and positions which have value. Conformity, on this level, may go beyond the gratification of fundamental belongingness needs to the search for a special kind of affiliation, one with an elevated position of status, and deep-rooted personal insecurity may generate a type of "status-dread"—fear of not

[2] According to this study on the Berkeley campus, sample subjects who reason from universal principles (as theorized by Kohlberg at levels five and six) are more active in political and social matters (particularly in protest) than those who reason at any other level. Their aim is the correction of immoral social injustice. However, males at level two are also politically active. This is the stage of "naive instrumental hedonism," at which motivation for moral decisions is the manipulation of goods and the rewards which are to be received from others. Their concern is "personally referenced," and a "generally politicized milieu" is required for protest to take place since it is a "fine expression of politicized IR's personal battles with a society which is seen as ungiving rather than immoral" (Haan, Smith, and Block, 1969, p. 29).

belonging to high-prestige groups. To the members of disadvantaged or low-status minority groups, this may mean nothing more than seeking admission into the more prestigious group which is the society at large.

From his study of institutionalized religion and prejudice, Allport (1968) suggests that conformers without intrinsic orientation for religion who attend church because of status-dread would theoretically be expected to be insecure and rejecting of others. If the specific institutional organization to which they belonged were manifestly antiprejudice, they would probably seek a different reference group of equal status or conform situationally, to attitudes not truly internalized, for the sake of maintaining their status there. Superficial and highly contingent, their acceptance of others would be based on acceptance of themselves in the high-status group.

The person motivated by the need for esteem from others is uncertain of his personal worth. The only self he has is the "looking-glass self" described by Cooley (1902). Without the image of value returning from the perceived judgments of others, he is lost. He seeks a level of acceptance of himself within his affiliations, or through them, which will justify his hope that he has value. By definition he is a social oligarch, since to have the same rank as others is not enough. His fearful preoccupation is to convince others so that they can convince him, and, as a substitute for self-respect and true autonomy, he may choose the power which high status brings (Bettelheim, 1960). Status insecurity, like the lower needs, affects his vision of the world and the type and variety of stimuli which he is capable of receiving from his environment (Mannheim, 1950, pp. 200–203).

Going to the root of the matter, we find that openness to change is only within reach of the person who really feels secure, and therefore is unafraid of losing either status or individuality by having his probity exposed to the testing powers of cooperation and exchange of ideas. In an authoritarian relationship it stands to reason that one of the parties has a higher status than the other and in his activities is concerned with maintaining that status, whereas in the ideal case of democratic partnership the question of status is ruled out by acknowledgment of essential equality: in other words, the desire for prestige stands less in the way of willingness to learn from another person than under an authoritarian system. Indeed, there is no greater obstacle to real learning . . . than the fear of losing one's status. A status-ridden person cannot really learn.

A seventeen-year-old boy in our study wrote, "I worry about not being able to marry and achieve true married happiness; not being able to have children; not being able to support them and send them to college; not being able to offer them the benefits of life I didn't receive; my lack of social participation; my overriding feeling of inferiority and uselessness; my continuing doubt of my abilities." Unwanted, unable, unliked in his own eyes, the individual without self-esteem perceives himself as deeply inadequate.[3] His reactions are rigid and defensive. Lack of self-respect restricts his perceptual field and his ability to initiate action, to undertake the decision-making "function which creates the ego and, once created, keeps it going and growing" (Bettelheim, 1960, p. 70). Because he has mastered nothing and known nothing that he could control, the sense of efficacy is lacking and with it, the belief that he may affect the environment and what happens to him during his transactions with it. As Shakespeare wrote, "Our doubts are traitors/And make us lose the good we oft might win, by fearing to attempt."

Apparently, as a group, the "well-adjusted" differ in political orientation from those who are not, and the subjective sense of control correlates highly with political participation (Campbell and others, 1960). Low self-esteem, however, may manifest itself either in apathy and withdrawal or in a type of participation which is a denial of selfhood. In studying adolescents in New York State high schools, Rosenberg (1962) asked a question which had been raised previously by Lasswell: "Do feelings of inadequacy produce striving for political power as compensation, or neurotic incapacity and withdrawal?" Those with low self-esteem were relatively less interested, less participant in discussions, and less likely to engage actively in them, as well as less likely to be asked their views or to take

[3] Combs and Snygg (1959) use the term *adequate* to correspond roughly to Kelly's *fully fulfilled* person and Goldstein and Maslow's mentally healthy person who may become a self-actualizer.

the lead. Sixty-two per cent of those with the lowest self-esteem, compared to 23 per cent of those with the highest self-esteem, rarely if ever took the lead. While high self-esteem by no means guarantees the adoption of active leadership roles, the adolescent with low self-esteem characteristically "manifests the behavior characteristic of the politically apathetic citizen" (Rosenberg, 1962, p. 209).

Where low estimates of the self are permitted to develop, the democratic character cannot develop (Lasswell, 1951). "Chaos within breeds a need for control without" (Lane, 1962, p. 126). (Chaos of a different order may generate a more positive product. See Frank Barron's [1963] studies on creativity.) Within the impoverished self, with its low self-acceptance and ego strength, are nourished the pathologies of undemocratic man. He loses his identity, becomes self-alienated and unwilling to explore his motives at the same time that he takes on self-referential qualities. He is anxious and irrational and lacks self-control. His interpersonal relations are characterized by misanthropy, constricted empathy, the coldness of a closed ego, conformity, and a polarized "We" and "They" orientation dominated by cynicism and the prevailing belief that the world is a jungle where men eat men.

If the opportunity occurs, this sad individual may be driven by his self-hate out of apathy and into mass movements. Eric Hoffer has said, "The less justified a man is in claiming excellence for his own self, the more ready he is to claim all excellence for his nation, his religion, his race, or his holy cause" (1951, p. 14). "A mass movement attracts and holds a following not because it can satisfy the desire for self-advance, but because it can satisfy the passion for self-renunciation" (p. 12). It "substitutes for the whole self or for the elements which make life bearable and which they cannot evoke out of their individual resources" (p. 13). (Ward H. Goodenough [1963], more positively, describes those who join revitalization movements, such as Moral Rearmament, as participants who are striving toward a more acceptable identity.)

Seeking some means of repairing his faulty and despised self, the individual who is motivated by the need for self-esteem does not realize that unification in a cause is a process of diminution, not addition. "His happiness and fortitude come from his no longer being himself. Attacks against the self cannot touch him" (p. 124).

Stripped of his distinctiveness, he "has been delivered from the meaningless burden of an autonomous existence" (p. 124) and has achieved dubious freedom "from the arduous responsibility of realizing [his] ineffectual [self] and shouldering the blame for the blemished product. [He does] not want freedom of conscience, but faith—blind, authoritarian faith" (p. 141). Hoffer goes on to say that, since his invincibility depends on a tenuous lifeline to the collective whole, "the true believer is eternally incomplete, eternally insecure" (p. 141). He accepts the movement or the cause and his place within it intensely but conditionally—lack of belief in himself prevents an enduring commitment or the open acceptance of others with whom and wherever he interacts.[4]

The individual with low self-regard is trapped in a dynamic web of rejection. Despising himself, he also tends to despise those who are foolish or mistaken enough to grant him worth where he knows he has neither competence nor mastery nor value, and ultimately his debased other-evaluation is likely to dislodge the foundations of esteem which others have for him. His insecurities betray him as an upstart whose personal forces expect to be challenged and deposed, and, following an old rule of battle, his defense is to attack—he rejects before he is rejected.

Many theorists believe that self-acceptance is positively correlated with acceptance of others. In a member of a despised minority group, individual rejection of self may manifest itself through deliberate affiliation with the majority and abandonment of origins which are seen as unbearably depriving. In a study of third-year

---

[4] Hoffer (1951, p. 85) describes the thin line between violent, extreme nationalism and treason. The chauvinist and the traitor are both fanatics. According to him, most World War II traitors were from the extreme right—swayed by some small contingency from violent patriotism to violent reaction. More recent examples of the relationship between extremes of political views are Whittaker Chambers, who moved from polar left—membership in the Communist Party—to right, and Karl Hess, who as a conservative intellectual, was the chief speechwriter for Barry Goldwater during the 1964 campaign. At that time, Hess was credited with the notorious phrase: "Extremism in the defense of liberty is no vice; moderation in the pursuit of justice is no virtue." In an article in the *San Francisco Chronicle* of March 5, 1970, he was described as a hippie intellectual who believed in "libertarian anarchy," in which the community—wherever people live—itself can govern. Hess was quoted as saying that he frequently met Goldwaterites who had taken a turn to the militant left.

medical students, William Fey (1955) found a relationship between acceptance of others and feeling and actually being accepted. Subjects with high self-acceptance tended to accept others and, even though they were not really accepted more than the subjects with low self-acceptance scores, felt themselves to be so. Rosenberg (1965) found that the lower self-esteem was in the adolescents he studied, the lower their participation and leadership also were. They also doubted that others liked or respected them and, in turn, handed back that low opinion to others.

In an interesting application of psychoanalytical theory to education, Richard M. Jones (1960) conducted an experiment through a course in psychology, the Self-Knowledge Workshop, which was designed to increase self-acceptance. Compared to the two control groups, the members of the Workshop increased significantly in their sense of self-worth. Most interesting, however, is the fact that, although no classwork had been designed to effect the change, acceptance of others (as measured on the Bogardus Scale) was also significantly greater, a difference which Jones attributes to the reduced need, over the period of the course, for its members to employ projective defenses to attribute to others their own failings. Most other research which has shown correlations between self-regard and acceptance of others has also involved college students or young adults, with the "other" either some generalized other or parents. (See Bills [n.d.], Berger [1952], Crandall and Bellugi [1954], Fey [1954], Henry [1956], Omwake [1954], Sarnoff [1951], Worchel [1957], Wylie [1957], and Zuckerman, Baer, and Monashkin [1956] for positive relationships. Zimmer [1956] and Zelen [1954a, b] show negative findings.) In a review of the literature, Marvin Goldfried (1963) concluded that, in general, a positive relationship exists between one's attitudes toward self and one's attitudes toward others and that maladjusted individuals tend to have more negative attitudes toward others.

Does class affect feelings of self-acceptance or self-worth? Ruth Wylie (1961) concluded from her survey of the literature—a total of four studies—that evidence for any relationship was inconclusive. Robert Ziller and others (1969) report a study of low caste East Indian schoolchildren whose objective social position apparently did not affect their high subjective ratings of self-regard.

Since these children were among a group carefully selected for the privilege of education, however, as Ziller points out, it may be that their level of self-esteem was a reflection of their special status among the members of their caste. Another possibility is that it is an effect of nurturance from a tightly woven primary group.

Pointing out that the social prestige rendered to small boys is ascribed to them rather than achieved by their own occupational efforts, Stanley Coopersmith (1967, pp. 82–83) suggests that upper-class children are still more likely to receive attention, respect, and self-esteem-enhancing treatment than lower-class children. He expected to find a positive relationship between high self-esteem and high social status. What he actually found was "no clear and definite pattern of relationships between social class and positive and negative attitudes toward the self." Persons in the lower-class are most likely to report lower self-esteem. However, there are "almost as many persons in this class who report high esteem as low esteem." Among the adolescents whom Rosenberg (1965) studied, those whose fathers were in authoritarian occupations such as the armed forces tended to be low in self-esteem. As we pointed out above, in his sample, degree of self-acceptance was distributed significantly according to social class, with males of upper socioeconomic status more likely to have high self-esteem.

The work of Martin Deutsch (1967), Ziller and others (1969), and Barbara Long and Edmund Henderson (1968) suggests a more negative self-image for the lower-class child and adolescent than for children of higher status. On the other hand, Anthony and Louise Soares (1969) and Judith Greenberg and others (1965), in studies using a rating scale to compare self-concepts of advantaged and disadvantaged children, found generally higher ratings among the lower group. In the present study self-esteem in the sense of mastery was not related to social class. However, esteem-from-others or social esteem was, with higher scores, found with low socioeconomic status. (Low status: $\overline{X} = 3.69$, sd 1.14, n = 81; high status: $\overline{X} = 2.39$, sd 1.40, n = 281, p < .001. The reader is reminded that high scores here represent needs, not their gratification.) The matter, it seems, is not to be settled by further collection of undifferentiated data, but by theoretical reformulation of the concept of self-esteem. We will return to this interesting question later, but, first, what is the effect of the face-to-face group on the developing ego of the individual?

Membership in an isolated subgroup simplifies choices since the ego identities which are formed are consistent with the values of the group, the group identity, and its basic ways of organizing experience. In such a situation, values are not caught in the type of conflict which occurs between interacting minority and dominant groups.

"Does the typical coal miner in Pennsylvania react as if he were overwhelmed by the complexity of modern conditions? Is the southern tenant farmer confused by social norms? Does the agricultural worker in Iowa experience constant conflict as a result of our variegated national cultural patterns? He may; but more often than not, he takes these differences in his stride. More important than cultural complexity in general is the amount of conflict and contradiction which the individual has experienced as a member of his family or neighborhood group" (Miller and Hutt, 1949a, p. 42).

In New Zealand Maori youth were trapped between the traditional dependency on friendship and the rugged individualism of the white invaders with its emphasis on upward mobility (Ausubel, 1961). On Okinawa, in contrast, the male, at least twenty years ago, underwent no such conflict. Pampered from birth and waited on all his life, he avoided the anxiety and test to his self-esteem which a break in regimen or the introduction of alien values would bring (Miller and Hutt, 1949b). In the modern world, few such isolated islands of consistency still exist. Social groups interact with other social systems large and small, and the social self and sense of worth that are developed by each individual are the outgrowth of these transactions. Self-esteem in both its manifestations—the sense of recognition and other-worthiness and the sense of personal mastery and self-worthiness—is closely linked to the need to affiliate and belong on a broad societal or secondary level, as well as on a more narrow or primary one, and is the product of an elaborate and dynamic network of interactions. The self-concept is a learned constellation of perception, cognitions, and values, an important part of which is acquired through observing the reactions of others and responding to them. "The self, that which can be an object to itself, is essentially a social structure, and it arises in social experience. After a self has arisen, it in a certain sense provides for itself its social experience, and so we can conceive of an absolutely solitary self. But it is impossible to conceive of a self raising outside of social experience" (Strauss, 1956, p. 217).

As we will say again, even the cognitive acceptance of societal or secondary group standards is based on an emotionally founded belonging. But not all belonging has the same saliency or power. Intensely close ties are more likely to exist between small group outcomes and values, including the value of the self, for the small group defines the self-view which the individual accepts. According to Wylie (1961), all personality theorists accord great importance to parent-child relationships in this development of self-definition.[5] By being loved and accepted, the child comes to love himself, and through the acquisition of accepted, that is, rewarded, behavior he comes to respect his own functioning. He learns the ideal standards of conduct which are associated with his role and status, some degree of realism in the acceptance of his limitations and abilities, including socially undesirable traits, and just how adequately he can trust his own judgment of his effect on others.

Not the whole society's evaluation, but that of the groups which are deeply and intimately referenced controls the balance in the psychic economy. The East Indian children cited by Ziller (1969) could ignore the culture-wide judgment when a valued reference group found them worthy. Jews, where a despised minority, have maintained an individual concept of self-value through in-group cohesion and the supportive shelter of the family. Where it occurs, Jewish anti-Semitism seems to be more a function of parental

[5] Wylie remarks that considering the centrality afforded parent-child interaction, there are few studies. These are inconclusive and correlational, rather than antecedent-consequent in design. She summarizes her findings thus: some evidence exists that children's self-concepts are similar to the view of themselves which they attribute to their parents. Limited evidence associates the child's level of self-regard with that of the parents' reported level of regard for him. Children, according to this survey, may see the self-concept of the like-sex parent as somewhat more like that of their own (than that of the opposite-sex parent) and, if they are maladjusted (judged by self-reports), believe their parents view them as different from themselves (pp. 135–136).

rejection than of direct experience with religious prejudice, although
it may also be seen as identification with the aggressor (Sarnoff,
1951).[6]

Among the southern subjects at Debouchement whose needs
and values are reported here there is a clear conceptual difference
between the esteem built by acceptance in the larger society and
the sense of worthiness which is the product of mastery and success
in an intimate environment. Black and lower-class, in a discrimina-
tory culture, these young people are characterized by a sense of personal competence and high self-esteem accompanied by a strong
need for esteem from others, that is, for the acceptance which the
larger social environment is most reluctant to give to a low-status
minority.

It is at this point, I believe, that the ambiguity and confusion
over contradictory reports relating low socioeconomic status to low
self-regard may be resolved: When primary groups support the opportunity for a sense of mastery and the growth of a positive self-
image, regardless of low socioeconomic status and external negative
pressures, a high degree of personal self-regard may be developed
and maintained. At the same time, however, the individual may
perceive clearly the extent of societal rejection and manifest his
awareness in an ungratified need for acceptance by others. This mul-
tidimensional conceptualization of self-esteem seems to explain conflicting findings which define the culturally disadvantaged child and
adolescent in terms of both a negative and a positive self-image.
Certainly, the data collected in the limited Debouchement sample
(n = 66) indicate strongly the need for a model of self-esteem which
is not unicellular.

Although Rosenberg (1965, p. 58), too, finds "no indication
of a linear relationship between an ethnic group's prestige rank and
the distribution of self-esteem in the group," cultural denigration of

[6] The self-esteem of women, too, is affected by this process. The cultural stereotype of males is more favorable and women accept this attitude,
apply it to themselves, and teach it to their female—as well as their male—
children. (The Women's Liberation Movement may change this—but not
before it ceases to be a male joke.) In contrast to the correlation cited
above between self-acceptance and acceptance of others, even when the
level of self-esteem is held constant, women generally tend to be more accepting of others than do men (Wylie, 1961, p. 147).

certain groups may take its toll in less direct ways. William Grier and Price Cobbs (1968) describe with power the filtering down process which may occur with devastating effect on some black Americans in the United States. Parental ability to build self-esteem in the child may be enervated by the parents' own, socially reinforced, belief in his relative inferiority. What the larger society suggests to the child, black parents may then drive home—sometimes even deliberately as a method of protection for their offspring—and the stubborn self-acceptance which is the outcome of supportive primary interaction is lost.

With low self-esteem, an individual would not, as we have seen, be likely to be accepting of others. Can an ethnocentric person who accepts ingroups highly and rejects outgroups equally strongly be expected to accept himself? An authoritarian, rejecting difference, accepts strongly, if conditionally, those groups with whom he can identify. A number of investigators have found high self-esteem associated with both ethnocentrism and authoritarianism, although, as usual, Wylie (1961) qualifies their findings by one study in which high self-rejection was associated with high F-Scale (Fascism) and E-Scale (Ethnocentrism) scores (Rokeach and Fruchter, 1956). Our findings support the dissenters: In the high school sample studied here, high- and low-esteem groups differed significantly $(p < .01)$ in dogmatism $(\overline{X} = 142.82, \ n = 251; \ \overline{X} = 167.18, \ n = 124)$. These means refer to scores on esteem-from-others (social esteem). No significant difference was found in self-esteem scores with their highly self-referential emphasis. High and low combined esteem groups also differed significantly $(p < .01)$ on dogmatism. (See Appendix C, Table 4.)

Measured by phenomenological report, a high acceptance score may be inflated by denial. It may, however, also be real and an indicator of the curvilinear relationship of this gratified need with mental health and healthy performance, for although it is generally conceded that low self-regard is indicative, and perhaps even a cause, of maladjustment, theorists are much less sure about the reverse proposition. High self-esteem may indicate either mental health or denial of problems (which may be more serious psychically than admission of low self-acceptance) or unsophisticated conventionality (Loevinger and Ossorio, 1959). Using an adjective check

list, Harrison Gough (1968, pp. 63–64) found that the identification of individuals manifesting a comfortable and imperturbable
sense of personal worth turns up egocentrism: high scorers are demanding, egotistical, opportunitic, and bossy. Self-confidence and
determination are associated with narcissism and indifference to others, manipulative behavior toward others, and defense mechanisms
against unconscious feelings of self-rejection.[7]

Like the black ghetto subjects of our sample who were characterized by high self-esteem in spite of their objective status within
the larger society, the young minority group boys whom Rosenberg
studied (1965) showed "unconditional self-acceptance" in spite of
poor grades and an objective failure to participate (p. 108). Rosenberg suggests that too much self-regard may be a deterrent to
achievement.[8] Ernestine Pannes (1963), from her investigation of
a large high school sample (n = 675), reported a significant positive
relationship between high self-acceptance and dogmatism: self-acceptance decreases with IQ while open-mindedness increases. Her
findings suggest that, at least in the upper reaches, high self-esteem
may be a detriment to the acquisition of tolerant attitudes and an
inhibition on the development of the kinds of self-critical abilities
which lead to personal growth. For several thousand years, other
writers have also seen the intimate connection between some bene-
ficial self-doubt and empathic and tolerant attitudes toward others.

Self-esteem, we may conclude, is the psychological product
of balanced, positive experience, both with oneself and with the reactions of others and the value which they attribute to that self.
According to Maslow, while its lack leaves the individual somewhat
less than healthy and fully human, its gratification moves him from
the range of human deficiency to its possible fulfillment, at a level
of being which is no longer simply supplying the gaps left by deprivation. Yet, there are "many societies where men are self-accepting

---

[7] Coopersmith (1967) disagrees: "Though high self-esteem may
occasionally be found concurrently with such characteristics as vanity and
arrogance, there is no social necessity for their relatedness and no objective
evidence that such a relationship exists" (p. 26).

[8] Although this may be so, it should be remembered that achievement
is here defined by the out-group. The in-group which helped to supply
gratification for the basic needs and to build self-regard may define achievement in entirely different terms.

and self-respecting, but where they are not capable of self-government because they are not self-governing" (Lane, 1962, p. 142). The sense of competence and the sense of significance are the necessary, but not sufficient, conditions for achievement; the individual who has them may be ready to govern himself, to actualize his potential, and to manifest his highest intellectual, creative, and humane gifts, but other factors may help to determine whether he actually does so.

We have been describing the needs which motivate the individual and lead him to develop certain superordinate values such as security, group acceptance, or status. But the personality, as we have seen, functions as a whole, and these needs, in their conative manifestations, express the feelings and control the cognitive aspects of that personality. Conceptually, these regions may be distinct. However, as Sanford (1967, p. 79)' reminds us, "Cognition, feeling, emotion, action, and motivation are easily separated by abstraction, but no single one of these can function independently of the others." What effect, then, do motivating values have on cognitive and affective interactions in our lives?

Chapter VI

On Values

Nameless, this nation of the Self
En tres partes divisa est
Where Plato mapped a psychic Gaul
In analytic humor, built
Land's end in learnéd spaces—
Good and True and Beautiful—
Fenced in meadows. Yet,
Not monumental burial nor barbs
Nor stone-based posts
Can separate a unity.
The whole organic country
Overgrows: two thousand years
The motive heart has thought;
The mind in operation felt
Its sensate lands in one.

                                    E. L. S.
                            The Solidary Psyche

Unless ye believe, ye shall not understand.
                                    St. Augustine

In the land of the blind, the one-eyed man is king. There is truth in the adage but falsehood too, for the one-eyed man may not be king, he may be an outcast and a menace. H. G. Wells says this very well when he has the people who live in the Valley of the Blind label the seeing stranger as insane. Sighted, his perceptions differ largely from those of the other members of the group; he is abnormal, a deviant, perhaps even a dangerous one. His troublesome difference shakes the pillars of the universe—the sense of reality.

Disagreement with fundamental notions is very threatening. For all of us, beliefs serve to place the world where it is and to define its contents. Through our beliefs we identify the objects, ideas, and feelings about which there is agreement. We identify the actions which are appropriate toward them. More even than identification—a cognitive map of the environment—belief is an emotional commitment to knowledge, common or personal, perhaps even what Michael Polayni (1958, p. 17) has called a "passionate participation in the act of knowing." It is a commitment which both produces and utilizes that directive force which we call valuing. Because they represent the activation of both the cognitive and the affective spheres, values are the filters through which beliefs about our universe are passed. For twenty-five hundred years since Plato's analysis, a false schism has divided these domains (and a third, the conative or directive and motivating). "In short, we must learn to remove the intellectual quality from reality if we are to be faithful to it," wrote Jose Ortega y Gasset in *Historia Como Sistema* (1962), yet this is not possible, for nowhere in nature is reality so separated. Inextricably interwoven, cognitive functioning is not apart from affective responses; one is the counterpart of the other. The two components vary together. They have an isomorphic, one-to-one relationship which adheres through the process of gathering data, testing, and transmitting it.

This relationship is not merely a matter of theory; it has been shown empirically. For example, an experiment in which the belief that Negro-white integration would lower property values was changed to the belief that it would raise them also demonstrated

71

changes of feelings toward Negroes. Conversely, changed feelings affect beliefs; feelings that were induced under hypnosis produced corresponding changes in cognition (Rosenberg, 1960). Our everyday experience supports these studies, for in the United States the persuasion professions have parlayed this unity into a multimillion-dollar public relations industry which attacks beliefs through feelings.

Values accumulate concurrently with concepts and their heavy equipment of affective sets and attitudes. (See Martin Fishbein [1967]. Both cognitive and conative [action] components of attitudes may be viewed as beliefs. Beliefs are not neutral; all contain some degree of favorableness or unfavorableness toward the object.) The tendency to cathexis, to value either positively or negatively, is made up of conceptual beliefs about the valued object. Furthermore, whether one values, how one values, and how strongly one values are all correlated with the content of the associated cognitive structure, with human emotion and thinking together forming a complex set of interactions.[1] It is almost as if, in the act of feeling, the individual were giving President Lyndon Johnson's famous invitation not to the citizenry but to his own integrated mind, "Come, let us reason together." The assimilative capacity makes meaning, in its deepest and most complex sense, possible.

Not all writers have followed the age-old dichotomy between mind and heart; sometimes they have patched it up one way and sometimes another. William James, for example, used the term *thinking* as a generic rubric for any kind of mental state (1890).

---

[1] See Asahel D. Woodruff (Fishbein, 1967, p. 80): "The perception of the positive or negative instrumental value of an object or a process, whether that perception is intuitive or clearly conscious, furnishes an input which becomes part of the concept of that object or process. This is the origin of value, both positive and negative. Instrumental value is the foundation of motive in all its forms: interest, sentiment, wish, major value, ideal, goal of any degree of immediacy or remoteness." See Milton Rosenberg (1967, p. 325): "When a person has a relatively stable tendency to respond to a given object with either positive or negative affect, such a given tendency is accompanied by a cognitive structure made up of beliefs about the potentialities of that object for attaining or blocking the realization of values states. . . . The sign (positive or negative) and extremity of the affect felt toward the object are correlated with the content of its associated cognitive structure."

Thinking, for him, included feeling. For Suzanne Langer (1967), the opposite is true—feeling is the subsumer. The "entire psychological field—including human conception, responsible action, rationality, knowledge—is a vast and branching development of feeling. . . . Value exists only where there is consciousness. Where nothing is felt, nothing matters" (p. 23).

From their genesis in this dual process, values serve as a relational linking between objects and the concepts which are formed of them. Once perceived, the value of an object or process, intuitively or consciously, becomes part of its construct or concept. Values may be brought to consciousness, but they are not found by using reason as a cognitive searchlight. They are attained through the satisfaction of needs and the socialization process, not by thinking through alone; nor is thinking "in the service of values" (Raths, Harmin, and Simon, 1966, p. 202). On the contrary, values are the implementors of thought; the cognizing process is done by means of the system of values we possess. Allport (1968, p. 164) put it very nicely when he said that a system of values was "meanings perceived as related to the self." It carries affective loadings and has motivational consequences since action—the conative factor—is also a part of belief. With this in mind, it seems almost ludicrous to suggest that the disadvantaged child would alter his values if he thought through the relationship between himself and his society. Like everyone else, such a child thinks with the values that he has, his beliefs about the nature of the world and his society; rational processes alone are little likely to change these loaded concepts, although they may clarify *why* he has learned to value and believe in certain ways by bringing his needs into consciousness—not at all the end desired by the value clarification process.

When an intrusive view or act violates an individual's private beliefs, the power of their cognitive function appears clearly in the chaos. Cognitive means—compartmentalization, changing one conflicting value, or redefining a belief or value—are sought by the individual to accommodate the painful discrepancy and resolve the imbalance. Early socialization or a later process may provide the violating discrepancy. Lipset (1959c), for example, points out how membership in democratic groups may override a predisposition to authoritarianism. Under liberal social pressures to act tolerant, confirmed bigots have been known to change their views as well as their behavior. Northerners moving to the South have become racial bigots, just as democrats living under Hitler's fascist regime were subject to cultural influences toward authoritarian behavior. As long ago as the seventeenth century, the philosopher-mathematician Pascal demonstrated how well he understood the integrating power of dissonance, just as William James (1890, p. 321) did when he wrote, *"We need only in cold blood ACT as if the thing in question were real, and keep acting as if it were real, and it will infallibly end by growing into such a connection with our life that it will become real."* (Italics his.) Pascal exhorted his readers to follow the way that other Christian converts had taken. Faithless, they had found their faith by praying, "by acting as if they believed." It is possible that, even late in life, some values, like attitudes, can be taught by deeply and continuously creating the dissonance which forces cognitive work. Humans seem to have a preference for consistency over chaos and they will go far on a painful road to maintain it.[2]

Values, then, are one aspect of the cognitive mediation of behavior. They mediate between internalized cognitions about the world and responses to it. In the process, they become, on the one hand, so differentiated as to apply to a few, limited situations and, on the other, so extensive as to apply to very broad areas of life. The raw material of our thoughts—our sensory data—is also sorted out by our values. Over and over, investigators have shown how deeply embedded in the field organization of an individual his values are. As Robert Oppenheimer once wrote, "The price of perceiving anything at all is that not everything is perceived that can potentially be perceived." Perceptions are automatically received, rejected, or classified on the basis of values.[3]

Like objects, action is perceived and interpreted on the basis of values. The Maori whose culture values friendship and a stable

[2] For a fascinating and well-written account (as well as the theoretical background) of these cognitive processes at work in a modern religious group, see Festinger (1957). Serious criticism of the methodology of cognitive dissonance experiments is presented in Chapanis and Chapanis (1964).

[3] One vivid laboratory example is described in Bruner and Goodman (1947), already cited. See also Bruner and Postman (1948), and Postman, Bruner, and McGinnies (1948).

place within a group, for example, will not find the same meaning in a situation as an American whose culture stresses values of individualism and upward mobility (Miller and Hutt, 1949b; Ausubel, 1961). In his discussion of Jewish reaction to the Nazi terror, Bettelheim (1960) points out that Anne Frank's father, like other Jews who made the disastrous choice for business as usual, was defining his environment and actions by compelling and no longer relevant social values. Children who do not survive to use them do not need to have middle-class possessions. They do not need to know their high school lessons; they need to learn how to stay alive in an intensely hostile and threatening environment. The values which had served Frank in the past distorted his perceptions of a changed situation.

Values, then, as the basis of conscious or unconscious choice, direct our thoughts, as well as our perceptions, into certain channels. They label, as Alfred North Whitehead said, "matters of importance" as opposed to matters of mere fact, define, limit, and delineate them. By providing an orientation toward the phenomenal world, they determine, indeed, whether a thought will be thought, whether an experience will be perceived and the stimuli received, as well as how it will be perceived, that is, whether positively or negatively. Values, it might be said, are a goodly portion of the stuff that thought is made of. How one feels about something, how strongly, and in what order of importance among the saliencies of life are all inextricably interwoven with the cognitive use that is made of values in the individual's map of reality. In this sense, values are much more than how things ought to be. They are also how things actually are. They represent the real—a view of the world, as well as of closer, smaller, matters. The concept or construct of justice, for example, could not be valued without the belief that operational referents of justice had existed sometime and somewhere (or that life would be unbearable without this possibility). The present study of adolescent values shows this very clearly. By and large, these youngsters believe in the American ideology of equality, self-reliance, tolerance, justice, and freedom. Their belief is part of a meaningful cognitive structure. These values exist as actual concepts, which are real in spite of the fact that the students sampled agreed overwhelmingly that these values, at this time and in this country, are not practiced. They are real because concomitant with belief in them is belief that they have been applied in the past or may be in the future.

As part of the reception we afford data or facts, values have a fundamental nature which is not merely normative or judgmental, because normative assumptions as to what is right and proper in a certain situation are never truly separated from their existential premises, from what people believe to be true. That is why Florence Kluckhohn and Fred Strodtbeck (1961) put great emphasis on the value orientation of the individual and the importance it lends to the person's decision-making functions and those of his culture. "Value orientations are complex but definitely patterned (rank-ordered) principles, resulting from the transactional interplay of three analytically distinguishable elements of the evaluative process—the cognitive, the affective, and the directive elements—which give order and direction to the overflowing stream of human acts and thoughts as these relate to the solution of 'common human' problems" (p. 4).

Truth and falsity, that is, beliefs, are a part of values subject to empirical verification, but they are rarely self-consciously tested. Indeed, deeply held beliefs may deliberately never be tried.[4] Under most circumstances, the more strongly values are held, the more likely it is that any statements which express them will be considered to be objective fact and not beliefs or acts of faith. In his study of the political life of American teachers, Zeigler (1967) reports how difficult it was for teachers to discriminate belief from fact when their democratic values were embodied in the statement "The American form of government may not be perfect, but it is the best type of government yet devised by man." They were unable to understand that an evaluative judgment was being rendered and not a conclusion drawn from data.

Why do so many of us worry about the influx of information which television has brought, except that it is accompanied by atti-

---

[4] Hook (1940, pp. 8–9) gives the example of Hitler's famous pronouncement after the military reoccupation of the Rhineland: "I go my way with the assurance of a somnambulist—the way which Providence has sent me." The dictator's early successes were due to shrewd and efficient avoidance of putting this belief to the test.

tudinal and valuational components? Meaningful information is never pure; it is heavy with values. Around the world certain books, courses, and speakers are feared or rejected because of the intuition that facts are also attitudes or that an emotional response leads to belief, to the cognitive acceptance of input.[5] As Rokeach (1960) showed in his study of open- and closed-mindedness, people with closed belief systems avoid receiving facts (information) from appropriate authoritative sources. They rely on secondary and biased reports. A member of the John Birch Society who violently rejects the United Nations will carefully avoid learning about its structure and how it functions. In order to maintain his hatred, he refuses to admit the materials which he needs to adjust his thinking. Since he cannot accept the cognitive without also accepting the affective aspect of the facts, and since maintaining hate is genuinely a matter of maintaining mental distance, he has no choice but to keep contrary information out of his environment. "Ethnic prejudice and/or authoritarianism are significantly related to rigidity, concreteness, and narrowness of thinking and problem-solving, to premature closing of perception, and to distortion of memory" (Rokeach, 1966).

Values describe for us what we accept or reject as appropriate thoughts or behavior toward other people or objects. Within a belief system, they are integrated into the total configuration of the individual as cultural traits are integrated into what Franz Boas called the "genius" of a culture. They are dynamic within the total personality. Expressed, they serve to define for ourselves what we are, and, for others, what we would like ourselves and our world to be, as well as, at least in part, what we actually believe it to be. Although they are weighted by our society in a very real sense, we are still free to choose from a range of values made available to us and to entrust them to the synthesizing function of the Ego which Erik Erikson (1968) describes.

Within a group some values become common property. They are shared by almost all its members and, even in a self-analytical age, represent Ruth Benedict's (1934) "unconscious canons of

[5] Dogmatism may be formalized by institutions (such as the Catholic church with its Index of proscribed works) or societies (such as the Soviet Union or Spain, where censorship limits the reception of available information) or it may be the product of personality variables within the individual.

choice." Then, too, when new personal feelings are acquired, for example, pride, social beliefs may be available to rationalize the affect—"Black is beautiful." These beliefs serve to translate, integrate, assimilate, and accommodate the feelings into the cognitive schemata of the person. In this transaction, attitudes and values born of feeling build an intellectual structure and, in return, are supported by its scaffolding. To the extent that this scaffolding retains its social base, it defines the group and its members and provides the overlap in reality which is standardized, the corresponding sum of expectations that Anthony Wallace (1968) describes and Polanyi (1958, p. 240) refers to as a "network of mutual confidence." The search for values is part of man's personal search for meaning—the compelling necessity that Viktor Frankl (1963) describes so movingly. Values, shared, provide the common cognitive framework of reference for perception and preference. It is this nexus which is the foundation of communication and understanding among people. Culture-wide and often wider, values are affect embedded in cognition, feeling in belief. They direct the process of thinking because they are its content. In the end, it is values which give significance to meaning, significance which wells into belief, attitude, and action from ontological and epigenetic sources of human need. It is here that we define our inquiry into the nature of motivating needs.

~~~~~~

CHAPTER VII

What is a Democrat

~~~~~~

Sometimes it is said that man cannot be trusted with the government of himself. Can he, then, be trusted with the government of others?

Thomas Jefferson
First Inaugural Address

We have examined the inextricable intimacy with which belief and values, needs, feelings, and thought interact, and now it becomes our task to bound the area of that mutual dependence which is of interest to us here. What, we must ask, is the nature of the ideal person in whose social and political functioning this interaction could be defined as democratic? Two broad and only somewhat divergent currents flow in the ocean of literature describing the construct of a democrat. The first of these is the capacity for trust, trust in the sense in which Erikson uses the word, originating deep in the intimacies of earliest familial life. The ability to trust oneself and providers, life and man, it is an underlying confident reliance which contains in it belief in the goodness of one's strivings and enduring faith in the kindness of the powers of the universe. The second, and derivative, current is participation, an orientation and commitment to personal action whose reasons and motivations are referred to, and shared by, others. Underlying this affirmation by deed are internally compelling values dependent on basic trust, the faith which makes action itself possible and shared action desirable. Deeply embedded in democratic political ideology, this assumption of positive human nature implies that, because man is good, men (and therefore representatives in positions of responsibility) can be trusted to look after the welfare of others.

The democrat as an ideal type not only believes, he hopes. His is an optimistic strength which Erikson describes as the lasting outcome of a favorable ratio between basic trust and basic mistrust (1963, p. 274). Unlike Hobbes's *homo homini lupus*, his view of human nature is not of men instinctively set one against the other, of man as a wolf to his fellow man, nor is the association of men, uncontrolled by authority, defined as the war of every man against every man: *bellum omnium contra omnes*. A person who has "deep confidence in the benevolent potentialities of men," the democrat has developed predispositions which enable him to survive conflict, violence, and disappointment—a range of negative experiences—without abandoning that confidence (Lasswell, 1951, pp. 497–499). He has "character strength"—the capacity to withstand environmental pressure adverse to his values.

He has, too, an underlying personality structure which is

80

capable of friendship and "unalienated from humanity"—detached, yet able to sense the feelings and viewpoints of others, rather than passionately attracted in an "intense and all-embracing sentimental bond" (pp. 495–496). This detachment is the human movement from wholly emotional trust to confidence in rational analysis as "authority based on the [logical and moral] principles of the human mind" which can be imparted to others by deliberation. According to Barbu (1956, pp. 178–179), reason includes the ability to grasp unity in diversity, order in change, and the capacity to compromise and make adjustments, shifts in behavior and thought which would not be possible without confidence in mankind and a strong feeling of security, both individual and collective.

Belief in human nature, to the democrat, signals readiness for cooperation with one's equals and faith in the wide distribution of responsibility. In his thoughts and his actions, the democrat is a moderate who can weigh alternative goals against each other, rather than an uncompromising absolutist in pursuit of a single value. "Let us speak of the democratic character as multi-valued rather than single-valued, and as disposed to share rather than to hoard or to monopolize" (Lasswell, 1951). This sharing extends to the rights of others to their lives and, along with the capacity to trust, has implicit in it a deep distrust of the imposition of will and of men who, under the cloak of authority, would inhibit the liberty of others. It means that "little significance is attached to the exercise of power as a . . . value" (Lasswell, 1951, pp. 497–499).

Madison, in *The Federalist No. 51*, ascribed this essential mistrust of the extremes of power to a darker side of human nature. Man, he said, was "unfit to be trusted with unlimited power" and, therefore, governments are necessary to prevent those in power from becoming "ravenous beasts of prey" just as they are necessary to prevent the rights and liberties of individual citizens from being infringed by other citizens. It is "of great importance in a republic, not only to guard the society against the oppression of its rulers; but to guard one part of the society against the injustice of the other part,"[1] to save "the rights of individuals, or of the minority . . . from interested combinations of the majority."

---

[1] See Arthur Koestler's *Darkness at Noon* for a classic fictional account of the tyranny of the minority—in this case, the Communist Party.

Ideally, then, the democrat is characterized by the capacity for trust and by loyalty which is qualified: it cannot rest entirely on the instrumental value of the political system—its effectiveness—because dependency on performance creates an unstable system. Participation should be neither purely instrumental nor purely affective and, according to Almond and Verba (1963), a balanced mixture of both these types of citizen gratification characterizes successful democracies. On the one hand, without loyalty and trust in rulers, the willingness to turn power over to them would not be created, nor a supraparty solidarity built which is based on nonpartisan criteria. On the other hand, abandoning Hobbes for a more positive belief in human nature does not mean a naive distortion of trust beyond the perception of evil when it occurs or the failure to recognize the necessity for control.

Democracy demands "an intelligent distrust of . . . leadership, a skepticism stubborn but not blind, of all demands for the enlargement of power, and an emphasis upon critical method in every phase of social life" (Hook, 1950, p. 290). It is trust, however, which advocates the minimal use of violence, pressure, or power, and intelligent skepticism which demands that, if power must be resorted to, it should be managed not by the few but by the many with "equal controlling influence" and an "integration of purposes." Central to Mannheim's view of democratic society, this integrative process is a creative transmutation of hereditary and social differences, of drives and interests which emerge as a new purpose and not simply as compromise or cooperation (Mannheim, 1950).

Just as democratic personality expects substantial enrichment from the process of absorbing these differences, so the behavior of democrats is combinatory and evolutionary and its archetype an integrative one. In his study of the movement of Middle Eastern traditional society into the modern world, Daniel Lerner (1958, p. 75) identifies this assimilative habit as empathy—a "high capacity for rearranging the self-system on short notice." This "psychic mobility" is a predominantly personal style only in modern society which he defines as "distinctively industrial, urban, literate, and participant," the kind of society which supplies the basic needs of its members and makes democracy a functional possibility.

In the personal economy of the democrat, the orientation toward participation emerges as a function of trust, profound inner security, and freedom from the crippling anxiety which prevents the mobilization of democratic patterns of value and of practice. Inkeles (1961), in a systematic attempt to relate national, rather than individual, character to political systems, argues that there is "substantial and rather compelling evidence" of a direct and regular relationship between personality and political behavior. While it is highly unlikely that a single character type is associated only with a specific form of government, nevertheless, he suggests, certain personality types may be more responsive and susceptible to certain kinds of influence. Conversely, certain personality types may be able to withstand certain kinds of influence.[2] Although Henry Dicks (1950), in a wartime study of German prisoners of war, found that the norms and ideals of fascism had been so widely preached that nonauthoritarian personalities had accepted them as well, he, too, describes political ideology as only in part a function of intelligence, indoctrination, or automatic group conformity. The more it fits unconscious need systems, the greater cathexis is given it by the individual; thus the repressed aggression of the deprived and insecure person becomes exacerbated by a harsh cultural ego-ideal. The socialization process alone has not made him an authoritarian, but it has exaggerated an already active process and provided him with socially acceptable means of acting out his inner reality.[3]

Like Lasswell's definition of democracy in the individual as "the maintenance of an open as against a closed ego" (Barbu, 1956, p. 288) and Mannheim's view of integrative behavior, Inkeles' description is of a personality which is both open to new ideas and experiences and also tolerant of diversity and differences. Belief in the dignity of others, stress on personal autonomy, and absence of the need to either dominate or submit—that is, a certain distance from powerful authority—lie at the core of democratic character (Inkeles, 1961, pp. 193–196). "The citizen of a democ-

[2] See Lasswell's emphasis on "ego" or "character strength."

[3] An authoritarian may cling to those patterns of thought and behavior under a democratic government, although, like Avis Rent-a-Car, he will have to try harder.

racy should be accepting of others rather than alienated and harshly
rejecting; open to new experiences, to ideas and impulses rather
than excessively timid, fearful, or extremely conventional with regard to new ideas and ways of acting; able to be responsible with
constituted authority; tolerant of differences and of ambiguity,
rather than rigid and inflexible; able to recognize, control, and
channel his emotions, rather than immaturely projecting hostility
and other impulses on to others" (p. 198). These are the qualities
of which a democrat, as an ideal type, is made. How does this construct differ from its opposite, that of the authoritarian?

Extrinsic factors such as education and socioeconomic status
may account for the explicit content of individual political orientation—what party a man belongs to or the labels by which he identifies his political life—but the style or form that political expression
takes is apparently largely determined by personality. In Inkeles'
view (1961) the typical authoritarian personality differs greatly
from the democratic character. It is marked by dogmatism and
rigidity, intolerance of diversity, suspicion and distrust of others,
xenophobia and hatred of the outsider, idolization of the powerful
leader, and a sense of guilt and alienation.

Taking his material from the Berkeley studies of the pre-
fascistic individual (Adorno and others, 1950), M. Brewster Smith
(1967, pp. vi–vii), in a vivid description of deficient and etiolated
functioning, both psychic and social, concluded:

*Authoritarianism characterizes the basically weak and dependent
person who has sacrificed his capacity for genuine experience of
self and others so as to maintain a precarious sense of order and
safety that is psychologically necessary for him. . . . The authoritarian confronts with a facade of spurious strength a world in which
rigidly stereotyped categories are substituted for the affectionate and
individualized experience of which he is capable. Such a person is
estranged from inner values and lacks self-awareness. His judgments
are governed by a punitive conventional moralism, reflecting external standards towards which he remains insecure since he has failed
to make them really his own. His relations with others depend on
considerations of power, success, and adjustment, in which people
figure as means rather than as ends, and achievement is valued*

competitively rather than for its own sake. In his world, the good, the powerful, and the ingroup merge to stand in fundamental opposition to the immoral, the weak, the outgroup. For all that he seeks to align himself with the former, his underlying feelings of weakness and self-contempt commit him to a constant and embittered struggle to prove to himself and others that he really belongs to the strong and good, and that his ego-alien impulses, which he represses, belong to the weak and bad.

Conceptually, authoritarianism as it is described here is an intraindividual construct with decidedly social consequences and etiology. It is marked by developmental processes. Beliefs and systems of beliefs which influence and interact with social forces reflect the central dynamics of authoritarian functioning. Although the concept is pejorative in a liberal democracy, it is not necessarily so— some Nazis, for example, believed its manifestations to be the highest flowering of Socialist manhood. In present-day Latin America, the image of the strong leader as the chief rule-maker is a positive one with deep historical roots (Blanksten, 1960).[4]

Past and present, the authoritarian is an easily recognizable social type; writers have long described him as alternating between submissiveness and aggression, a fawning underling who is at the same time a tyrant to those under him. The authoritarian is the individual with the bicyclist personality: "Above he bows, below he kicks."

As Greenstein (1965b) points out, the basic construct of authoritarianism is old. What is new in the twentieth century is the specification of a constellation of psychological correlates of the tendency and the elaboration of a theory of psychological dynamics and genesis. Freud's psychoanalytical description of the anal character (typified by orderliness, parsimoniousness, and obstinacy) and

---

[4] "I have never been an enemy of monarchy, as far as general principles are concerned. On the contrary, I consider monarchies essential for the respectability and well-being of new nations. . . . The new states of America . . . need kings with the name of presidents" (Simón Bolívar, quoted in Blanksten, 1960, p. 488). Upon achieving independence, Mexico and Haiti adopted monarchical systems which later failed; the reign of a Brazilian monarch—Emperor Dom Pedro II (1831–1889)—is still regarded as Brazil's Golden Age.

his theories of obsessional neuroses and paranoia have influenced the growth of personality theory which places emphasis on early childhood experience. Whereas Freud's revolutionary insights underlay much of the development of the theory of authoritarian character, Fromm's discussion of its social genesis seems also to have been highly influential.

Fromm, in *Escape from Freedom* (1941) describes a person of sadomasochistic character as authoritarian because of his attitude toward power: "He admires authority and tends to submit to it, but at the same time he wants to be an authority himself and have others submit to him" (p. 186). There are, for him, two "sexes": the powerful ones and the powerless ones. In his hostility toward influences from above, he becomes a defiant rebel, never a true revolutionary, who seeks destruction instead of change and the compensation for his feelings of powerlessness through his battles with authority. "He has belief in authority as long as it is strong and commanding. His belief is rooted ultimately in his doubts and constitutes an attempt to compensate them. But he has no faith, if we mean by faith the secure confidence in the realization of what now exists only as a potentiality. Authoritarian philosophy is essentially relativistic and nihilistic, in spite of the fact that it often claims so violently to have conquered relativism and in spite of its show of activity. It is rooted in extreme desperation, in the complete lack of faith, and it leads to nihilism, to the denial of life" (p. 195).[5]

Can the authoritarian be identified by certain social characteristics? Membership in a particular group does not necessarily indicate an authoritarian disposition. The evidence which relates educational level to this orientation is ambiguous, partly because people of high educational levels tend to reject the extreme-sounding unsophisticated statements of measures of authoritarianism (such as the F-scale used in the Berkeley studies) at the same time that those high in authoritarianism tend to agree with the lofty aphorisms these statements present. In their review of studies corre-

---

[5] It is tempting to find a parallel with some modern American grass roots movements on and off campus. Without cause, plan, or project, some aspects of the "revolution" appear only as rebellion—painful screams against failure, doubt, and fear which are aimed at institutions showing cracks of vulnerability.

lating authoritarianism, child-rearing practices, and development of children's beliefs, John Kirscht and Ronald Dillehay (1967) suggest that individual differences in belief are best treated in ways which relate them to the social structure in which they occur.

Is the authoritarian a healthy, well-adjusted personality? Fromm described this type of personality as "normal" in certain societies, but since the *Authoritarian Personality* (Adorno and others, 1950) studies at Berkeley, considerable debate has been waged over the mental health of the authoritarian. Although maladjustment has been found to be associated with the tendency,[6] no conclusive empirical evidence exists which makes it possible to characterize all authoritarianism as pathological. Because the common criteria of mental health vary from group to group, traits considered abnormal in one society may be culturally supported in another or at another time. The Puritan divines, for example, would hardly fit the ideal pattern of American personality today. Benedict wrote of extreme forms of ego-gratification in our contemporary society, citing the unbridled egos of some law officers, business men, and paterfamilias: "They are not described in our manuals of psychiatry because they are supported by every tenet of our civilization" (1934, p. 277).

In spite of this cultural variation, however, according to Kirscht and Dillehay, most students of authoritarianism believe that, in the psychological sense, its presence is costly—a belief which is substantiated by the highly significant correlation found in the present study between dogmatism and anxiety. ($n = 412$; $r = .264$, $p < .001$.) Generally conceived of as the product of intrapsychic conflict, authoritarianism arises from defects in socialization. The outgrowth of an unsuccessful attempt to resolve problems of psychic need, it appears to be generally maladjustive for the individual.

What does the authoritarian believe? Ultimately, nothing. As Fromm has made clear, whatever he believes is tenuous and held conditionally. Politically, he may express his dogmatic closed-mindedness at either end of the spectrum by adhering to either extreme

[6] See, for example, Jensen (1957), a study of student subjects in which prejudice as measured by Gough's *Pr* scale was found to be related to MMPI clinical scales of maladjustment.

left or rightist views.[7] In *The Open and Closed Mind* (1960), Rokeach suggests that the specific views held are not important for defining the authoritarian. What is crucial is the way in which these beliefs are held. Intolerance, for example, is a key concept in authoritarianism, but the specific criteria for the rejection of others may vary greatly. (See Kirscht and Dillehay [1967, p. 92], "any learned social discrimination could function in the service of authoritarianism." In the present study, Rokeach's Dogmatism Scale and Gough's *To* Scale showed a high negative relationship [n = 412; r = −.641, p < .001].) Rokeach goes on to conclude, however, that under modern political conditions, the closed-minded person is most likely to be extremely conservative. At least in this country, membership in a particular party does not seem to be related to the degree of authoritarianism held, although change from Democratic to Republican identification seems to indicate a relationship between authoritarianism and the party chosen. (See, for example, Campbell, Converse, Miller and Stokes [1960].)

Beliefs are not necessarily correlated with political activity, however. Authoritarian persons may not be interested in politics or they may be bound by the potent restraints of social structure; membership in a group with a particular, salient ideology may override a personal predisposition and prevent its expression. In his review of theories of authoritarian and democratic character, Greenstein (1965b) points out that social authoritarianism does not necessarily mean the holding of fascist beliefs. Neither does it invariably lead to particular types of political activity. The forces by which social movements or institutions are initiated and maintained are complicated and numerous. Greenstein reiterates the point made above that many social and cognitive factors mediate between personality and the behavior of individuals. Nevertheless, on the whole the authoritarian as both rebel and conformist will adjust his behavior to the social situation, especially if those exerting pressure are powerful.

Paradoxically, M. Wagman (1955) found that change in the direction of democratic attitudes could be brought about by authoritarian suggestion if the subjects were authoritarian. Within

---

[7] See Shils (Christie and Jahoda, 1954) for a criticism of the original Berkeley F-scale studies as measuring right-wing manifestations only. For middle-of-the-road views see, for example, Barker (1963).

small groups, dogmatic subjects showed their dependence on leaders by their anxiety and compulsive behavior. In a further study by S. Zagona and L. Zurcher (1964), consensus reached by a dogmatic group disappeared after the instructor, presumably acting as an authority figure, challenged it.

What, then, is authoritarian character? Let us (following Greenstein) conclude by summarizing it in three aspects: its phenomenology (its observable, external manifestations), its genesis (the etiology of these occurrences), and its dynamics (or inner workings). The behavior of authoritarians is characterized by dominance of subordinates, deference toward superiors, sensitivity to power relationships, and adherence to whatever values are conventional in a particular setting. Unable to tolerate ambiguity or disorder or a chaotic universe, the authoritarian perceives the world in a highly structured fashion and seeks to control it by excessive use of stereotypes (Greenstein, 1965b, p. 87).

For many students of personality, authoritarianism as a syndrome develops primarily within the family or during other early interpersonal relationships. Insecurity, lack of a sense of community, lack of affection, and lack of opportunity to develop a social self adequate to provide esteem needs—the fundamental organismic needs described in Maslow's hierarchy (1954)—are the result of interpersonal failure at an early age, and they are the origin of the nondemocratic personality. Else Frenkel-Brunswik's studies of prejudice in children (Adorno and others, 1950), for example, showed that the homes of the unprejudiced children were characterized by warmer, closer, and more affectionate interpersonal relations. Prejudice was associated with "strictness, rigidity, punitiveness, and rejection vs. acceptance of the child" (pp. 482–483). Although causality cannot be assumed from the relationships found in the current study, findings here, too, show an association between social gratification of needs and development of democratic personality and values.

Others have described the genesis of authoritarianism as social in a different sense. D. Stewart and T. Hoult (1959), for example, have developed a social psychological theory which delineates authoritarianism as a concomitant of the degree of skill attained in mastering roles—taking them on and learning to play them appropriately. To the importance of family background and early childhood experiences are added certain situational and social structural factors which influence role behavior—education, age, restrictiveness of environment, and minority group membership. As we have said, Lipset (1959a, b, c) attributes authoritarianism, at least in part, to social structure, in particular, to placement on the socioeconomic hierarchy. In his analysis, studies in Germany, Japan, Great Britain, and the United States have borne out the fact that tolerance increases with moves up the social ladder. Citing the relative lack of economic and psychological security in lower-class family life, Lipset (1959c) goes on to say that low education, low participation in organizations, little reading, isolated occupations, economic insecurity, and authoritarian family patterns are all elements which contribute to a predisposition toward authoritarianism. "Noneconomic liberalism is not a simple matter of acquiring education and information; it is at least in part a basic attitude which is actively discouraged by the social situation of lower-status persons" (p. 103).

Two principal theories account for the dynamics of authoritarianism. One has been called "ego-defensive" and describes a strong but ambivalent disposition toward powerful authority figures. According to this theory, inadmissible hostility is repressed into blind acceptance which results in rechanneling toward the weak and powerless. Ego-defensive authoritarianism also creates in the individual a diffusely negative view of man as evil, the environment as treacherous, and surrender to feeling or impulse as dangerous. Fear leads to the stunting of cognitive capacities: the authoritarian is "unable to face the prospect of canvassing his own psyche" for fear of what introspection may yield, and therefore becomes highly dependent on external sources of guidance which are carefully selective (Greenstein, 1965b, p. 88).

Not only his view of himself but his view of the universe becomes warped by the intellectual liabilities associated with this personality type. Kirscht and Dillehay (1967) conclude that the most useful way to define the concept is probably in terms of cognitive style: closed-minded cognitive functioning characterized by both the inability to deal with novel material and the search for rapid closure which is heavily dependent on external authority for support of the belief system. At least in our culture, certain domains of belief serve as foci for this closed-minded style: areas of personal functioning such as sex and aggression, institutional areas such as politics, and religious outlets, especially those of fundamentalist sects and institutionalized authority. Ethnocentrism, constantly maintained barriers of social distance, and intolerance also provide behavioral channels for the authoritarian.

    A second theory of authoritarian dynamics relates to the correspondence of inner and outer reality. Sometimes "patterns of expression and behavior that have been characterized as authoritarian are based upon simple learning of the conceptions of reality prevalent in one's culture or subculture." These patterns "also may to some extent be accurate reflections of the actual conditions of adult life faced by some individuals, rather than having the labyrinthine roots in reaction formation suggested by the ego-defensive theory" (Greenstein, 1965b, p. 89). These authoritarian persons are neither psychopathic nor maladaptive. The world they inhabit is actually, in many respects, a jungle and the attitudes they have developed are realistic in view of its dangers.[8] In an insecure, uncontrollable, and treacherous world, survival itself may demand a particular adaptive pattern of acting which, in its behavioral manifestations, may resemble that of the psychically warped individual who imposes his own inner chaos on the external environment in which he lives.

    In a very real sense, the social behavior of the individual manifests what he is and, indeed, all that he can be within his psychic environment. If he is a democrat, given a cultural situation in which such behavior is elicited or even possible, his actions result, directed and motivated, from the frame of mind described by Barbu (1956, pp. 12–21): an ecology of reference whose crucial elements are maintained in flux by the deliberate interaction of individuals. To him, personal and communal life is in a state of permanent transformation and readjustment. Power and authority are unstable and relative and holding them "implies the concession made by one

---

    [8] See, for example, Miller and Riesman (1961) on working-class authoritarianism.

part to another part of the community," the sharing, always temporary and shifting, which is the "process of delegation."

Unlike the authoritarian who believes he is caught in the web of unchangeable fate, the democrat believes that he can, at least in some measure, control his universe. Change is neither inadvertent nor accidental; it is the result of the activities of persons. Through the very nature of individual differences, participation contains within it the nutrient of change, for society "grows from within, by the activities of its members, individuals and corporate bodies." Each "individual is a maker of his own society" (Barbu, 1956).[9] "The food of feeling," John Stuart Mill said, "is action. . . . Let a person have nothing to do for his country, and he will not care for it," and what the philosopher arrived at through reflection has been supported by the empiricists: citizen allegiance to the democratic rules of the game is positively related to political participation. Merely becoming involved in the workings of a political system tends to increase one's commitment to the nature of those workings (Cnudde and Neubauer, 1969, p. 521)'.

According to the norms of democratic ideology, the personality model to be found in the successful democracy is that of the rational activist. The successful democratic system requires that many citizens be involved, active in politics, and influential. Decision-making, especially of actual voting decisions, must be done on the basis of careful evaluation of evidence and weighing of alternatives. Activity, involvement, and rationality define the role of citizenship; emphasis is on aspects of participant behavior rather than

9 And may also be its destroyer. Bennis and Slater (1968, Chap. 1) relate the survival of social systems under conditions of chronic change to the adaptability of their members and deeply held democratic values which include: (1) full and free communication regardless of rank and power, (2) reliance on consensus rather than the more customary forms of coercion or compromise to manage conflict, (3) the idea that influence is based on technical competence and knowledge rather than on the vagaries of personal whims or prerogatives of power, (4) an atmosphere that permits and even encourages emotional expression as well as task-oriented acts, and (5) a basically human bias, one that accepts the inevitability of conflict between the organization and the individual but that is willing to cope with and mediate this conflict on rational grounds. According to these writers, democracy is inevitable—a functional necessity—if the changing social system is to survive (p. 4).

on passive, subject behavior on the part of the governed. Almond and Verba (1963), describing the development of democratic character in Great Britain and the United States—two relatively stable and successful democracies—found that citizens in the two countries differed somewhat from this ideal. Although the informed, active, involved citizen is more frequently found in successful than in unsuccessful democracies, citizens anywhere rarely live up to the ideological model and the process by which they arrive at voting decisions is "anything but a process of rational calculation" (p. 338).

Furthermore, they point out, being a citizen in a democracy implies the passive role of subject as well as the active role of citizen-participant. The passive orientation modifies the intensity of the individual's political activity down to a relatively unimportant part of his concerns.[10] Is this discrepancy between ideal and actuality an indication of malfunctioning in the political system? Is democracy a failure if people are not ideal active citizens? Almond and Verba suggest that these apparent contradictions—what Harry Eckstein has called "balanced disparities"—are necessary in a successful democracy. "On the one hand, a democratic government must govern; it must have power and leadership and make decisions. On the other hand, it must be responsible to its citizens" (Almond and Verba, 1963, p. 340). Through the drive toward opposing goals, a balance is developed between consensus and cleavage, affectivity (or emotional attachment), and affective neutrality which permits both power and responsiveness. "Thus the democratic citizen is called on to pursue contradictory goals; he must be active, yet passive; involved, yet not too involved; influential, yet deferential" (pp. 343–344). Activity and involvement are balanced by a measure of passivity and noninvolvement.

This balance between the active influential role and the pas-

---

[10] However, the citizen-participant sleeping too soundly underground may have serious impact when he awakens; voters who almost never voted brought Hitler to power. "The same underlying factors which predispose individuals toward support of extremist movements under certain conditions may result in total withdrawal from political activity and concern under other conditions. In 'normal' periods, apathy is most frequent among . . . [those who have suffered from hostility and lack of love since childhood], but they can be activated by a crisis, especially if it is accompanied by strong millennial appeals" (Lipset, 1959b, p. 116).

sive spectator role is maintained in two broad ways—by the distribution of persons within a society who devote themselves to one or the other of these roles and by the existence of inconsistencies within the attitudes of the individual which make it possible to adopt both these roles at the same time, so that he is affecting the course of policy and yet, at the same time, noninfluential to the extent that he makes it possible for political elites to make decisions independently.

In both Great Britain and the United States, Almond and Verba found substantial proportions of subjects who are believers in the "democratic myth," that is, they consider themselves able to influence local or national government, although this sense of efficacy is not matched by their actual political behavior as allegiant subjects. Neither is the amount of participation matched with the strength of the sense of obligation to participate.[11] Because the democrat is a believer in the rationality-activist myth, he is part of a reserve of citizenry power which can create political structures in time of need. "He is not the active citizen: he is the potentially active citizen" (p. 347)'.

The comparative infrequency of political participation, its relative lack of importance for the individual, and the objective weakness of the ordinary man allow governmental elites to act. The inactivity of the ordinary man and his inability to influence decisions help to provide the power that governmental elites need if they are to make decisions. But this maximizes only one of the contradictory goals of a democratic system. The power of the elites must be kept in check. The citizen's opposite role, as an active and influential enforcer of the responsiveness of elites, is maintained by his strong commitment to the norm of active citizenship, as well as by his perception that he can be an influential citizen. This may be in part a myth, for it

[11] Fifty-one per cent of American respondents reported that the ordinary man ought to take some active part in the affairs of his community; only about 10 per cent reported that they spend their spare time in this way. It is interesting to note that within these two successful democracies, the balance between active and passive citizen roles is differently weighted with Americans at the active-participant pole and Britons tending somewhat in the direction of the subject-deferential pole (Almond and Verba, 1963, pp. 360–361).

involves a set of norms of participation and perceptions of ability to influence that are not quite matched by actual political behavior. Yet the very fact that citizens hold to this myth—that they see themselves as influential and as obligated to take an active role— creates a potentiality of citizen influence and activity [p. 346].

To be an effective political force, the democratic myth that ordinary citizens ought to participate in government and that they are, in fact, influential cannot be pure myth. It must be an idealization of real behavioral patterns which is accepted by both the citizens and the elite decision-makers. Because the belief has some truth in it, it indicates real behavioral potential to which the elite respond. The anticipation of citizen reaction acts as a mechanism to control the operation of power. Responsive behavior is designed not only to cope with active demands but also to keep citizens from becoming active.

Enlarging on the conceptual framework of the democratic mind, Barbu suggests that democracy is not a specific idea or theory but rather a cultural climate, just as, years before, John Dewey had also expressed the affective and cognitive unity of the democratic personality in social terms.[12] In *Democracy and Education* (1916, p. 87), he said that democracy is more than a form of government. It is "primarily a mode of associated living, of conjoint communicated experience." Within this cultural climate or conjoint experience, a type of person is nurtured who holds specific views of human nature and the actions which are appropriate toward and among human beings. Personal experience and social forces interact to produce extremes of democratic or authoritarian personalities and all the varying possibilities between.

An amalgam of genes, situational factors, and cultural past

[12] See also Hook (1950, p. 294): "Democracy is an affirmation of certain attitudes and values which are more important than any particular set of institutions." These include values such as the belief in the intrinsic worth or dignity of each individual and a commitment to the resolution of value conflicts and the tentativeness and flexibility which permit change in policies and practices—dogmas as generalizations held lightly and without burdening reverence. Note once again the recurrent themes of participation and trust, the relationship between individual attitudes and values and the cultural ambient as a whole.

specific groups of which he has been a member, the individual thinks, feels, and acts in certain well-integrated ways, a social object whose consciousness of self is shaped by the "generalized other"— the social groups—of which he is a part (Mead, 1934). If he is a democrat, his view of man is positive but not naive; his belief in himself and others is strong but not aggrandized; his dependence in a contingent but not malevolent universe rests with himself and not with unknown or unknowable forces. Above all, his private preferences are consistent with the role requirements of the democratic social system. "He *wants* to behave in the ways he should behave, if the functioning of the democratic system is to be successful" (Greenstein, 1965b, p. 94). Participant, trusting, and sharing, he refers "his own action to that of others, and . . . consider[s] the action of others to give point and direction to his own" (Dewey, 1916, p. 87). That, we believe, is the answer to the question with which this chapter began.

CHAPTER VIII

~~~~~~~~~~~~~~~~~~~~~~~~~~~~~~~~~~~~~~

Who is a Democrat

~~~~~~~~~~~~~~~~~~~~~~~~~~~~~~~~~~~~~~

It is personalities, not principles, that move the age.
Oscar Wilde
The Picture of Dorian Gray

Participant and trusting, the democrat is a person whose view of human nature is basically positive, who knows in the darkest recesses of his being that the forces of the universe are shaped by a generally rational and trustworthy humankind which refers its personal wants and goals to those of others. From studies and comment in such diverse fields as political science, philosophy, anthropology, sociology, and psychology, these characteristics of the democratic individual have been identified conceptually. But our concepts must have empirical relevance and our construct must have application in human terms. To isolate abstractly and theoretically is one matter; to define behaviorally is quite another. To translate our general definition into specific terms, it is necessary to crack its contents into five fundamental beliefs, each operationally defined as a range of scores on one or more of a series of scales: The first is belief in human nature as fundamentally good and trustworthy, as measured by the Rosenberg Faith-in-Human-Nature Scale. The second is belief in the ability of the individual to control his environment, his life, and his future, as measured by Rotter's Internality-Externality Scale. The third is belief in the individual as capable of choosing rationally for himself, rather than relying on the judgments of others, as measured by Hogan's Survey of Ethical Attitudes. The fourth is belief in the validity of the experiences and opinions of others—that is, acceptance and openness, as measured by Gough's Tolerance Scale and Rokeach's Dogmatism Scale. And the last is belief that the rights of other human beings are to be respected, as measured by Gough's Socialization Scale. Together, these beliefs constitute a view of human nature and the appropriateness of action toward human beings which approaches the theoretical view given above.

Our most important task was to see whether the subjects of our study do indeed hold these beliefs and whether the degree and strength of the beliefs are related in any consistent way to the level and type of psychological needs of the subjects. Our major hypotheses may be stated in simple terms: First, psychological deprivation is negatively related to democratic socialization. Second, psychological deprivation is positively related to cognitive closure. Elaborating, we set forth a number of more minor predictions to be tested

98

as well: First, direct expression of ideological values is not significantly related to type or degree of psychological deprivation. Second, direct expression of ideological values is not significantly related to democratic socialization. Third, race is significantly related both to psychological deprivation and to democratic socialization. Fourth, socioeconomic status is significantly related to both psychological deprivation and democratic socialization.

In this report, psychological or psychic health means the gratification of the basic needs hypothesized by Maslow, that is, the presence of no deficiency needs as they are operationalized here. At this stage, growth needs such as the drive toward self-actualization manifest themselves. Psychological or psychic deprivation refers to the presence of one or more ungratified basic needs of any type. Cognitive closure refers to the degree to which the belief system of the individual is closed to new stimuli, new experiences, new information, and the experiences of others are accepted as valid. It is defined operationally as scores on the Dogmatism Scale (Form E) developed by Rokeach. Democratic socialization is used here as the transmittal of democratic social norms from the culture to the individual. It is defined operationally as scores on the Faith-in-Human-Nature Scale, the Survey of Ethical Attitudes, the Tolerance and Dogmatism Scales, the Socialization Scale, and the Internality-Externality Scale. As we have said above, we find the foundations of political democracy in the underlying dimensions of its social infrastructure and the psychic manifestations which are the work of these dimensions.

Race and socioeconomic status (SES) are to be understood here, as in other psychological studies, as constructs which define groups whose members have experienced certain equivalent psychic realities.

Ideally, a study of deprivation and belief which is based on personality and environmental variables should use a variety of measuring techniques, including oral interviews and projective tests, as well as written questionnaires. Practically, it was impossible to adopt this multi-method approach and still draw a nonrandom sample large enough for the results to be meaningful heuristically. For this reason, the measures were limited to the use of a written self-report multiple-answer questionnaire (the Needs and Values Inventory) incorporating scales measuring democratic beliefs or values, an index of psychological deprivation (the IPD), another measure of psychic distress (the shortened Manifest Anxiety Scale), and a number of direct ideological questions with two projective questions to be answered narratively. (For a description of the measures see Appendix A. Intercorrelations of the measures of democratic values and the measures of psychic needs may be obtained by writing the author.)

Although this method of measurement may not be ideal, its usefulness may also be defended. Herbert McCloskey and John Schaar (1965), for example, believe that the written self-report measure is superior to the oral interview for some types of personality assessment. "It combines survey and clinical testing procedures in a way that can enhance both" (p. 764). Inkeles and Raymond Bauer (1961) used both oral interviews and written questionnaires to study forty-six Soviet subjects in the United States. From their experience, they concluded that the written self-report minimizes the tendency to slant answers in which the subjects' prestige or that of the interviewer may be involved.

An issue clouding the development of self-report measures has been that of validity: Can subjects who answer such inventories be expected to respond honestly? For forty years, investigators such as Maller (1930) and Olson (1936) have expressed doubt that this was a reasonable expectation if the subjects were asked to sign their names. More recently, however, evidence has appeared on the other side. When L. J. Perlin (1961) used a self-administered questionnaire in his study of hospital personnel and gave the respondents the option of anonymity, he found that 38 per cent of the return (86 per cent) was unsigned. In his analysis of responses, he found that anonymity made no apparent difference where judgments were required about an objective situation. This was true even when the questions presented a situation which might be assumed to represent a threat, for example, criticism of the administration of the hospital in which they were employed. (Interestingly, he did find certain personality traits to be characteristic of nonsigners: they were low scorers in self-esteem and faith in people.)

Objectivity in the canvassing of one's own attitudes and beliefs, however, may be difficult and the possibility of fakery should be considered. There are three aspects to faking phenomena: the attempt to "fake good" in which subjects attempt to present themselves in the most socially desirable way, the attempt to "fake bad" in which respondents exaggerate their bad qualities, whether consciously or unconsciously, and random, or "scrambled," responses which indicate disinterest, carelessness, or intent to deceive. The first two of these have been thoroughly discussed by Allen Edwards (1957) and P. E. Meehl and S. R. Hathaway (1946). The latter suggest that such fakery may be controlled principally in three ways: by obtaining internal contradictions through the repetition of items, by the inclusion of items which appear to be favorable yet "almost certainly could not be true," for example, "I never tell a lie under any conditions," with which the objectivity of the subject is tested, and by the empirical derivation of a "fake" scale by making use of item shifts between naive conditions of testing and a retest in which the subjects are instructed to fake.

In this study, students were not asked to sign their inventories, but were asked to mark the two halves in some identifying way. Random or scrambled fake responses were controlled by the inclusion of items from the Communality (Cm) Scale of the California Psychological Inventory. No inventories were discarded on the basis of Cm data from the first (Bayamo) sample. In subsequent samples, the scale was eliminated in order to fit the administration of the entire inventory into two class periods.

The sample of 412 subjects in this study is not random in any mathematical sense. As many educational research samples are, it was chosen through connection, acquaintance, and nonsystematic chance. It is composed of three subsamples which vary in size, location, social class, race, and some of the psychological dimensions being reported. Nevertheless, each of these segments has in common with the others certain unifying characteristics, both social and psychic: the subjects are all American, all in midadolescence, all in American public schools, and all attending social studies courses within those schools. The prediction was made (and supported by the data) that the full range of basic psychological needs would appear within each group and, on some level, be related to the presence of democratic values as operationalized here. This is an exploratory study whose data are largely of heuristic interest. On these grounds, summarizing the data for each subsample separately while discussing the findings for the total sample seems to be justified.

In the spring and fall of 1969, the Needs and Values Inventory was administered in the field to social studies classes in the three public high schools. On two days, over approximately an hour and a half, the subjects recorded their responses in separate booklets. The data were then coded and keypunched for scoring and statistical analysis at the University of California, Berkeley, Computer Center. Data analysis used the Pearson r product-moment correlation to determine an association between democratic values and psychological deprivation. Univariate analysis of variance (anova)' was used to show differences between single- and two-factor socioeconomic and racial group means and the f-ratio and level of significance reported. The significance of dichotomous need/no-need group means was measured with t-tests, and percentage tables reporting Chi-Square were analyzed to determine whether relationships exist within the sample between certain demographic characteristics and needs, between expressed value preferences based on American ideology and their enactment in specific measures of democratic belief, and between these preferences and levels of psychological deprivation.

Maslow theorizes that much of the time most human beings are motivated primarily by one need, although the level of motivation may vary briefly and situationally. This hypothesis was supported by data gathered using the Index of Psychological Deprivation (IPD). The range of scores on each subindex was recoded into need-no need categories formed according to the following criteria: physiological needs were defined as scores greater than 3; security needs as scores greater than 5; belongingness needs as scores greater than 5; esteem-for-others needs as scores greater than 3; and self-esteem needs as scores greater than 3. Psychological deprivation was defined as a score of one or more needs.

Almost 60 per cent of the subjects operate at the level of one of the lower deficiency needs or (beyond the stage of psychological deprivation) at the level of health when motivation by self-actualization growth needs becomes possible. An additional 25 per cent have no more than two basic needs. See Table 1 for complete data.

But perhaps more important than the scarcity of gratification within the psychic economy is the nature of satisfactions when they appear. As may be seen in Table 2, deprivation type is distributed unevenly throughout the sample. High percentages (32.5 per cent) of the needs—physiological and security—which are essential for survival in a sample heavily biased toward upper social

Table 1. Subjects' Needs
(in percentage[a])

Number of needs	Tramontane (n = 232)	Bayamo (n = 114)	Debouchement (n = 66)	Total sample (n = 412)
None	34.91	25.44	7.58	27.9
One	34.05	30.70	27.28	31.9
Two	21.54	24.54	36.39	24.8
Three	5.60	15.80	18.20	10.8
Four	0.43	1.76	9.10	2.2
Five	0.00	0.00	1.52	0.2

[a] Because of rounding, columns do not add to 100 in tables.

and economic rank support Maslow's assertion that psychological deprivation due to lack of gratification for needs, although exacerbated by objectively harsh socioeconomic conditions, is by no means confined to individuals of low socioeconomic status.

In Maslow's theoretical description, individuals will tend to be motivated by the need for recognition or belonging only after lower, prepotent needs for physiological satisfactions and security have been at least partially gratified. Hungry, a person does not seek love. Afraid, a person does not customarily find in affection and community the stuff with which to combat a terrifying and unpredictable world. In a life prolonged on the ragged edge of survival the need for esteem rarely emerges as a motivating force.

Table 2.   TYPE OF NEEDS
(in percentage)

Needs	Tramontane (n = 232)	Bayamo (n = 114)	Debouchement (n = 66)	Total sample (n = 412)
Physiological	1.82	9.65	27.28	8.0
Security	16.37	27.19	48.49	24.5
Belongingness	45.69	48.23	45.46	46.4
Esteem from others	20.69	34.21	68.18	32.0
Self-esteem	13.37	18.42	9.10	14.1

Almost half (46.4 per cent) of our sample shows evidence of belongingness needs. Although physiological and security needs are defined internally—as psychic reality—in this study, nevertheless, the high socioeconomic status of many of these subjects makes motivation on this high level of need both expected and plausible. Most of these families can satisfy needs for consistent food and shelter and outer personal safety, whether they do or not (although inner safety and the conviction that love, food, and shelter have been satisfactorily supplied may be another matter). A fifteen-year-old boy with belongingness needs wrote in answer to a question about how he would define a good life: "To have a fair amount of good friends. Live in a community where I feel comfortable. Feel good about people and not base my life on material objects, but enjoy the material possessions I do have."

According to Maslow, if needs have been adequately gratified in the past—in our society usually through the affectionate intimacies of nuclear family life—they should not emerge with great force later. The fact that they do, in this sample, seems predictable from the large body of literature suggesting that the adolescent shift from home to community through the peer group carries with it a sense of alienation and estrangement from collective reinforcements.[1]

[1] See especially Erikson (1968) on the adolescent identity crisis.

The high percentage of belongingness needs may, in short, be an artifact of the age of the sample. (Using the f-test, belongingness mean scores did not differ significantly across the three subsamples.) The tension generated in this adolescent shift showed up clearly in a high positive correlation ($r = .396$; $p < .001$) between anxiety as measured by Bendig's shortened version of the Taylor Manifest Anxiety Scale and the Belongingness index scores.

In the theoretical framework employed here, physiological and security needs have been closely linked. Beyond their gratification, on the next level of functioning, a qualitative change takes place from needs whose at least partial gratification is required for individual or group survival to needs which are social and personal in nature. Although organismically based, these belongingness and esteem needs derive much of their satisfaction and some of their origin from human interaction. Like the need for belongingness—inclusive membership in a group with whom one shares goals, beliefs, and customs—the need for esteem from others can only be satisfied by other people. The social self, or "looking-glass self," that Cooley (1902) defined is linked closely to the atttainment of self-respect and self-esteem—a sense of worthiness in the eyes of others.

Here are the pathetic words of a fifteen-year-old girl who is lacking in self-esteem: "There is no friend that I am really close to and that understands me, and I am not the type of person I would like to be." Beyond the need to know that one is respected by others, and dependent on it, lies the deeper region of respect for oneself and one's own capabilities. Acceptance and recognition from others appear to be necessary preliminaries to valuing one's own self and to actualizing individual potentialities in a psychically healthy way. (It was among the West Indian fishermen with self-esteem needs, and not among the canecutters with lower needs that Aronoff [1967] found traces of the need for self-actualization.)

In operationalizing the hierarchy of needs, each item of the IPD was judged for its construct validity and retained or discarded on that basis. Further confirmation that the surviving items are indeed tapping levels of psychic distress is seen in Table 3. In every case, the mean anxiety scores of those who were characterized by a psychic need differed significantly ($p < .01$ for all needs, except security: $p < .05$) from those without these needs. (See Table 4.)

Table 3. Anxiety and Psychological Deprivation (r)

Need indices	Manifest anxiety
Physiological	.184***
Security	.163**
Belongingness	.396***
Esteem from others	.201***
Self-esteem	.289***
Combined psychological deprivation	.418***

$*$ p = .05　　　$**$ p < .01　　　$***$ p < .001

If Maslow is right and the fundamental needs he delineates do indeed form a series with decreasing strength and necessity, we would expect to find increasing gratification and mental health as the individual moves up the ladder of psychic satisfactions. From the level of physiological need to the level of the need for self-esteem, the mean scores of the psychically deprived should move in the direction of decreasing anxiety. This does not occur. Nor is the presence of a particular need associated only with that of contiguous needs. We conclude, therefore, that the group of basic needs here delimited is most appropriately described as a typology rather than a hierarchy—at least above the survival level.

Anxiety, wrote Kurt Goldstein (Piotrowski, 1959), is the result of an active encounter with opposing environmental forces, "a necessary though by no means sufficient condition of self-realization in health, and self-preservation in illness." In its beneficent form, it has an all-pervasive role as a dynamic factor driving toward certain goals. But when "the environment is dreaded as a whole because it is felt to be unreliable, mendacious, unappreciative, unfair, unjust, begrudging and merciless . . . a menace to . . . development and to . . . legitimate wishes and strivings" (Horney, 1939, p. 75) and when the torturings and tensions of anxiety are

Table 4. ANXIETY OF NEED–NO NEED GROUPS: T-TEST

Need type	Need			Manifest anxiety No need			p
	$\overline{X}$	s.d.	n	$\overline{X}$	s.d.	n	
Physiological	9.73	4.22	33	8.29	4.29	367	.10
Security	9.14	3.95	100	8.15	4.38	302	.05
Belongingness	9.78	4.06	187	7.13	4.04	214	.01
Esteem from others	9.87	4.20	128	7.71	4.17	274	.01
Self-esteem	10.98	3.67	56	7.98	4.24	348	.01
Combined esteem	10.63	4.52	83	7.81	4.04	319	.01
Combined psychological deprivation	9.38	4.11	284	5.92	3.61	114	.01

not fantasy but are well founded on the reality of the environment which produced this psychic state, it is no longer motivation toward vital striving and the joy that successful trial gives to the striver. Where such massive and debilitating anxiety occurs, the individual becomes a psychological cripple, a defective organism which, as Goldstein reminds us, by following a universal law of behavior regains order and organization only "through an appropriate constriction of its milieu" (Piotrowski, 1959). Through rigidity, repetition, and perseveration, anxiety is reduced. It is not surprising, then, to find this paralyzing reaction to stress associated with cognitive closure, lack of acceptance, belief that the world is ruled by fate rather than consciously or rationally controlled, and a distrusting disbelief in the rights of others (see Table 5).

Table 5.   Anxiety and Democratic Values (r)

Value scales[a]	Manifest anxiety
Faith-in-human-nature	−.188***
I-E	.245***
SEA	−.010
Dogmatism	.264***
To	−.445***
So	−.277***

[a] I-E = Internality-Externality Scale; SEA = Survey of Ethical Attitudes; To = Tolerance; So = Socialization.
* p < .05; ** p < .01; *** p < .001.

Age, language spoken at home, head of the household, number of siblings, and residential mobility were not significantly related to level of need as measured by the IPD. As may be seen in Table 6 (collapsed for clarity), sex was associated with one level of need, but only for the Tramontane sample. Regardless of other social characteristics, women in our society, at least until recently, appear to have been somewhat more uniformly socialized into a generalized

Table 6. SEX AND ESTEEM-FROM-OTHERS[a]

Sex		No esteem-from-others need	Esteem-from-others need
Male	n	92	31
	%	39.7	13.3
Female	n	90	17
	%	38.8	7.3

[a] $df = 7$; $X_2 = 14.666$; $p < .02$.

role of sex-specific behavior than are males. These young people are already playing out well-differentiated sex roles and apparently this is being done with a minimum of distress and rejection. Where expectations of secondary rank meet reality, the need for status to be granted may be muted. If the individual expects himself to be rejected and believes he should be, he is not likely to feel deprived.

The economically insecure inhabit an objective world with precariously few guarantees for survival needs, and on these grounds alone, without the suspicions and depreciating regard of their status-conscious fellows, we would expect to find greater psychic deprivation than among those receiving a larger share of distributed economic and social values.[2] Anxiety, as measured by the shortened version of the Taylor Manifest Anxiety Scale, was found to be related to socioeconomic class at the .089 level; see Table 7, Appendix D. (In this study, the term *socioeconomic class* refers to occupational role. High social class here has nothing to do with inherited wealth, private school education, or measured, shared norms per se. Its importance lies in the implication of capacity to provide need gratifications of an equivalent nature to the members of a particular group.) When race is controlled, differences in anxiety remain

[2] See Hollingshead and Redlich (1958) for a comprehensive community study which relates social class to the genesis and treatment of mental illness.

among blacks (low SES $\overline{X}$ = 9.23; high SES $\overline{X}$ = 6.12), although
not among nonblack subjects (low SES $\overline{X}$ = 8.83; high SES
$\overline{X}$ = 8.16). For blacks, a crucial variable intervening between experience and anxiety appears to be position on the socioeconomic
ladder. Controlling socioeconomic status, significant differences disappear between racial groups. (See Appendix D, Tables 1 and 2,
for data.)

Using as a gross measure the mean scores of the combined
IPD, we find in Table 7 a steady decrease in psychological depriva-

Table 7. SES AND PSYCHOLOGICAL DEPRIVATION

| SES | Psychological deprivation | | |
	$\overline{X}$	s.d.	n
Low	19.22	3.22	81
Middle	17.81	4.35	16
High	16.20	3.86	281

tion from low to high social class. For each of the subindices of
psychological deprivation, the association between need level and
social class is less clearly marked. Lower means (and therefore less
need) are associated with higher socioeconomic status and the psychic support which may be the product of objectively easier environmental conditions. However, differences between groups are
most significant (p = < .015) at the basic level of need, the physiological, and at the level of esteem-from-others needs. In this sample,
low socioeconomic status is confounded with race, but when socioeconomic status is controlled, black and nonblack groups still differ
significantly on the survival needs, that is, on physiological and
security needs. (Using the f-test, physiological needs: low SES
p = .008; high SES p = .051. Security needs: low SES p = .065;
high SES p = .414.)

The need for acceptance by others and for their regard
which blacks manifest in this study is in sharp contrast to the needs

which nonblacks, whose expectations of acceptance begin higher, exhibit. When socioeconomic status is controlled, differences between nonblack and black groups remain ($p = .011$ at the low level)', a finding which suggests strongly the reality of the varying psychological conditions which these two groups confront. The need for self-esteem is the exception to the generalization that higher scores are associated with low socioeconomic class. In our sample, heavily biased toward blacks on the lower socioeconomic level, low status is associated with higher self-regard than is high status. In our discussion above of the genesis of high self-regard within the supportive confines of intimate groups, we attempted to account for the development of a sense of mastery and self-worth among the members of the protective southern black enclave at Debouchement. How clearly social dimensions other than socioeconomic status affect this psychic state is shown when socioeconomic status is controlled and differences ($p = .040$) remain between black and nonblack groups at the lower level.

Going up the ladder of socioeconomic status, faith in human nature increases ($p = .064$) and greater internality appears (ns). (See Table 6, Appendix C.) Belief in autonomy and a personal reference of authority are highly associated ($p = .005$) with socioeconomic status, as is tolerance ($p = .013$). Low dogmatism and high socialization, while increasing in the expected direction, are not significant. When nonblack and black groups are compared within each socioeconomic level, significant differences appear between low status groups on faith in human nature, locus of authority (with the black group strongly based in the contractual authority of man-made laws), dogmatism (nonblacks $\overline{X} = 138.67$; blacks $\overline{X} = 179.49$; $p = .025$), and tolerance (nonblacks $\overline{X} = 18.50$; blacks $\overline{X} = 11.97$; $p = .006$). Within middle socioeconomic status, the groups differed significantly only on faith in human nature ($p = .029$) and, in comparing blacks and nonblacks of high status, significant differences were approached only in closed-mindedness ($p = .064$) with blacks more dogmatic than nonblacks ($\overline{X} = 155.50$; $\overline{X} = 126.95$).

Is socioeconomic status significantly related to psychological deprivation? When status is considered together with race, differences appear significant only with physiological and esteem-from-others needs at the lower socioeconomic level, although approaching significance with security needs and with physiological needs at the higher socioeconomic level. See Table 8 for data.

Socioeconomic status was significantly related to democratic values (faith in people and man-made contracts as a basis for choice of action, dogmatism, and tolerance at the lower level; faith in people at the middle level; and dogmatism approaching significance at the higher level) when race and socioeconomic status were considered together. See Table 9 for data. The reader is encouraged to take the sociological data presented here with the spice of scepticism and a grain of salt. Not only was the total sample biased heavily toward high socioeconomic status, but status was confounded with race and location since most subjects of low socioeconomic status were black and from the South and most subjects of high socioeconomic status were nonblack and from the West. In considering the relationship between race and status, psychic needs and democratic values, the number of subjects in each cell varied greatly and in several cases did not exceed six (see Tables 2 and 3 in Appendix C). I believe, however, that the data reported here generally support evidence gathered by others which indicates a strong relationship between socioeconomic status and needs, especially at the lower end of Maslow's hierarchy. (See, for example, Knutson [1968] and Aronoff [1968, 1967].)

Within the three subsamples at three locations there is a well-defined sociological continuum which corresponds almost isomorphically with a psychic one. At one pole lies the predominantly white, upper-middle-class, college-bound student body of traditional Tramontane; at the other lies the black, lower-class ethnic enclave of Debouchement, surrounded by a wall of rejection which as much shapes as contains it. In between these extremes are the students at Bayamo, in a state of change, whose transitions have brought together races, social classes, educational levels, the conserving and the innovating. The extent to which the sociological context of each subsample's situation affects the psychic disposition of its members is implied clearly in the continua of belief and deprivation mean scores of Table 10 which move evenly from the socially accepted and secure to those who are rejected and afraid. The students at Tramontane, for example, are more democratic than those at either

Table 8. RACE: NEEDS

(Two-factor nested design: nonblack-black groups)'

Needs	Low SES		Middle SES		High SES	
	f-ratio	p	f-ratio	p	f-ratio	p
Physiological	7.190	.008	.005	.941	3.840	.051
Security	3.430	.065	.567	.460	.669	.414
Belongingness	.200	.655	1.930	.166	.367	.545
Esteem from others	6.520	.011	.275	.600	1.660	.199
Self-esteem	4.250	.040	.327	.568	.270	.601
Manifest anxiety scale	.044	.833	.264	.607	1.670	.197

Table 9. RACE: VALUES

(Two-factor nested design: nonblack-black groups)

Values	Low SES		Middle SES		High SES	
	f-ratio	p	f-ratio	p	f-ratio	p
Faith-in-human-nature	7.640	.006	4.82	.029	.225	.636
I-E	.550	.458	.36	.548	1.040	.308
SEA	11.810	.001	.28	.594	.002	.969
Dogmatism	5.060	.025	.121	.728	3.450	.064
Tolerance	7.660	.006	.642	.423	2.020	.156
Socialization	.430	.511	.600	.439	2.130	.145

Table 10. MEANS AND STANDARD DEVIATIONS: PSYCHOLOGICAL NEEDS AND VALUES

	Tramontane (n = 232)		Bayamo (n = 114)		Debouchement (n = 66)		Total sample (n = 412)	
	X̄	s.d.	X̄	s.d.	X̄	s.d.	X̄	s.d.
Needs								
Physiological	1.73	.75	2.07	.98	2.83	.99	2.00	.95
Security	4.10	1.46	4.73	1.40	5.39	1.32	4.49	1.50
Belongingness	5.44	1.50	5.39	1.41	5.41	1.30	5.42	1.45
Esteem from others	2.33	1.39	2.80	1.37	3.91	1.03	2.72	1.44
Self-esteem	2.18	1.11	2.65	.90	1.82	1.14	2.25	1.10
Combined esteem	4.52	1.95	5.45	1.60	5.73	1.52	4.97	1.87
Combined needs	15.80	3.91	17.63	3.56	19.36	3.23	16.89	3.94
Manifest anxiety scale	8.48	4.44	7.68	4.36	9.20	3.35	8.38	4.29
Values								
Faith-in-human-nature	6.15	2.66	5.31	2.56	3.03	1.64	5.39	2.74
I-E	10.81	3.78	11.59	3.96	12.50	2.97	11.31	3.76
SEA	17.95	5.19	16.82	5.98	23.47	4.40	18.55	5.76
Dogmatism	143.43	19.35	146.83	24.80	180.11	17.02	150.87	24.78
Tolerance	21.07	4.54	18.13	5.10	11.91	3.98	18.75	5.67
Socialization	31.08	5.24	28.80	5.33	27.85	5.27	30.20	5.40

Bayamo or Debouchement. They have more faith in people, more tolerance, and less closed-mindedness. They are more likely to respect the rights of others and to have a sense of efficacy—to believe that they can control their environment and that what they do makes a difference.

The one exception to smooth parallel movement of social and psychic dimensions of value lies in the locus of authority as measured by the SEA. Whereas the Debouchement subjects believe most strongly that the authority for their actions comes from the agreements which men, as social animals, make, it is the Bayamo, and not the Tramontane, sample which centers the origins of decision in the autonomous, reasoning individual. It seems likely that this reverse may be explained by situational factors, for a high degree of autonomy[3] may be a cultural expectation in an environment of intensified political and social awareness. Activism has been found to be related to autonomous and principled judgments (Haan, Smith, and Block, 1969). It is surprising, in fact, that, given the dynamic and varied social milieu of Bayamo, the direction of scores toward natural law and autonomous principles was not stronger; its weakness may indicate the balancing effect of other personality variables on the cultural context.

In keeping with our prediction of a relationship between democratic values and psychological need, the young subjects at Tramontane also have less psychic deprivation than the members of the other subsamples: 34.91 per cent have no needs, as opposed to 25.44 per cent at Bayamo and 7.58 per cent at Debouchement. The importance of the perceptual field of the individual is shown in the higher (than Bayamo) percentage of Tramontane subjects with physiological needs. Among this well-to-do sample, high scores represent a sense of relative deprivation. Consider, for example, the discrepancy between actual occupational ranking of heads of household and perceived ranking of income level within the community which was mentioned in the introduction. Mean need scores descend along the sociological continuum for every type of deprivation (except belongingness in which the three adolescent groups do not dif-

---

[3] Or, at least, suspicion of, and nonconformance with, existing social contracts, whether norms or laws.

fer significantly, and self-esteem in which, for reasons which we have discussed above, the Debouchement group at the lower socio-economic pole is less deprived). We see here, then, the first indication as to how our primary question may be answered: Are the basic needs which men share related to the values which they hold?

CHAPTER IX

~~~~~~~~~~~~~~~~~~~~~~~~~~~~~~~~~~

Psychic Needs and Democratic Values

~~~~~~~~~~~~~~~~~~~~~~~~~~~~~~~~~~

Let us agree that man is never the proper means of any purposes other than those rooted—actually or potentially—in his own individuality. Man himself is the only end. As I understand this principle, it should mean that the maximization of every man's and woman's freedom—psychological, social, and potential— is the only proper first-priority aim for the joint human efforts that we call political.

Christian Bay
The Structure of Freedom

118

If basic deprivation is related to the values and beliefs which the individual has internalized in his psychic economy, we would expect to find significant differences in democratic value scores between the deprived and those whose needs have been gratified. To test our expectations, we sorted our subjects into dichotomous need and no need groups (the need group included all who showed at least one need), compared the means of the two groups, and tested the significance of their variance using the t-test. *For almost every subtype of need, mean scores for each democratic value differed significantly between those whose deficiencies had been gratified and those who were still motivated by lack of satisfaction* (Table 11). Nonsignificant differences (using a criterion of $p < .10$) were found on the I-E Scale and the SEA at the level of physiological needs, the SEA at the belongingness level, and Dogmatism within self-esteem—no self-esteem needs groups. (See Appendix D, Table 4 for complete tables.)

Within the distribution of scores found during this research, less faith in human nature and less externality, more locus of authority in social contracts, more closed-mindedness, more intolerance, and less regard for the rights of others are all associated with higher scores of psychological deprivation as measured by the combined IPD, as indicated in Table 10. Furthermore, when the continuum of scores for each democratic value is sorted into high and low categories,[1] we have unambiguous confirmation that it is quantity, rather than quality or type of deprivation, which affects the individual's receptivity to democratic beliefs. As shown in Table 12, *in the case of every value, the percentage of subjects who hold it declines as the number of total needs which motivate the individual increases.* The one exception to this pattern occurs in the relationships found in the SEA. The percentage of belief-holders decreases evenly as the number of needs rises except at the level of three and

[1] We remind the reader that scores of democratic values, like those of psychic deprivation, represent an incremental continuum which has been dichotomized somewhat arbitrarily. Like baldness and locating the loss of hair which separates the bald man from the one with hair, it is hardly possible to find the threshold of, say, tolerance which divides the accepting person neatly from the unaccepting one.

119

Table 11. Values and Combined Psychological Deprivation: T-Test

Value scales	Needs			No Needs			p
	$\overline{X}$	s.d.	n	$\overline{X}$	s.d.	n	
Faith-in-human-nature	4.90	2.68	268	6.59	2.51	110	.01
I-E	11.73	3.72	274	10.29	3.72	112	.01
SEA	19.09	5.77	286	17.21	5.53	112	.01
Dogmatism	156.73	24.20	264	136.80	20.49	109	.01
Tolerance	17.40	5.58	284	22.01	4.48	113	.01
Socialization	29.44	5.60	286	32.04	4.52	113	.01

Table 12. PSYCHOLOGICAL DEPRIVATION AND DEMOCRATIC VALUES[a]
(in percentage)

No. of needs	Faith-in-human-nature		
	Low	High	n
1	41.0	59.0	100
2	57.8	42.2	116
3	76.5	23.5	85
4	81.6	18.4	38
5	88.9	11.1	9
Total	60.9	39.1	348

$(df = 4; X_2 = 35.56; p < .001)$

No. of needs	I-E scale		
	Internality	Externality	n
1	58.8	41.2	102
2	56.9	43.1	116
3	44.7	55.3	85
4	39.0	61.0	41
5	11.1	88.9	9
Total	51.3	48.7	353

$(df = 4; X_2 = 13.54; p = < .01)$

[a] Criteria for dichotomizing values scores were as follows (high category given): Faith-in-Human-Nature ≥ 7 (belief in human nature as basically trustworthy); I-E Scale ≥ 12 (belief in fate, luck, uncontrollability); SEA ≥ 21 (belief in authority of social contracts, rather than of the individual); Dogmatism ≥ 154 (closed-mindedness and cognitive constriction); Tolerance ≥ 22 (belief in acceptance and open-mindedness); Socialization ≥ 34 (belief in the rights of others).

Table 12. PSYCHOLOGICAL DEPRIVATION AND
DEMOCRATIC VALUES* (cont.)
(in percentage)

No. of needs	SEA		
	Natural law	Positive law	n
1	68.3	31.7	101
2	65.9	34.1	123
3	47.7	52.3	88
4	59.5	40.5	42
5	33.3	66.7	9
Total	60.6	39.4	363

$$(df = 4; X_2 = 12.87; p = < .02)$$

No. of needs	Dogmatism		
	Low	High	n
1	75.3	24.7	97
2	63.7	36.3	113
3	44.3	55.7	79
4	19.5	80.5	41
5	0.0	100.0	9
Total	55.5	44.5	339

$$(df = 4; X_2 = 55.14; p = < .001)$$

* Criteria for dichotomizing values scores were as follows (high
category given): Faith-in-Human-Nature ≥ 7 (belief in human
nature as basically trustworthy); I-E Scale ≥ 12 (belief in
fate, luck, uncontrollability); SEA ≥ 21 (belief in authority
of social contracts, rather than of the individual); Dogmatism ≥ 154 (closed-mindedness and cognitive constriction); Tolerance ≥ 22 (belief in acceptance and open-mindedness); Socialization ≥ 34 (belief in the rights of others).

Table 12. PSYCHOLOGICAL DEPRIVATION AND
DEMOCRATIC VALUES[a] (cont.)
(in percentage)

No. of needs	Tolerance		
	Low	High	n
1	44.1	55.9	102
2	58.5	41.5	123
3	77.0	23.0	87
4	97.5	2.5	40
5	100.0	0.0	9
Total	64.3	35.7	361

$$(df = 4;\ X_2 = 50.19;\ p = < .001)$$

No. of needs	Socialization		
	Low	High	n
1	56.4	43.6	101
2	65.3	34.7	124
3	75.9	24.1	87
4	85.4	14.6	41
5	100.0	0.0	9
Total	68.5	31.5	362

$$(df = 4;\ X_2 = 19.12;\ p = < .001)$$

[a] Criteria for dichotomizing values scores were as follows (high category given): Faith-in-Human-Nature ≥ 7 (belief in human nature as basically trustworthy); I-E Scale ≥ 12 (belief in fate, luck, uncontrollability); SEA ≥ 21 (belief in authority of social contracts, rather than of the individual); Dogmatism ≥ 154 (closed-mindedness and cognitive constriction); Tolerance ≥ 22 (belief in acceptance and open-mindedness); Socialization ≥ 34 (belief in the rights of others).

four needs. An increased emphasis on natural law—autonomy and decision-making rooted in the self—may be tentatively explained as a denial mechanism which asserts, against the evidence of experience, the outer independence of the seriously deprived individual who, building his own neurotic safety, rejects the shelter of the protective group and man-made contracts collectively formed.

Recurrent through the literature of democratic political philosophy is the theme of trust and confidence. He who does not believe that human beings are fundamentally trustworthy is not likely to believe that the majority can rule either their private or their public lives by themselves. He is likely to think that guidance and control must come from some unquestionable authoritative source, institutionally based and historically removed from the decision-making powers of living men, which will keep the weak and the bad in line. Repression of personal freedom and civil liberties may seem justified on the grounds that people cannot judge on their own and do not know what is good for them.

Disenchantment and social alienation are revealed in the negative correlation $(-.301; p < .001)$ found between generalized psychological deprivation and low belief in man, between the inner state of lack and the sense that man somehow is responsible for not being all that he should be. Somewhat more strongly $(-.330; p < .001)$, a sense of acceptance and worthiness in the eyes of others is related to the growth of belief that people in general may be trusted—a reciprocal interaction which supports earlier research reported above: the individual who believes himself worthy of respect is likely to find others so. A strong correlation $(p < .001)$ also appears at the level of self-esteem for Tramontane subjects, although it does not reach significance $(p < .05)$ for the combined sample.

Unlike the sense of esteem-from-others, which derives from outgroup acceptance, belongingness is gratified only by membership, by a sense of completion and integration within a community of shared meanings, values, and norms. Perhaps the lack of a significant relationship between this type of deprivation and belief in man's goodness may be best understood by recalling that membership and the sense of belonging need not be positively based on affection and the belief that the other members of the group are good or loving (although a certain measure of reliability may be demanded)'. Community is a shelter, a base, and a psychic home, but it may be one in which this quality is its sole positive attribute. *In every case, then, except belongingness and self-esteem needs, a highly significant ($p < .001$) relationship exists between psychological deprivation and belief in human nature as fundamentally good and trustworthy.* (See Appendix D, Table 5, for complete need-value correlations.) Significant ($p < .0001$) differences in belief in human nature occur between nonblack and black groups. Considering race and socioeconomic status together, at the highest level these differences disappear, indicating that the illusive cultural quality called race (as well as other variables) may have some effect on these value scores.

Trust, turned inward, provides the sense of power in oneself—confidence in capability and the capacity of one's actions to shape the environment. What people do and the amount and quality of their participation in social life and political activity are functions of the expectancy that their actions will have effect, that is, that a powerful source of control is internal. When the reinforcements which occur to the individual are perceived as a matter of chance or luck and not the result of his ability to control, he is little likely to try to adjust or regulate the evolution of change in the world around him. With such self-abandonment, he becomes fatalistic and superstitious. In the social world he is liable to acceptance of the status quo and the neglect of conscious choice as a force in the achievement of goals. In the political sphere he assumes the inevitability of outside control by the "they" who have power which cannot be challenged by either individuals or their combination. The forces which shape what happens to him and to other members of his political systems are external to his own will.

It is not surprising, then, to find *a positive correlation between the continuum of internality-externality (with its poles of efficacy and fatalism) and the continuum which describes the satisfaction of needs* ($r = .265$; $p < .001$). For each of the subneeds except self-esteem ($r = .113$; $p < .05$), the relationship is significant at the same level. The anxious and fearful, lacking in a sense of self-worth and community and, on the most basic level, lacking freedom from fear for survival itself, are not likely to believe that their own actions may help to mold a world which has proved so dangerous to them. Efficacy is not a value to the psychically deprived. (For this sample, feelings of efficacy are not related to socioeconomic status or to race [alone or controlled for socioeconomic status]. See Easton and Dennis [1969] and Hess and Torney [1967] for studies which find a relationship between this variable and both socioeconomic status and IQ.)

As tested here, the relationship between the value of principled autonomy and psychic health is by no means unambiguous. *When all the needs are considered together as a total score on the Index of Psychological Deprivation (IPD), we find correlation in the expected direction (r = .244; p < .001)*. The less needful an individual is, the more likely he is to believe in natural law and to accept himself and his fellow men (as independently functioning units) as a proper source of authority for decision-making. However, a highly significant negative relationship (r = −.169; p < .001) occurs between the need for self-esteem and the continuum of scores indicating the range of belief from natural to positive law. (This negative direction also occurs with belongingness needs, although the relationship does not reach significance.) High self-regard is associated with belief in positive law—belief that the authority for judgments rests in the laws and norms which men have developed collectively. This reversal may be explained by considering the specialized derivation of both self-acceptance and a sense of belonging from social groups. Accepted memberships and highly gratifying interactions within intimate, primary associations might be expected to root the individual's sense of authority to the groups which satisfy his needs, rather than to his own autonomous powers.

Physiological (p < .01), security (p < .001), and esteem-from-others needs (p < .001) are all positively related to belief in man-made contracts rather than the principled decisions of the individual. However, in support of our theoretical conjectures above, the latter need has the strongest relationship (r = .404) with the natural law-positive law continuum. Without acceptance by others and worthiness in their eyes, the individual cannot respect his own capacity for judgment or rely on his own powers. (The SEA was chosen to measure the locus of authority of the respondent; the I-E Scale, to measure the sense of efficacy or expectations of controllability. Since perception of the self as a source of power for decision-making is conceptually related to perception of the self as able to implement these decisions, we might expect these instruments to be somewhat correlated. They are not. The SEA is not related to the Socialization Scale, either.)

As a democratic value, we concede, it may be argued that either end of the spectrum measured by the SEA fits within the confines of political philosophy. Men unite with their fellows directly or through representatives to make the contracts which serve as laws and rules and, as long as opportunity to participate, however oblique, is open to the majority, we may call this process democratic. Yet the essence of participation is individual decision-making and action (although these qualities are tempered by group influences) and the belief that each man can decide by himself. Autonomy is grass roots equality. We believe, as we did when establishing our premises, that a belief in natural law is more consonant with democratic personality as a whole. This belief as measured here, however, is not clearly related to each of the types of need studied nor to anxiety ($r = -.010$; n.s.). (At the lowest socioeconomic level, significant ($p < .001$) differences remain between nonblack and black groups when socioeconomic status is controlled. See Appendix D, Table 3.)

Dogmatism, as the term is used by Rokeach (1960), refers to a total configuration of ideas and beliefs which are organized into a relatively closed system. It means a style of cognitive functioning, not the specific content which is manipulated in the thinking process. It "is not so much what you believe that counts, but how you believe" (p. 6). According to Rokeach, the personality of the individual—and the ideology represented within his psychic structure—consists of an organization of beliefs or expectancies with a definable and measurable structure. His cognitive activities are the processes and changes which take place within this already formed system of beliefs. When an individual operates within an extremely narrow field of experience and is unable to assimilate new stimuli and data within his belief system, when he is intolerant of ambiguity and tentativeness and seeks a fixed and authoritative answer to questions and problems, he may be unable to cope with the demands for adaptability, accommodation, and openness made by democratic political or social systems. Basic to democratic functioning is the ability to compromise, to adapt one's wishes and requirements to those of others equally valid.

In theory, inflexibility and closed-mindedness seem highly maladaptive traits under any social conditions, for, as Roger Brown (1965) points out, all societies, even fascist ones, need creative thinkers. We would expect to find these traits strongly related to mental health and degree and kind of psychic deprivation as measured by the IPD. Indeed, a strong relationship appears ($r = .538$; $p < .001$) between the continuum of open- and closed-mindedness and that of basic need. The need for esteem-from-others is most highly correlated with dogmatism ($r = .553$; $p < .001$), although the correlation holds at the same level of significance for the sub-needs as well, with varying degrees of strength.[2] Clearly, the individual without basic gratifications, without security or membership or status, who has been rejected by the "generalized other" which forms an important reference group for the growth of self-worth, may be seen as retreating and closing off a depriving world.

In earlier studies, high self-esteem has been associated with high dogmatism and with low. For our combined sample, the association between closed-mindedness and high self-esteem does not hold, although the correlation is in that direction. Responses from subjects at Tramontane indicate a relationship ($r = .234$; $p < .001$) between need for self-esteem, that is, lack of a sense of self-worth, and closed-mindedness. We infer from this reversal that the psychic defense elicited by this need is being managed in varying ways or, more simply, that some variance occurred in the respondents' perception of the testing instrument.

In its most passive form, tolerance implies nothing more

[2] Knutson (1968) also found a strong relationship between dogmatism and self-esteem needs. Dogmatism was highly related to number of needs (private communication, 1970):

Number of needs	Dogmatism		n
	Low	High	
1	48.1	51.9	189
2	26.5	73.6	68
3–4	6.2	93.8	16

$$(df = 20; \chi^2 = 96.51; p < .001)$$

than endurance or, perhaps, freedom from prejudice or judgmental rejection of others. As a democratic value, it includes openness and positive acceptance of man in the aggregate without reference to specific biological or cultural traits.[3] Consistent with our self-esteem dogmatism findings, tolerance here is not significantly related to self-esteem. With every other subneed, correlation with belief in tolerance was significant at the .001 level. Anxiety ($r = -.445$; $p < .001$) and combined IPD scores ($r = -.501$; $p < .001$) were correlated with those indicating this value. We may say, then, that the less deprived an individual is, the more likely he is to be accepting and nonjudgmental toward others; the less his needs have been gratified, the greater likelihood that he will not be tolerant.[4] Significant ($p < .013$) differences appeared in mean socioeconomic status scores and race scores ($p < .0003$). With socioeconomic status controlled, differences remained significant ($p < .006$) only at the lowest level.

Democratic theory, with its components of mutuality and equality, implies the existence of individual rights, both social and political, in the protection afforded to minorities. One man, or a small group, may not stand against his fellows, but if these others have internalized a view of man which grants him the privileges required by the self, his rights to survival, property, and order may stand without jeopardy. Gough (1968, 1960) found a sociological continuum ranking roles to correspond to the continuum of mutual expectancies or norms operationalized in scores on socialization as a personality variable. In the present research, socialization differences between racial groups, with no socioeconomic status controls, were significant at the .0003 level. However, with socioeconomic status controlled, differences between socialization scores for nonblack and black groups no longer reach significance; differences may not be attributable to race.

With both total scores of deprivation—as measured by the

[3] Tolerance as measured by Gough's scale is not the reverse coin of dogmatism or the same as faith-in-human-nature, although the scales have mutual components.

[4] Tolerance, as measured by Gough's scale, is highly related to Rosenberg's faith-in-human-nature scale ($r = .547$; $p < .001$).

IPD and by the MAS—and subscores on each of the types of need comprising the Index, significant negative correlations are found with socialization. The man who believes in the rights of others is likely to be an individual whose basic needs have been gratified; the more he lacks psychic health, the less he is likely to grant to others the freedom of personal respect. (Socialization, as measured by Gough's scale, is highly related to tolerance [$r = .523$; $p < .001$].)

The subjects were asked to rank six cultural values from traditional American ideology: justice under the law, tolerance for all, freedom to govern yourself without interference, equality for all, self-reliance, and equal freedom for everyone. In their reflection of the social characteristics of the school communities, the values chosen as most important personally are interesting in several ways. (See Table 13.) Among the upper-middle-class, mostly nonblack subjects who attend Tramontane, conservative expectations and beliefs are expressed through comparatively high valuation of justice, self-reliance, and tolerance. In no case did the majority of these students believe that basic democratic values were enacted within the school or the larger society and in only one case (justice) within the community. Equality was perceived as a culturally enacted value by fewer than 10 per cent. In an interesting confirmation of the cynicism apparent here, the self-transcendent definition of the good life did not appear in the projective protocols of these subjects. Socially sheltered, their values differ from those engendered in the changing political climate of Bayamo's mixed social classes, races, and social as well as political activism—an involvement expressed in the high degree of agreement on equality as the most important value. In the examination of protocol answers to the question "What do you think you need to have a really good life?" an interesting new category of values emerged in a few (3.63 per cent) Bayamo respondents: the definition of the good life as self-transcendent.

Members of a black, low socioeconomic enclave in the South, the students at Debouchement demonstrate dramatically their personal rejection of tolerance with its implication of coexistence and mutual acceptance—a rejection substantiated by comparatively high dogmatism and low tolerance scores.[5] Regardless of the private ca-

---

[5] We mean, of course, a comparison within this study. Rokeach

thexis of specific ideological values and rejection of others, the De-bouchement subjects were less cynical than either of the other groups in their perception of whether these values are enacted within the society as a whole. It should be noticed, however, that neither of the other groups reached the 50 per cent level. Among all subjects there is very little belief that these culturally taught values are en-acted.

Our hypotheses, however, involved more than the expression of conventional ideology or the degree of perceived enactment. We were interested also in determining whether, for this age level and these political and social values, an old truth still holds: between words and action, no relationship necessarily exists.[6] Furthermore, although we thought it unlikely, we wished to know whether a pre-dictive association might be found between the expressed values and total psychological deprivation or the particular stages of the need typology. To find the support we sought, expressed values were run against both the democratic value scores and the indices of psycho-logical deprivation and the results analyzed in percentage tables, using Chi-square as an indicator of association. The results followed the prediction: in no case was a relationship found between total psychic deprivation or needs of any type and expressed values, nor between these personal values and democratic beliefs as operation-alized by these scales. Interestingly, our findings supported an earlier empirical study of registered voters in college communities, in which agreement on abstract principles of democracy (including the belief that it is the best form of government, that the majority should rule, and that the rights of the minority should be protected) was unre-lated to agreement on these principles when expressed in situational terms. The investigators (Prothro and Grigg, 1969) concluded that

---

(1960, p. 90) found mean scores higher than this for one group at Michigan State University (182.5), among English college students (219.1), and the old and infirm in a Veterans Administration domiciliary (183.1).

	Dogmatism $\overline{X}$	Tolerance $\overline{X}$
Tramontane	143.43	21.07
Bayamo	146.83	18.13
Debouchement	180.11	11.91

[6] See Hartshorne and May (1930) for a classic study of character education which demonstrated this old saw empirically for ethical values.

Table 13. EXPRESSED AND ENACTED VALUES

(in percentages)'

	Most important personally			Perception of enacted values		
	Tramontane	Bayamo	Debouchement	Tramontane	Bayamo	Debouchement
Justice	11.6	6.36	6.1	41.8	40.00	53.0
Tolerance	12.1	3.64	00.0	18.1	12.73	19.7
Freedom	12.1	13.64	12.1	22.8	13.64	24.2
Equality	35.8	60.91	54.5	9.9	17.27	22.7
Self-reliance	15.1	7.27	7.6	42.7	25.45	50.0
Equal freedom	9.9		19.7	13.8		25.8

any political theory that implies consensus of specific principles is empirically invalid.

Let us return now to a consideration of our major hypotheses and the meaning of the data: First, psychological deprivation is negatively related to democratic socialization. Each of the democratic values studied has been found to be highly related (p < .001) to generalized psychic deprivation as measured by the IPD. With few exceptions, (belongingness and self-esteem needs for belief that man is trustworthy; belongingness need for belief in the capability of the individual to decide autonomously; and self-esteem for intolerance) each of the value measures which define democratic socialization are significantly (p < .05 or less) related to individual subindices of need types. Second, psychological deprivation is positively related to cognitive closure. Scores on our measure of closed-mindedness, the Dogmatism Scale, are highly related to generalized psychic deprivation (r = .538; p < .001) and to all subneed types, except self-esteem.

And what is the effect of our findings on the subhypotheses? The first was that direct expression of ideological values is not significantly related to type or degree of psychological deprivation. This prediction was supported by the findings: in no case was a relationship found between expressed values and quantity or quality of needs. The second was that direct expression of ideological values is not significantly related to democratic socialization. As operationalized here in value scales of personality variables, democratic socialization was found to be unrelated to expressed values. The third was that race is significantly related both to psychological deprivation and to democratic socialization. Considered alone, this variable is significantly related to deprivation on levels of physiological, security, esteem-from-others, and self-esteem needs, and not of belongingness needs. For this sample, it is highly related (p < .0001) to democratic values. However, in both cases, differences between nonblack and black groups generally disappeared when socioeconomic status was controlled. The fourth was that socioeconomic status is significantly related to psychological deprivation and democratic socialization. For this sample, socioeconomic status is significantly related to physiological needs and approaches significance for esteem-from-others needs and anxiety. Intolerance, belief in man-made rules as the authority for decisions, and low faith in the goodness of man are associated with low socioeconomic status.

We have returned full circle to the question with which we began this work: What are the factors which may predispose an individual to incorporate certain values into his value system? In our theoretical formulation, we answered, "his needs," asserting that existential belief systems, that is, values, are the product of biogenetic needs acted on by the social environment. If this is so, we reasoned, prediction of values should be possible from knowledge of need states; in the process of testing this prediction, we have empirically explored certain relationships between psychic variables and historical correlates of democratic belief. Although we have found these relationships to be highly suggestive, we have not studied directly the etiology of democratic socialization, its wellsprings and sources. Confirmation of causality must wait for further study.

We have, nonetheless, modified an index into a new instrument (the IPD) which has tentatively been shown to have some predictive power to describe potentially enacted values—values which cultural and situational factors may bring into play. If antecedent-consequent research supports the findings here presented, there will be widespread and serious implications for social education. If continuing, formal, institutional socialization, however reinforced, will not alone induce democratic values, we must find another answer, an answer which may lie in an environment which is deliberately planned, as an integral part of a curriculum commitment, to gratify the basic human needs of the child.

If the antecedents of democratic values are indeed the satisfaction of these needs, and a major objective of the school is democratic political socialization, the school must be prepared to contribute far more than it has in the past to the gratification of these needs. It might not be too much to say that it must feed the child when he is hungry, let him sleep if he is sleepless at home, offer him quiet if his world is riotous, in short, provide him at whatever cost with a secure center of gravity in a perilous world, offer him membership which is not contingent on his abandoning his self, and render automatically the respect and recognition of individuality and competence which form the basis of self-esteem.

CHAPTER X

Personality
and Society

Insofar as American education has tended to regard its chief business as that of conveying information and training skills, it has tended to store its values, so to speak, in the educational attic. The result is that values . . . are more often treated with a kind of sentimental deference . . . than critically and constantly reinterpreted as of importance to the whole theory and practice of education in a democratic culture.

Theodore Brameld
Cultural Foundations of Education

135

$\mathbb{E}$ducation is behavior. It is not ideas or feelings, not plans or theory but actions, the patterns and arrangements of behavior which occur between the already established institution and personal variables—those individual tendencies which make up the attitudes, values, beliefs, and behavior of persons. It includes, as Robert Gagné (1965) has clearly pointed out, the past and prior experience—what has been learned before—yet behavior is a function of the situation in which it occurs, the time and place, people, physical environment, even the ambience or ethos[1] and the management of this formal situation provides the social structure of institutions, including education. There are no learners and no teachers, no delinquents and no saints, no failures and no successes, except those which occur in time, place, and situation.

To the extent that a culture is unwilling to leave learning entirely to chance, the time and place and situation in which it occurs are controlled, although the extent and direction of that control may vary greatly over space and time. Seen in this perspective, asking teacher and administrator to become more innovative and autonomous, more accepting, and more supportive, is not relinquishing authority but merely shifting its location and emphasis. Education as a structured process remains essentially, as it has been, a management of experience based on decisions at various status levels about the qualitative and quantitative nature of that experience. That these fundamental decisions vary widely in the face of a substantial, and increasing, body of empirical evidence about the nature of learning seems to be another sad example of human nonutilization of available knowledge. At a time when the relationship between emotional and social stability and cognitive development is beginning to be well understood, scholars,[2] practitioners, and par-

[1] For a comprehensive exposition of this field theory of behavior, see Yinger (1965, 1963).

[2] See, for example, Ausubel (1969) who is particularly contradictory in stressing cognitive learning ("the primary and distinctive function of the school in our society is . . . to foster intellectual growth and the assimilation of knowledge" [p. 411]) and pointing out at the same time that the damage done to socially deprived children at an early age may be irreversible (pp. 190, 246).

136

ents alike still emphasize strongly the intellectual function of the schools. The social limitations of this behavior are readily observable—the dropout rate, the teen-age drug problem, young mothers pregnant from ignorance, the chronically unemployable, and acting-out in its more violent manifestations are all on the increase. When disregard of other responsibilities leads to the ultimate stunting of intellectual capacities, it must be considered a malfunctional shortcut. Education is situational and contemporary, yet it includes history and the effects of the past on the individual, the institution, and the society. We believe that the individual cannot be taught without considering his past environmental encounters and their effects on him.

If the primary goal of the school is teaching children to think, then the most economical method of attaining that goal should be through the satisfaction of demonstrably a priori requisites—psychic needs and mental health. But the setting of culture-wide goals in a complex society is by no means a simple matter and, once they are set, as we have seen, goals expressed as values are not always those enacted. Even when they are, they may be corrupted through the process of organizational goal-displacement which Robert Merton (1957) describes, for bureaucracy in any form effects certain changes on the personalities of its members which encourage tendencies to adhere rigidly to rules and regulations for their own sake. When this happens, past policy becomes the prevailing criterion for decision, and the original goals and purposes of the organization are distorted or disappear. Adherence to past policy itself becomes the functional goal of the organization; what were means become ends. (For a succinct statement of the problems of school organization as they impinge upon change and innovation, see Elton McNeil [1967].)

If the chief institutional goal of education has been the conveying of information and training in intellectual skills, that goal has been thoroughly displaced where the social structure of the schools has been maintained for its own sake. Definition of teachers as bullies of the intellect, authoritarian administrative hierarchies, lack of integration between the needs of the child and those of the culture and beyond, the rigidity which automatically inserts humans who have nothing more in common than age into a single timetable, emphasis on cognitive learning ripped from its proper context of values and feeling—all these contribute to the inward dislocation of educational goals. By defining their function in terms of the status quo, the schools have been restricting change on the basis of formal limitations which do not necessarily exist, limitations of institutional and cultural adaptability to present knowledge about the nature of learning.

The problem of self-imposed limitations which may not derive from reality affects the substantive curriculum as well, for those who believe that innate ability is the essential learning variable. For if biological factors are the ultima causa movens, education is quickly defined or made futile. As Freud said about therapy, what is determined by biology cannot be changed. It might be easier to despair and to educate by the rigid inevitabilities of genetic typing—if we knew what the types were and who belonged in them—but above all, education as an American institution has an obstinate and optimistic commitment to belief in corrigibility. Like De Tocqueville, we recognize "society as a body in a state of improvement, [and] humanity as a changing scene in which nothing is or ought to be permanent" (Inkeles, 1961, p. 197).

Fifth century China and the countries where Islam has flourished were committed to fatalism and the belief that foreknowledge and effort could prevent nothing that was destined. For hundreds of years, disease and early death went unperceived in Africa because it did not occur to anyone that life could be different. But in our active, dissatisfied society, disparities between ideal and actual tend to lead to change. We know that there are genetic boundaries, but also that their definition has changed over time. This is not to say with that prototypical environmentalist Ortega y Gasset, "Man has no nature, only history." It is between man's nature and his environment that history is born. Not everything can be changed, even by awareness and belief coupled with technical and scientific knowledge. However, it is under these conditions of expectancy that knowledge of shared problems, their causes, and efforts to cope with them tend to become public responsibility and a moral obligation. (They may also become private responsibility. See Rosenthal and Jacobson [1969] for a fascinating account of the effect of teacher expectancy on pupils in the classroom.)

To the extent that individuals within the public at large accept that responsibility, problems become manifest rather than remaining latent or suppressed, and with that manifestation comes the active attempt to find their solution. That, I believe, is what is happening now in many countries, including the United States, England, and Germany. I do not believe that the changes we are seeing would have been possible during the Great Depression of the thirties or the war years of the forties. In spite of the war in Southeast Asia, the bomb, racial conflict, crime in the streets, pollution, and revolution against the Establishment, unemployment has stayed below its 1950s peak and more Americans than ever before may take the gratification of their physiological needs for granted. Many of our children have grown up in an affluent society; more are better fed and, in some important, immediate ways, more secure, in spite of rapid social change, than most humans have been in the past and so they are freed to seek the satisfaction of higher needs. It seems to me that younger teachers and administrators who have known neither economic deprivation nor war are less afraid and less anxious than their older colleagues and less likely to carry internal threat into the external environment.

In the educational institution, as well as in the society at large, a different personality type seems to be emerging, one motivated by higher needs and the expectation that their gratification can be achieved. What we are witnessing, I believe, is a restructuring of vital socioeconomic institutions based in part on psychological determinants working directly on the cultural system. To explain this process and the results of its transactions, in turn, for observable personality variables, Joel Aronoff (n.d.) has postulated a scheme of "reciprocal exchange" between sociocultural and psychological organizations, in which historical sociocultural institutions, environmental determinants, and psychological determinants form a matrix from which personality variables and sociocultural institutions emerge. The latter, in turn, act upon each other to produce new forms.

Aronoff (n.d.) hypothesizes that both personality variables and sociocultural institutions are the final product of three factors: environment, past sociocultural institutions, and organismically based psychological needs.[3] The model is explained by suggesting that

specific environmental features create the possibilities and set the limits of cultural and personality development. The cultural institutions introduced to the setting adapt to its requirements to produce preliminary institutional forms. However, while this first arrangement will gratify the basic needs of the individual on some levels, it may deprive them on others. If the early social forms provide only limited degrees of gratification, they will leave deficiencies in other needs not yet provided for. As basic psychological needs must find some form of gratification, these deprived needs exert their influence on the general cultural system and restructure the initial institutional forms in such a fashion as to get as much gratification as is possible in that setting.

Reciprocal interchange is seen as the restructuring process in which the relationship between the three factors is altered into some variety of resolution which is observable both individually and institutionally.

For nine months in 1962, Aronoff studied villagers on the island of St. Kitts in the British West Indies. Two groups within the village were compared, fishermen and sugarcane cutters. Although the basic personalities and subcultures of these groups differed markedly, the results of the original study showed that the maintenance (economic, political, and social) systems and family organization in each group were strongly influenced by personality

[3] Earlier Whiting (1961) suggested that psychological predispositions may serve culture in an integrative function. In his linear model, maintenance systems are the basic customs surrounding the nourishment, sheltering, and protection of the members of a society—for example, the economic, political, and social organizations. Projective systems are systems of psychological defense, any feature (art, music, religion, ideology) "not immediately and practically involved in the satisfaction of basic biological needs." Emphasis is focused upon the cultural determinants of personality: the maintenance systems determine child-rearing practices, which, in turn, determine the personality of the child—an intervening hypothetical variable which is finally reflected in the projective systems. In contrast to Aronoff, Whiting does not consider organismically based psychological needs or the possibility that they may influence the cultural system directly.

variables, as measured by a sentence completion test based on Maslow's theory of personality and the hierarchy of needs. In 1966, Aronoff returned to St. Kitts to observe the psychosocial changes which had occurred in the interval, changes in which one of the proposed three critical determinants (the psychological one) had varied naturally and influenced the social system.

Following his model of social change as the outcome of reciprocal interchange, Aronoff suggests that a number of social variables such as better medical care and lower emigration rates contributed to the increased psychological security of the canecutters. The younger cutters were no longer a physiologically deprived and anxious lot operating on very basic levels of motivation. From an authoritarian work gang in 1962, the canecutters' group had shifted toward a democratic social structure, until by 1966 it had become an individually-oriented gang. Aronoff concludes that personality factors, as well as environmental determinants and historical sociocultural institutions, must be allowed causal status in the structuring of a social system.

We know of no systematic basis for comparing psychological variables either in students or in the managers of the American educational establishment over a period of drastic social change such as the one today. No panel study has been done, and we are left without the possibility of finding an empirical analogue to Aronoff's research. However, contemporary records show an increasingly complex technology, the growth of affluence, and the social changes which have accompanied them. We see the pattern of gratification and infer from private and public action the cultural and personal transactions which follow Aronoff's model: if the needs of the individual are met, both he as an individual and his society as a structural system will be changed.

Where, then, does the school, as an observable, contemporary sociocultural institution, stand in this anastomosing river of change? Product of the historical past, the physical and social environment, and the personalities which have acted upon it, it is set to task to bear witness first to a widespread public commitment to superordinate values which include those of human survival, the reduction of interpersonal hostility, and the development of individual powers, and second, to the use of the most recent available knowledge of methods of implementation of these values, including the effects of gratification upon needs and motivation.

A commitment such as this is a defining vehicle for goals, as well as an expression of belief. The supreme norm becomes Rollo Handy's (1969, p. 160) "greatest possible satisfaction of the needs of those involved in a given situation." In different situations, quite different needs may be prepotent, but "In principle, we can identify the group concerned, diagnose the needs involved, determine the most adequate way of satisfying these needs, ascertain the costs, etc., all by means of the normal processes of scientific inquiry." The problem, as Arnold Rogow (1969, p. 285) has written, is "how to make the world safe for democratic character development and unsafe for those authoritarian and destructive tendencies that threaten an end of the human experience. In short, the most urgent question . . . is the question of man's survival itself." No statement makes clearer the fundamental social mission of all the culture's institutions—survival—and the futility of stressing subordinate cognitive goals within the schools to the exclusion of others which are interdependent and superordinate. There is no entry to existence through that door, and it is pointless and dangerous to teach a child to open a door to nowhere.

Just as the cognitive, conative, and affective are interdependent in the personality, their behavioral counterparts must be integrated in our institutions. The inhibition of destructive, antisocial tendencies begins with a socialization process far more fundamental than the acquisition of cognitive skills or a body of substantive knowledge. It begins with transactional processes, the environmental encounters and interactions which build health, lessen vulnerability under stress, and provide the ability to cope with normal life crises so that the developing child may become what both he and a democratic culture most wish him to be—and what he must be if both are to survive.

CHAPTER XI

Structures of Intimacy

Truth is within ourselves; it takes no rise
From outward things, whate'er you may believe:
There is an inmost centre in us all,
Where truth abides in fulness; and around,
Perfect and true perception—which is truth;
A baffling and perverting carnal mesh
Which blinds it, and makes error: and, "to know":
Rather consists in opening out a way
Whence the imprison'd splendour may dart forth,
Than in effecting entry for the light
Supposed to be without.

Robert Browning
Paracelsus

143

The "light supposed to be without" gave way to "imprison'd splendour"; the metaphoric funnel by which knowledge was poured into pupils was replaced by the pump. Today such simplistic visions appear distorted. They fade before a more sophisticated conception which sees the child as the active agent of his own learning, practicing processual skills in the acquisition of substantive concepts. Truth is within ourselves, having arrived there by social means, and—given the poet's hyperbole—"perfect and true perception" which is rendered defective by debilitating life experiences. The developmental unfolding of maturity can no longer be taken for granted as a primary factor of school success, either. "A child's background for school functioning such as his maternal and familial environment; social, cultural and economic status; cognitive development; constitutional status; intellectual endowment; and developmental status can be considered predictors of school functioning" (Lambert, 1967, p. 433). His past, like his genetic inheritance and all that he has formally learned, comes in the door with a student at any age. Surely it seems as reasonable to continue the socialization process from where he is, as an individual, in terms of his particular pattern of need gratification as to do it in terms of his present stage of intellectual development.

But, by and large, schools are still group- not person-oriented, unlike institutions whose function is exclusively to deal with mental health.[1] Within their boundaries, even today, individuals tend not to be noticed unless they are deviants from the norm. At this time, then, the problem is less matching the individual child to the social situation which will meet his needs at the level which is most vital for him than it is the provision of a therapeutic social system acting both to prevent deficiencies and to heal them for all persons in the subsystems within its charge.

Society, as Fromm (1955) has written, must adjust itself to

---

[1] As we have shown, the conventional service roles of the two institutions overlap. The ability to cope with normal stress in life crises is perhaps one measure of institutional success in either case. For a case study which describes their functional linkage, see Glidewell and Stringer (1967). A viable, developmental interconnection was found in the focus on prevention of both academic failure and social-emotional breakdown.

man's needs and not vice versa, if man is to become truly productive and humane; the basic needs which each individual has are
superordinate values for him. All else falls heir to these. Within a
social structure which is designed for intimacy and the face-to-face
supportiveness of primary interaction, provision must be made for
relief from fear, for the gratification of lower needs which provides
healthy motivating values. Here, above all, except in the privacies
of the family, exists the necessity for the civilization-wide preservation of small group traits, of close interaction without threat.[2] Interpersonal relationships, as we have seen, condition the development
of high ego-strength which may be characterized in both affective
and cognitive ways: as a strong positive sense of self and as intellectual coping mechanisms and skills. The teacher truly stands *in
loco parentis* and classmates *in loco familiae*. Where widespread
liking occurs in a classroom, as in a home, warm emotional climates
are engendered; pupil involvement affects the self-perception of
position within the peer group as well as the utilization of ability
in academic learning (Lippitt, Fox, and Schmuck, 1967).

When teachers delegate responsibility and power to their
pupils and provide them with a high degree of emotional acceptance, the effect has been to "(a) stimulate more pupil-to-pupil interaction; (b) reduce interpersonal conflicts and anxieties; (c) increase mutual esteem, rapport, and self-esteem; (d) induce a wider
dispersion and flexibility of peer social power as manifested by a
greater tolerance for divergent opinions in the initial phases of decision-making and a greater convergence of opinion in the later
phases of decision-making; (e) increase moral responsibility, self-
initiated work, independence of opinion, and responsibility, in im-
plementing accepted assignments" (Glidewell and Stringer, 1966,
p. 232). Beyond the satisfaction of hunger and the need for physical
security, here success on other levels becomes as possible as it is indispensable—success in discovering that persons may, by their own
effort, influence the environment, success in recognizing that they
have status as members of various groups, as well as value, success

[2] See Mathews (1949, pp. 47–49) and Silberman (1970) for two
among many advocates of democratic interpersonal relations within the
schools, and Mannheim (1950, pp. 200–203) in our earlier reference to the
learning obstacles faced by status-ridden persons.

through experiences with faith which pay off in a reasonably trac-
table and beneficent environment.

Tolerance toward personal or group differences in a therapeutic community is not enough, if tolerance implies a distaste which
is being overcome. A genuine allowance for deviance must take into
consideration the wide variations in orientation which children
bring into their classrooms (Kluckhohn, 1967). It must welcome,
not merely admit, the contributions of the abnormal—the creative,
the foreign, the introvert, the extremes in intelligence—to the flux
and variation of human life. Consideration of the resources which
others contribute to the group, the needs of others, and the effects
of actions on others are all part of a supportive atmosphere. Important, too, is the ability to endure ambiguity in life situations and
an attitude which does not see uncertainty as stupidity.

Two dimensions of school adaptation are needed for the
enactment of a therapeutic community; one is attitudinal, the other,
structural. The first is necessary to affect basic orientations and beliefs which control the role perceptions of teachers, superintendents,
administrators, students, and members of the community—all who
are charged with the arrangement and management of education
and who are most closely affected by it. The second is necessary to
revise and reconstruct the organizational forms and procedures by
which the school community is joined. As we have seen, the two
dimensions overlap as, in a transactional circularity of personality
and culture, democratic structure depends on the democratic beliefs, attitudes, and values which underlie and support it.[3]

Certainly it is not possible to overlook the systemic circularity of democratic practices, once formalized, for the mental health
of both students and teachers. However, a substantial handicap to
the initial development of classroom structures of intimacy lies in
the presently existing attitudes which themselves bear the marks of
the need deficiencies a therapeutic community is designed to lessen.
These are characterized by generalized closed-mindedness, rejection
of differences, intolerance of ambiguity, an authoritarian orienta-

[3] The individual becomes what he is because of what he perceives
and perceives what he does because of what he is. "A hero is never a hero
to his valet; and that is not because the hero is not a hero, but because the
valet is a valet" (Hegel).

tion, and a definition of the teaching or administrative role which emphasizes resistance to change or innovation. Above, we discussed the close relationship between feeling and belief and the effect that changing one has upon shifts in the other. In a study of teacher-pupil relationships, O. J. Harvey and others (1968, 1966) examined the conceptual or belief systems of teachers and their influence on classroom environment and student behavior. Abstract, open belief systems were related to pupil behavior characterized by greater cooperativeness, involvement and activity in pursuit of relevant goals and by achievement at a higher level. Pupils of teachers with concrete belief systems were somewhat more likely to seek guidance and approval. Abstract systems were also related to less teacher authoritarianism and punitiveness in dealing with students—a finding which supports earlier studies connecting dogmatism and authoritarianism. The degree of teacher open-mindedness, then, may affect the school environment. What other immediate forces may be brought to bear on the intrapsychic state of the individuals directly involved in classroom teaching?

To answer that question we must first consider that attitudes, like beliefs, serve two important functions: one, the definition of the universe and of the self and, two, the definition of self to others. Some attitudes are rooted in existential beliefs or values which have their origins in early childhood and the gratification of basic needs and, as personality variables affecting a total orientation, may be difficult indeed to change in maturity (Maslow, 1954; Rokeach, 1960). Others, less fundamental, are maintained or created by shifts in cognitive structure which occur when new information is received and the definition of the universe must be modified. There are three principal cognitive models of attitude change which attempt to account for the way this modification takes place—congruity, balance, cognitive dissonance.

In C. E. Osgood's congruity model (1960), objects and sources of information are evaluated as good or bad. Conflicting attitudes may be held without incongruity only so long as they are not brought into relation to each other. If they are, pressure to regain congruence and internal consistency will bring about attitude change. For example, President Kennedy might be admired and decreased farm subsidies disliked, but if Kennedy were perceived to be in favor of decreased subsidies, the incongruity would force a shift in attitude toward either disliking Kennedy or liking subsidy decreases. How strongly attitudes are held determines which attitude will change and in what direction. The basic postulate of the balance model, developed by Fritz Heider (1958), is that if people seek balance or congruence between their beliefs and their feelings about objects, attitudes can be changed by modifying either one or the other. The disruption of structural consistency between affective and belief components of an attitude is a basic condition for the occurrence of attitude change, as persuasive communications—new information—from others will be accepted to the degree that they help to resolve these imbalances.

According to Leon Festinger's cognitive dissonance theory (1957), to be consonant, attitudinal components must imply each other. When they do not, a motivational tension, or dissonance, is generated. As in the congruity theory, the amount of dissonance is a function of the importance of a cognition and that of the one with which it is dissonant. Dissonance may be reduced by decreasing the importance of certain beliefs or attitudes or through change of certain of the relevant elements. All three theories are concerned with the pressure produced by persuasive communications which disrupt cognitive structure and create inconsistency. The change in attitude is seen in terms of a strain toward consistency and, in the theory of cognitive dissonance, the ability of the individual both to create dissonance through his behavior and to resolve it. They suggest the usefulness of clarification techniques in effecting short-range attitudinal change in both teachers and students—techniques which would help make inconsistencies self-evident and so develop the motivational tension and discomfort which is needed for change.

A public expression of belief can be a commitment, as well as a vehicle for self-expression or the definition of goals, since it is backed by the need for social rewards and approval. With his opinions on record, an individual is likely to feel that they cannot be altered if he is to appear consistent and honest to those with whom he interacts (Hovland and Mandell, 1952; Deutsch and Gerard, 1955). Beliefs, values, and attitudes are strengthened by placing them in the public eye. Conversely, we might add, change agents or groups interested in effecting change would do well to avoid forcing a recalcitrant subject into a defiant public expression of his views. As we have said above, continuing interaction with others produces the definition of self to oneself and others, a "social self" seen and judged by the actor himself as well as by those around him, who also assign him to categories loaded with evaluative components. These categories are a function of the roles available within the culture, of the perceptions of the actor, and of those with whom he interacts in various groups. In each case, however, social relationships form the foundation for attitudes which are attached to these classifications.

Because of overlapping memberships in various groups and the varying saliency of memberships as well as individual differences, individual teachers may perceive their professional roles differently. When role perceptions differ, role definitions and values may be ambiguous, and the actor may be made extremely uneasy about what expectations he should have for himself and what are held for him by others. Obscure boundaries between perceived professional commitments and the limits of autonomous behavior may cause considerable role insecurity. Ambiguity or closeness of roles, for example, ruler and ruled in a democracy or dispenser and receiver of knowledge in a democratic classroom, may be confusing and cause the immature, the needful, or the anxious to flee in psychic retreat to authoritarianism. Attitudes of acceptance and openness to change probably depend on the clear definition of expectations in a particular group, for roles well-defined in a specific situation come with reassuring built-in attitudes, group values, goals, and norms which are developed by practice and identification with some one figure who sees his own role and the teachers by this light. In a conflicting or ambiguous situation, such leaders are vitally important as models with whom to identify.

As Paul Lazarsfeld (1967) has pointed out, the starting point for most sociological analyses of school systems is to view them as organizations of goal-directed social systems composed of positions linked together by a division of labor and a system of authority. However, since individuals differ in intelligence, personality, and metabolism, as well as in the amount and type of learning they have acquired, both their perception of the roles which comprise these positions and the actual "fit" of the roles may vary greatly. What is a social mold for one person may be a strait jacket for another (Thomas and Biddle, 1966). The problem of person-role fit is likely to occur to everyone in some degree over the course of a lifetime in a complex modern culture, but it may be greatly exacerbated if the social definition of the role itself changes rapidly, as it is doing for the class of persons called "teacher." Today some teachers feel unhappily that the unitary role for which they trained has been subdivided into three others, those of therapist, politician, and entertainer.

Under conditions of extreme and accelerated change, malfitting is bound to occur, and this nonconformity to altered circumstances will cause conflicts which produce pressure and strain—the "felt difficulty in fulfilling role obligations" (Goode, 1960, p. 483). One result of strain may be "uncommonly discontinuous transitions" (Thomas and Biddle, 1966, p. 62), that is, the individual may be forced out of his role by high personal costs at the hands of others whose conceptions and actions conflict with his own. Since the purpose of innovation in the school system is to effect social change toward structures of intimacy, and not to eliminate the present players of the teacher role, counteraction which prolongs the transitional period from one definition to another may temporarily relieve some of these felt difficulties. On the other hand, the effects of massive change may be just insupportable enough to produce sufficient alteration of attitudes, beliefs, and behavior through the various processes of cognitive dissonance to permit the individual to adapt readily to new role expectations. Margaret Mead (1964) has suggested that change in preliterate or folk societies has been easier when, rapidly and comprehensively, it has affected many interlocking cultural traits, and it is possible that sudden, overall redefinition of role, and the attitudes attached to it, may facilitate acceptance of its modified form.

Albert Cohen (1966) has suggested a developmental theory of role learning with both cognitive and affective approaches. The cognitive basis is the acquisition of new knowledge and new experience; the affective, with three major thrusts, rests first on the positive joy which exists in the confirmation of some valued part of our identity, that is, the pleasure which is present in the acceptance of a new role. Second is the "propaganda," that is, the emotionally charged knowledge which is received from reference groups; and third is the reinforcement for learning which is provided by reference groups. Just as the role was initially learned, its modification may be internalized through the interplay of these forces. However, roles and the expectations attached to them cannot be treated as nonproblematic, since their rights and obligations are not necessarily matters on which there is consensus. Lack of agreement may serve as a lever for change, just as agreement may, and, whether agreement exists or does not, it is also possible that ignorance about what is expected may prevent change or cause it. This may be the result of failure in communication which keeps individuals or groups from knowing accurately what the attitudes of other members or groups within the social system may be.

Biddle and his associates (1966) refer to these shared inaccuracies as social phenomena that are the result of processes acting jointly on a number of individuals. Teachers in a school or a community may share certain inaccuracies of attributed role concepts. An important source of failure to change may exist in these distorted ideas of one another's norms. They may, for example, erroneously believe that teachers are expected to behave in certain ways and attempt to conform. They may mistakenly attribute norms for their roles as teachers to those—the community, the principal, the superintendent—who are in a position to judge their role performance and, although their own norms may differ in the direction of openness to change, shared inaccuracies may prevent these norms from manifesting themselves behaviorally.

Problems of shared inaccuracies are by no means limited to teachers. From research on the actual and ideal images of contemporary high school students, S. Goldman (1962) found that many adults perceived youth as a class with a monolithic stereotypic image. Teachers, parents, and students agreed reasonably well on the ideal image of the graduate, but varied greatly in their views of how closely reality approaches the ideal; teachers were most negative and students were least so in their view of the actual adolescent.

As Biddle and his associates have said, "Many persons [including teachers] may assume that the public continues to think of teachers in terms of the values of small-town America when they listen to the criticisms of the superpatriots and those interested in a 'classical' education." They go on to point out that teachers are particularly vulnerable to "inaccuracies due to their ambiguous position of giving personal service in a public institution and their inability to form strong professional organizations that would set and enforce standards for their profession" (p. 309). However these shared inaccuracies develop, these authors believe that they are maintained by two principal mechanisms—restriction of communication and restriction of performance observation, with a concomitant low level of discussion about performance standards.

Confusions about the norms or expectations of school officials are further compounded by mistaken (or accurate) beliefs about the views which these officials hold regarding the conservative norms of the community. The official representing the school to the public may publicly appear authoritarian and traditional at the same time that he is attempting to encourage his teachers toward open-mindedness and flexibility. When the social structure of the school organization is strongly hierarchical and the maintenance of staff authority depends on social distance between officials and the teaching faculty, communication may be complicated and shared inaccuracies may increase.[4] Thus, in an unfortunate paradox, teachers who are conscious of the public image may in fact share norms with school officials and yet be "burdened with satisfying a set of standards which they don't believe in and which are not shared by school officials" (Biddle and others, 1966, p. 309).

It seems likely, then, that since school leaders may underestimate the willingness of the public to change (and teachers may do the same for their superiors and supervisors), change in teacher attitudes may be facilitated by sampling opinion regarding expectations about the teaching role on a regular basis. Loosening the restrictions on performance observation, discussion, and communication on all levels, in short, faster and more accurate access to information about what is wanted, may also facilitate change if its principal impediments are inaccuracies in attributed role norms.[5]

> [4] Wheeler (1961) reports similar findings.
> [5] It should probably be added here that deception may have a real value for attitude change when the deceiver holds norms which are contrary to those of the position which he—for whatever reason—wishes the teachers

Furthermore, Biddle and his associates suggest that shared inaccuracies may be more likely with immature persons and with increased social distance between roles so that, for example, teacher understanding of community expectations may be more distorted than teacher understanding of the expectations of democratic supervisors or administrators with whom they associate constantly in their work. If that is the case, decreasing social distance between judges of performance and performers may increase accurate communication of mutual role expectations. Such a communication failure may also be repaired through the offices of an agent, such as a sociologist, external to the social system. In this case, players of particular roles may find their definitions of specific groups altering in the light of new and more accurate knowledge regarding what others expect. If teachers are informed about the role expectations of other social system members through some form of careful extramural assessment, their self-expectations may be altered too.

The basic assumption here is that perceptions, values, and attitudes are derived, as we have said, from interaction with other human beings. Just as housewives originally rejected such labor-saving products as prepared cake mixes and instant coffee, apparently out of fear that others would consider them lazy, teachers may be extremely reluctant to innovate where members of the community may find them rebellious, immodest, or socially radical if they do. Sociologists have found, in research on new farm practices, that the effectiveness of publicity, advertising, and personal communication (in this case the county agent) in persuading the farmer to adopt new improvements in farming methods is mediated by the farmer's position in the rural social system (Glock and Nicosia, 1967). Innovators are usually mavericks whose reference groups are outside the farm community and whose status in the community is not high. For this reason, their example is not immediately copied by most other farmers, nor is it likely to be until high-status farmers have observed the innovation in use, consulted professional opinion about it, and decided to adopt it. Since these high-status farmers function as opinion leaders for the majority, widespread adoption usually follows. In an educational parallel, it may be that innova-

to adopt. This deliberate deception may result in shared inaccuracies which facilitate change in the direction desired.

tions which depend on attitude change in teachers may occur after adoption of these practices by other teaching professionals of high status.

The adoption of new drugs by physicians has been found to follow generally the same pattern. Arthur Cohen (1964, p. 119), for example, cites "the pervasiveness of personal influence . . . and . . . direct contact with a doctor who has already used it" as the single most important factor in the widespread adoption of an innovation. Initial adoption of a new drug is tied to social integration within the medical community.[6] In fact, as an index of early innovation, social integration is a more important variable than age, medical school, patients' income, or readership of medical journals. The investigators hypothesize that, whereas change agents or other outsiders (professional magazines or the media) act as informational sources, social support within the group provides security against the risks of innovation and legitimizes it. It seems possible that attitude change and openness to innovation are also functions of the degree of social integration within the social system of the school, as measured by indices of friendship and discussion partnership. If this is true, then, conversely, increased social interaction in a group, through friendship or discussion or on another level should produce greater social confidence and willingness to innovate or to accept and implement changes which others have initiated.

Although medical influentials are likely to be readers of professional journals, to value them more than noninfluentials, to attend more out-of-town professional meetings, and to have contact with a greater diversity of medical institutions and societies, persuasive communications (stemming from the mass media and from authoritative communicators) are not by themselves a sufficient condition for producing attitude change in them. The effect of new, if authoritative, information is filtered through a nexus of mediating factors and influences such as individual predispositions, selective perception, selective exposure, interpersonal relations, group pressures, and personal influence. Again, drawing a parallel based on assumptions of some institutional equivalence between medicine and education, it may be that teachers whose attitudes are open and

[6] As defined by the frequency with which the innovators are named by colleagues as friends or discussion partners (Menzel and Katz, 1955).

democratic will be those whose reference groups extend beyond the immediate boundaries of the local educational social system to include regional, national, or even international systems. If this is so, it may then be hypothesized that deliberate extension of reference groups beyond the local educational system, through contact and other means of education, will be accompanied by increased openness on the part of the teacher.

The latter statement suggests the effects of one possible route for changing attitudes, that is, through modifying or extending group identification for the individual to include groups with attitudes in the desired direction. When expectations are made clear to them and positive values are attached to membership in a new group (for example, the group of those who are open to change or who approach the teaching of classes as a problem of individual learning), individual teachers may, in Merton's term, "anticipate their socialization" and adopt the norms and values of the new group concurrently with, if not actually prior to, its formation. This procedure is functional for both the initiate and the new group, as it admits him early to the embryo group and assists the genesis and consolidation of the group itself. Adoption of new norms means defection from old ones, weakening of solidarity among those who hold them, and loss of morale. Where the social situation is in a state of flux, those adhering to old values are likely to contrast their situation with that of the defectors and shape their self-appraisals accordingly. If they are in the majority, the changer may be considered an outcast and a renegade, and the solidarity of the group he has left may be deepened. When defectors become the majority, however, pressures increase for all remaining members to abandon their attitudes and norms and adopt new ones—a variation on the old theme "If you can't lick them, join them."

Induction into the second group depends on a breakdown of the patterns of socialization which were previously developed in the original group, the group which then places a value judgment ("bad") on this lack of conformity to its norms. Once an individual begins to change his exploratory lack of conformity, he may precipitate a further breakdown or deterioration of social relations with the members of his original group. As might be expected, this estrangement is experienced as repudiation by the members of the group and may well evoke a hostile response which still further alienates the individual who is shifting away from his former associates. Since his behavior is changing, he no longer receives the customary social rewards of group conformity—he is not conforming to their norms— and the accumulating detachment of the seceding member is the result. Extension of his newly learned behavior classifications to the actions of others tends to perpetuate in a self-sustaining way the norms and mores of the social group to which the recently socialized member now belongs. If this classification, or set of norms and the values attached to them, is extended specifically to former associates and past like-minded colleagues, the pressure may facilitate change on their part in the same direction in which the defector has gone (Merton, 1957).

From Merton's observations and those of other writers on intolerance—for example, Stember (1961)—we may deduce that using direct methods of education to increase openness and acceptance and to reduce intolerance in the classroom is a complex problem. Sociological evidence suggests that the effect of education may be strongest if the individual is separated from the previous group or subculture whose norms reinforced the prejudiced belief and is transferred to a group offering opportunity for contact with open-minded individuals. There is a strong possibility that an authoritarian personality, once developed, cannot be made to change except under conditions of persistent socialization and continuing reinforcement. However, change, once accomplished, may tend to persist if it is strengthened through consolidation, repetition, rediscovery, and application to one situation after another. As in other learning situations, opportunity for practice and the application of patience, time, and hard work are essential, as well as the opportunity to transfer learning, that is, to use it in a variety of new and different contexts. The avoidance of failure-producing or threatening, anxiety-producing encounters may also be critical. Freud wrote that there were two emotional responses to danger—anxiety, with a quality of diffuseness and uncertainty which paralyses the individual into helplessness, and fear, which is specific and direct and produces the ability to cope. For teachers, as well as students, anxiety- or failure-producing situations may act as deterrents to learning new attitudes.

We have discussed one possible route to changing attitudes—
extending the individual's group identification to include those with
attitudes in the desired direction. Another route, which James Coleman (1961), Muzafer and Carolyn Sherif (1964), and Kurt Lewin
(1952) have advocated, involves changing the attitudes of the original ingroup, or reference group, as a whole. Lewin, for example,
believed that social change is most effective when it is the result
of group decision, that is, decisions which are firmly locked into reference groups so that change in each person is supported by the
approval and advocacy of the group. Under these circumstances,
the individual acts as a member of the group and not solely on the
basis of his own preferences. *"The act of making a decision* [as a
member of the group] *and the degree of group consensus* perceived
by the individual, taken together, appear to account for the effectiveness of group decision in influencing action" (Cohen, 1964, pp.
103–104; italics his). Within a group, pressures of various kinds are
set up to conform to group norms, including newly adopted ones.

Two classic experiments illustrate the influence of the group
toward the conformity of its members. One (Sherif, 1935) utilized
the autokinetic effect to study both whether the group affected the
judgment of individual members and whether this influence carried
over into novel situations. The results showed that social norms
are the product of shared frames of reference which are built up
through interaction among individuals. When the individual faces
the world alone later, in an ambiguous situation, these common
norms, once established, are used as a standard for judging what
he perceives. In other words, if members of a group, in ambiguous
situations, together adopt a set of response ranges or norms, the
norms may be incorporated as individual predispositions and attitudes which may be applied in other situations. In the second experiment, Solomon Asch (1951) designed an experiment to test
some of the conditions under which individuals tend to resist or
yield to group pressures when they believe the group is wrong. The
fact that about 40 per cent of the subjects yielded to the group and
modified their judgments to conform with those of the majority
illustrates the power of these group influences. The degree to which
subjects retained their independence was a joint function of the

clarity of the stimulus, the unanimity and number of the opposition, and the personalities of the subjects.

Other factors may also affect the type and degree of influence which the group has upon its members. One of these consists of personality variables such as the level of needs hypothesized by Maslow. Another consists of the internality-externality component of personality hypothesized by Rotter. In Rotter's view, the externally-oriented individual believes that he has little control over his environment. It would be very difficult to persuade such a person to change his behavior or his attitudes on his own since he does not believe such control is possible. However, since he is expecting control from the outside, he will be less resistant to external suggestions or guidance than internally-oriented subjects who will resist external influence if they believe an attempt is being made to manipulate them.[7] Jerry Phares (1965), in a study of female subjects, found that significantly more of them changed their attitudes when the experimenters attempting to influence them were internally-oriented, as measured by Rotter's I-E Scale. His results suggest that attitude influence on teachers and other school personnel will be more effective if also attempted by individuals or groups who believe that they can effect change and control the environment.

Another factor which affects group influence is the kind of leadership which appears in the group. In a study done in the 1930s, Ronald Lippitt and Robert White (1952) looked for the effect of authoritarian, democratic, and laissez-faire leadership on arts and crafts work in four different children's clubs. Achievement and group satisfaction were the focal points. The laissez-faire group was lowest on both counts, although great differences were found among the groups. Authoritarian leadership consistently produced both aggression and scapegoating.

Furthermore, Lester Coch and John French (1952)', in a study of resistance to technological change in a factory, found that democratic participation in the orientation, retraining, and planning program greatly facilitated change. The group informed outright by the factory management that the change would take place failed

___

[7] When they perceive the advantage to themselves, internally-oriented people, too, will conform, willingly and consciously, without losing control of the situation.

to adjust. Its members fell behind in production, and personnel turnover as well as the number of grievances went up. Although these results were convincing, the investigators strengthened them through a follow-up study a few months later in which members of the maladjusted group were compelled to change jobs again. This time, they were informed of the change and the reasons for it and were also encouraged to design and plan the new jobs as well as the retraining. Successful adaptation to the second change ruled out personality factors as the basis of the previous failure to adjust.

Amitai Etzioni (1964, p. 38), summing up one view of organizational management, includes these experiments and the writing of Elton May and Kurt Lewin as part of the "human relations" approach. According to him, three postures emerge as particularly important to this managerial method: First, communication between the ranks, that is, explaining why action is taken; second, participation in decision-making; and third, democratic leadership which is "nonarbitrary and concerned with the problems of workers, not just those of work." Techniques which have so influenced industry may also be applicable to educational management and to building the therapeutic community. The opportunity for participation and effective communication, for recognition of the teacher as psychological and social rather than merely physical entity, may greatly facilitate attitudinal and behavioral change in the direction of openness and acceptance in the schools. Democratic leaders, it seems, are, in Etzioni's term, the "cultural engineers" who are necessary for initiating enduring change. Prolonged social change requires cooperation even if it is initially installed by force, and lasting cooperation cannot be elicited by authoritarian means.

In considering here a number of answers to the questions of how teacher perceptions and attitudes may be altered, we have concerned ourselves most directly with the problem of generalized closed-mindedness and resistance to change. Durkheim (1902) has written that "new norms arise when people interact in fluid and extraordinary situations where behavior alternatives increase beyond those in the compelling grooves of daily routine" (p. 108). Yet "fluid and extraordinary situations" are only necessary and not sufficient conditions for even temporary change, let alone that which lasts. From the literature, it appears that attitudinal or behavioral change is, for all its complexity, the personal outcome of environmental transactions, of productive activity and the joy which accompanies it within the experience, and shaped to the needs, of each individual.

In the long run, new ideas, attitudes, and ways of behaving cannot be presented, enacted, or imposed by others, whether groups or individuals, students or teachers. Acceptance and open-mindedness must be "meanings perceived as related to the self" (Allport, 1968, pp. 164–165). Whether it is possible for all teachers to internalize a fluid and open-ended definition of role or to behave supportively and in a nonjudgmental manner toward students of varying cultural background and personal capability remains an open question. Personality variables and, above all, the level of ungratified needs for security, belongingness, and esteem which motivate that personality may well be factors of far greater importance than immediate social reinforcements in determining whether such change is possible.

The other possible kind of change is structural change. Alienation, as Wallace (1967, pp. 86–87) has written, either may be the experience of private loss of a satisfying identity with its social roles and the norms which attach to them or it may be a "recognized group characteristic" which leads to organized action. Hostility and destructiveness are likely to be the group's chief aims in what may become a struggle against the Establishment for identity. (Wallace points out that left and right factions both attack the same Establishment—big corporations, big universities, and big government—the one for deprivation [forbidding marijuana, attempts to censor, criticism of sexual indulgence] and the other for intrusiveness [high taxes, fluoride in drinking water, Communist subversion].) Although, for some, group alienation means only making common outcry against what exists, revitalization and active work for restructuring are possible among such groups. Demands for admittance to planning and control by college and high school students appear to be attempts at self-determination and the creation of a humanistic learning situation in which needs for security, belongingness, and esteem may be met.

Change, and the possibility of change, do not include alteration in the fixed juxtaposition of teacher-learner roles. At any given moment, knowledge is unevenly distributed, and it is a mistake to believe that, whatever their age, the ignorant can by themselves produce the content for their own learning. The permanence of this aspect of structure need not, however, interfere with the satisfactions available to the child. Nor should it obscure what may, and should, be altered.

What are some of the formal conditions necessary to successfully create an environment in which the basic needs of students can be gratified? Certainly, rigid adherence to the status quo in rules, subject matter, and an authoritarian hierarchy of administration, inflexible schedules, curricula which fail to enlist the interests, experience, and abilities of the individual child, and, above all, a greater provision for failure than for success are unlikely to effect the dynamic fulfillment of needs necessary for ego-development. Consistent and compelling denial of human reciprocity in the classroom, especially through the adolescent years, will hardly produce fulfillment either. The child who is not free to behave toward the teacher as she does toward him, that is, with consideration and interest, is being excluded and diminished.

Prestigious goals which are established at a level where only a few can achieve them set the stage for widespread feelings of inferiority and self-rejection. Grades which, on the one hand, provide a concrete means of recognition from others and respect for oneself, on the other inhibit learning because they commonly represent success at competition rather than achievement. Is it not possible to structure school organization so that the individual's betterment is dependent upon the betterment, and not the denigration, of others?[8]

We know now that continued failure on any level is a deterrent to both cognitive and affective learning.[9] While implementation of the nongraded school ideal presently labors under a gross load of

[8] See Handy (1969, p. 163) for a discussion of the importance of social organization for the satisfaction of needs and the resolution of value conflicts.

[9] For some views on the effects of failure, see Goodlad and Anderson (1959, pp. 37–39) and Caswell and Foshay (1957, pp. 387–394).

testing and other paperwork, its conception—which incorporates emphasis both on success and on the differentiated potential of each individual—appears highly therapeutic. We may yet have an end to what John Clausen has rightly called "education by cohort." Access to information regarding the affective state of the individual is not easy to come by, although it has been shown that teachers'-clinicians' opinions correlate on the general health of a particular child even though the particular symptoms are not equally significant to both groups. As we have said, however, this information should not be considered indispensable to the preventive and healing system we are suggesting here. According to Maslow's theory, all children have these needs and, in a generalized sense, the school should be able to contribute to the gratification of all of them, regardless of the level of psychological deprivation of the individual child.

An authentic classroom partnership which involves all those within its boundaries and becomes their mutual responsibility probably means some knowledge of group dynamics and utilization of some of the interaction techniques used in encounter groups and T-groups of various kinds, but only when the purposes of these processes are clearly related to social, that is, shared, need gratification and the furtherance of educational aims, both affective and cognitive, within the group. Under these conditions, the intrinsic learning which the child undergoes about himself and his ability to experience and control his emotions, as well as his intellect, serves as a roadbed for the extrinsic learning which is his cultural heritage.[10] From the outside, a faculty-administrative team which seeks

[10] Unlike other varieties of encounter groups which are intended to enable participants to experience intimacy and emotions closed to them in their daily life without enlisting the service of their capacity to think, rational encounter, developed at the Institute for Advanced Study in Rational Psychotherapy in New York City, includes conscious examination of value systems and a plan of action for changing behavior which has proven detrimental in the past. Although it is intended to include individuals who are distinctly disturbed, its holistic, problem-solving focus appears potentially useful for the education of the healthy individual. In a disciplined and humane book, Jones (1968) has established classroom guidelines for integrative cognitive-affective education. Schutz (1967) and Brown (1968) are two writers who have suggested methods of increasing individual awareness and a sense of cohesion within groups.

change may provide much needed reinforcement for revisions in classroom management which are aimed at producing emotional supportiveness (Lippitt, Fox, and Schmuck, 1967).

The educational system is splitting and steaming with signs of internal movement; throughout the country, therapeutic structural changes are being slightly tried and greatly discussed. A fairly comprehensive list of innovations would have to include free public education from three years through twenty, increased emphasis on study which uses community resources and depends upon district-community communication, twelve-month employment for teachers and the extension of the school year, flexible teacher assignment among schools and grade levels and freedom for curricular experimentation, ungraded and multigraded classes with the competitive grading system eliminated, flexible student scheduling, and use of teacher aids and multiple texts (Hanna, 1970, pp. 225–230). Modified patterns of behavior such as these, if they become institutionalized, may provide structural support for changed attitudes, beliefs, and values.

But whatever systematic shifts occur, above all, change in social structure, if it is to contribute substantially to basic need gratification, should add a new dimension to the lower reaches of the school. From the review of studies reported here, it seems clear that the impact of deprivation on the very young makes a psychic dent far greater than that in later years. The damage, as Cervantes (1965, p. 201) has said, has "already been done to the child even before he has entered first grade." Unlike ad hoc, patchwork repair programs such as Headstart, a systematic, institutionalized nursery and preschool program, planned on the therapeutic model and incorporating practice in cognitive skills, should help to provide the social and psychological resources which parents and siblings may not be able to supply. If there is a tide in the affairs of men which must be taken at the flood, it is this one—the gratification of basic needs at a time when the lack most profoundly affects the primitive structure. Therapeutic and prophylactic, the educational community should affect the child in such a sustaining way that he will carry with him, internalized, the change in his environment.

"Any subculture of society that directly or indirectly promotes mental health and democratic citizenship . . . is one that not only treats those who are ill; it seeks to prevent illness by establishing an environment that is supportive of health, rationality, and creativity. Oriented toward the whole man and not merely one of his roles or functions, a therapeutic community helps develop in everyone the potential for neurosis-free behavior in both the personal and social setting" (Rogow, 1969, p. 288). Out of acceptance, openness, and a participation which is backed by earned value and power, come security, a sense of belonging, and self-esteem. It is, as Horney (1939, p. 289) has written, a "precondition of happiness to have the center of gravity within oneself." Freedom, quite literally, grows from relief from unnecessary pain and the constant need to supply emotional deficiencies—freedom to utilize situations and to develop capacities both interpersonal and personal. Structures of intimacy are built of warmth, acceptance, well-defined limits—that is, clear-cut, unambiguous goals with managerial rather than punitive procedures for sanctions—and the realization that democracy means not indistinguishible likeness, but respect for differences of experience, ability, and personality. Such structures are a prerequisite to learning. Within their psychic shelter an environment may be arranged to provide the substantive concepts and processes which may be carried away to build the bridge between the affective and the cognitive within the individual. This is our goal and to effect it, educators, as Barbara Biber (1967, p. 124) has written, need a "binocular perception of the learning child" which involves both his intellectual and his emotional life.

Although a healthy person is equipped to deal with his world in ways which are qualitatively different from those of the psychically underprivileged, the direction and management of that enriched outer world, as well as of the droughted one of the deprived, are also a necessary function of the school.

As a whole, we are a generation of men so estranged from the inner world that many are arguing that it does not exist, and that even if it does exist it does not matter. Even if it has some significance, it is not the hard stuff of science, and if it is not, then let's make it hard. Let it be measured and counted. Quantify the heart's agony and ecstasy in a world in which, when the inner world is first discovered, we are liable to find ourselves bereft and derelict. For with-

out the inner the outer loses its meaning and without the outer the innner loses its substance [Laing, 1967, p. 33].

The satisfaction of needs does not happen in isolation; something must be there to be perceived, manipulated, and enacted into the structure of the individual. The solution of basic deficiencies must culminate in the opportunity for achievement and growth—emotional, intellectual, and aesthetic.

CHAPTER XII

Opportunity of
Environment

Man should not ask what
the meaning of his life is
but rather must realize that
it is he who is asked.
                    Viktor Frankl
            Man's Search for Meaning

Man is a creature who needs to know. Tendencies toward outreach and exploration appear to be inherent in the human organism and by no means to be explainable simply as tension-reducing drives. Unless these tendencies are blocked in the course of maturation and the accumulation of experience, as they may be for the psychically deprived, they will continue to operate in a wide range of situations (Hunt, 1961). According to Maslow, in the deeper sense the need for knowledge for its own sake—the pure and healthy joy of inquiring and devising answers from either inner or outer experience—does not occur unless this blocking is prevented and the basic needs have been at least partially gratified. The need to know may also function at lower levels but there its propulsion derives from the necessity of influencing the unknown in order to provide the food, shelter, safety, affection, and esteem which are needed. On the lowest level, the physiologically deprived person needs to understand his environment, whether it be the barren altoplano or the ghettos of American cities crowded with competition for economically scarce resources. The insecure individual seeks knowledge of his social and physical surroundings in order to defend himself; deprived of his sense of membership in a group, he uses his senses, his mind, and his skills to find a route to acceptance. Learning becomes a means to an end at the esteem level, too, where the outward manifestations of the need for achievement may cover its neurotic uses.

It is only at a healthy level of functioning that the individual pursues information because he has to, because he feels he must, because the need to know is vital and hardly to be denied. Education as a human institution, with the function of restoring or preserving the highest that is man, must not repress these higher needs. It must safeguard them by gratifying the lower ones which permit psychic access to those whose implementation depends upon such satisfaction. "Education, civilization, rationality, religion, law, government, have been interpreted by most as being primarily instinct-restraining and suppressing forces. But if our contention is correct that instincts have more to fear from civilization than civilization from instincts, perhaps it ought to be the other way about (if we still wish to produce better men and better societies) : perhaps it should be at least one function of education, law, religion, etc., to safeguard, foster, and encourage the expression and gratification of the instinctoid needs" (Maslow, 1954, p. 145).

The word *safeguard* is used here advisedly. Generally, the higher the position of the need in the hierarchy, the weaker and more suppressible it is. The healthy need for self-actualization, the need to know for the sake of knowing, the need for beauty—all are peculiarly vulnerable to man's inability to satisfy his most fundamental needs. The extent of this threat to some of man's unique qualities is considerable. "The possibility of the destruction as a species character of these higher needs is a terrible one and one that is especially important today. We have reason to believe that the man who has known true freedom will not willingly give it up. However, men have been enslaved and some have never known freedom. In individuals we know that the higher needs can be effectively destroyed. If, in addition, some situations occur in which those who survive are mostly those who do *not* carry these needs as genetic characters or who carry them only weakly, it may well be that the combination of little need and no chance for even that much need to appear will result in the emergence of men without enough desire for self-actualization and freedom to make any effort to achieve it" (Roe, 1956, p. 30). The higher needs, although truly instinctoid, may not occur at all in some human individuals: "A [genetic] character in process of evolution does not typically appear in every member of the species, and even a fully established species character may be lacking in some individuals, although at this stage the lack is usually pathological. It is not only possible but also probable that these higher needs are later evolutionary developments in man" (Roe, 1956, p. 30).

Obviously, it is not possible to expect the environment to gratify needs which do not exist or individual members of the species to be motivated by needs they do not have. Since mental health cannot be defined with a constituent trait which is missing genetically—at least, not if health is a possible achievement of all human beings—this seems all the more reason for describing the level of the satisfaction of basic needs—physiological, security, belongingness, and esteem—as the stage of health. If Anne Roe is correct, not all children can benefit from the same education for genetic reasons quite apart from their general intelligence, but without first gratifying lower needs, how are we to know the higher needs which may exist in the healthy child? Since the environment is controllable, at least within certain limits, it is the ability to manipulate need level which makes Maslow's theory relevant to educational practice. If the needs for self-actualization, knowledge, meaning, and beauty do not occur, is it possible that they may be induced if the tutoring generation cares enough to keep alive this cultural inheritance of values?

From the supporting or rejecting climate the child derives his primitive beliefs. These are the preconditions for the learning of values. Beyond this point, the specific content of his psychic structure depends on exposure, on the opportunity to learn, which occurs, as we have said, within a specific situation, and which is made effective through the reinforcements of social rewards and punishments provided at that time. Value criteria must be, and, indeed, are in one way or another, applied to the whole curriculum. Cultures educate their young in order that they may learn what the society wants them to know and, beyond the provision for basic need satisfaction, what they learn depends on the specific experiences to which they are subjected and how they are asked to handle them. Although this is changing, the classroom still exists as the basic source of what is known beyond the immediate environment. If mastery, intelligence, and goodness are correlated—as both Socrates the philosopher and Edward Thorndike the scientist are supposed to have believed—it may be simply because a certain level of ability is necessary to learn what is expected even when it is presented.

Clarification methods[1] which expose the value issues may serve the function of enhancing self-esteem by strengthening the ego-definition the child has. They may also succeed, not because he is truly offered options within which to find his own values, but because he is made more aware of shared, cultural values when these techniques are used. Even more important, he gains the essential opportunity to compare his subjective frame of reference with the values of the culture (Miller and Hutt, 1949a). Acceptance is gained for beliefs prized by the community and is strengthened by

[1] See, for example, Raths, Harmon, and Simon (1966).

the learner's belief that he has not chosen heteronomously but by himself. Certainly, if he is going to learn a value he must know it exists, however it is perceived, although words and actions may be copied separately and, as expressed and enacted values, may, as we have seen, not be at all isomorphic in fact. Beyond knowing, he must have the opportunity to practice what is perceived whether directly or inferentially and to relate it, as Martin Trow (1953) suggests, to its consequence. Pattern practice, as the linguists refer to this type of repetitive learning, may take place through either role-taking or actuality practice.

Value systems, as preference patterns, are a recurrent type of behavior which can be objectively described, assigned to a class, and dealt with predictively. What the child perceives in common with other children, and the reciprocal expectancies which grow from mutual experiences, is cultural. Role-taking produces not simply an empathic reaction but also covert modal perceptions and expectations. Roles, as the child encounters them, are a cultural concept or generalization—certainly nobody in reality holds only one role or fulfills all its norms as the ideal type. Identification, however emotionally involving, is not with the unique particular but with the general and the abstract—the hollow, three-dimensional cultural model. It seems likely that role-playing in the classroom is highly effective because it displays a culturally approved generality to which the idiosyncratic observers and participants are invited to subscribe. It is an invitation to convergence, an invitation which, if accepted, helps to maintain mental health by developing explicit social values which all subgroups of society can integrate as part of their identities and by teaching each individual about the objective complexity of cultural patterns (Miller and Hutt, 1949a).[2] Where role-playing is used as pattern practice, it should probably aim at

[2] This is the hazard, as well as the attraction, of role-playing. Putting yourself in another's place is not the same as being him in his place. Buber (1947, p. 97) makes the distinction between empathy (the former) and inclusion (the latter). In his place you remain yourself. The business of science is classification or stereotyping—a valuable antidote to confusion and abundance but poisonous if overingested. When empathy is standardized, it becomes objective and therefore unreal. Without nuance and subtlety, the person disappears and the category remains—a classification filled with an idea but not flesh, nomothetic spirit but not ideographic heart.

empathy with others in specific functional roles in particular situations so that the individuals involved learn the social meaning of the roles from the self-other patterns which are developed (Cottrell, 1942).

Emergence of age-specific modes of behavior has been attributed to ontogenetic factors rather than to social stimulus contingencies (Erikson, 1963; Flavell, 1963). It is our view, following Maslow, that developmental changes are not merely or even primarily the unfolding of genetically programed response predispositions, but are, rather, the result of social satisfactions and the reinforcements derived from interaction with other human beings. Imitation of models in actuality practice appears to be an important part of social learning, as it involves the living through of attitudes and specific classes of behavior. Albert Bandura and Frederick McDonald (1963), in their study of the effect of social reinforcements and models on moral behavior, found that the type and complexity of judgments in children could be altered by the provision of models alone, without the addition of reinforcements. According to Coopersmith (1969), successful modeling is based on seeing the model cope with specific situations. Values and attitudes originate in small groups where most agree to the ideology and are committed to it, where there is respect for minorities and open-mindedness about the techniques to be used for solving problems, and where there are people who function as models in this way.

Expressing opinions backed by evidence and decision-making are two other important aspects of reality practice. Students want teachers to have opinions and to render judgments (Zeigler, 1967) against which conflict may build ego-defining structures. As we have stressed earlier, understanding grows from the interaction of values, opinions, attitudes, feelings, and beliefs. The person who is neutral has none of these things. He has not attached a conceptual meaning to the referent object or issue and, without belief or knowing, affect dissolves. Like the girl in Yeats' poem who wanted to be loved for herself alone and not for her golden hair, objects are to be valued for their conceptual reality, their cognitive meaning, as well as for the valence and intensity which they arouse. Neutrality means emptiness of the knowledge that is attached to affect. That is the emptiness of "pure" fact and "pure" generalization—the meaninglessness which is all golden hair and none of the affect attached to it, or all noumenal affect and no phenomenal object. Education depends on the consideration and control of both affective and cognitive meanings held toward objects and events.

But discussion of external (or internal) events is probably not enough. Along with practice in developing informed opinions and making decisions must come specific ability to implement views and choices when they are made—that is, power.[3] Student bodies must have the enabling support, both psychological and economic, of the administration for projects which they choose; they need encouragement to assume responsibility for carrying forth the educational purposes which are the function of the school—public debate, newspapers, tutoring, community service—to include the immediate environment and beyond. In the classroom, individual decision and a variety of "contract" learning—when the child is helped to carry it through and not left to sink or swim by himself through the watery maze—provide practice in self-direction. Access to the communal life of the school—the teams, the dances, various leadership positions—must be possible to all, and it should be the business of the school not only to make this so, but also to make the students believe that it is so. A balanced sense of power, that is, the feeling that one has at least some ability to influence or control the environment, seems to be a necessity for mental health.[4] The day is fast disappearing when symbols such as student body officership or even a silent seat on the school board can offer a satisfactory substitute for a true share of control.

Actuality practice has another aspect of some importance. That is the realization that the repeated manipulation of numbers, words, artifacts, chemicals, plant and animal life, and so forth is not done for the future but is practice, in a sense, for its own self:

[3] Pflieger and Weston (1953, pp. 105–106), for example, stress the negative relation between maladjustment and failure of the sense of efficacy and good citizenship, which they found in a study of Detroit school children, and suggest that the attempt to influence events has its basis in success at real control.

[4] See Bettelheim (1967, 1950) for accounts of autistic children at the Orthogenic School of the University of Chicago. These young people have shut out a world in which no effort on their part could make any difference.

the use of sensory equipment and all of man's technological pros-
thetic devices for the further, competent creation of moments of
exploration and use. "Noetic illumination," as Maslow (1968) has
written, does not do the job of education by itself, any more than
therapy does (although Freud originally thought it did). It needs
repetition, consolidation, rediscovery, and application to one situation after another. Working through is a necessary part of an environment which provides the opportunity to learn. After the pro-
phetic flash of imagination come the necessary cultural processes
of restriction: practice in controlling oneself emotionally and in
structuring thought rationally, and, the equally important ego-
function, practice in mastering the external environment. The demands of learning do not exclude its delights, nor vice versa. "We
have made it clear that the kind of school that we should like to see
is one in which the delights as well as the rigours and demands of
learning are built into the whole life of the place, so that there is
little or no need for the stimulus of marks" (*Children and Their
Primary Schools* [*Plowden Report*], 1967, p. 269)'.

Working through should imply a promise of success in one
of the many areas which a multi-valued society provides and the
realization that competence, even in a competitive society, can be
measured objectively, judged by others, as the ability to cope with
and transcend a wide variety of situations. The success of one person need not be destructive of the success of others; its purpose is
the strengthening of constructive reactions to ordinary life crises
through conflict and striving, and that success appears to be a necessary plinth for the development of self-esteem and mental health.
The very core of ego-strength is competence and the feeling that
one is competent (White, 1963)'.

The opportunity which the educational environment gives
should yield what is known of both outer and inner worlds: the institutional routines and their effects, the physical world, the self
and its relationship to all about, and the processes which join them
all effectively. Mastery means utilization as well as awareness, and
it means, somewhere beyond the therapeutic community and individual competence of techniques and tackle, the opportunity to find
means for transcending the self—to put personal mastery and health
to the service of others.

Intervention is the means of education—interrupting and interfering with the random increment of experience. Its goal is not the same as interpersonal therapy which has as its sole end the reduction or elimination of inner conflict or tension. Therapy, at least as Carl Rogers (1964) describes it, has no concern for social origins, implications, or context of behavior. Education, on the contrary, means an intervention which has as its infrastructure the agreement of behavior with cultural expectations, but it extends beyond such agreement to awareness of the objective shortcomings of socioeconomic systems, their effect on the lives of people, and the possibility of their modification and elimination.[5]

Productiveness, as Fromm describes the defining characteristic of the healthy personality, involves transcendence of self. By this we mean neither the highly personal Emersonian meaning of knowledge attained intuitively from supersensual, spiritual sources nor the lonely drug-taking which expands the senses in idosyncratic experience. We mean moving beyond the self to contribute to its larger element: communality. Maslow (1968, p. 25) describes the self-actualizer as a person with a fuller knowledge of, and acceptance of, his own intrinsic nature. He is motivated to actualize his potential, capacities, and talents. He does what he must, not because he wishes to but because it is his duty, his calling. It is unclear whether these goals do not solely serve the egocentric purposes of the individual rather than larger social purposes and therefore are not transcendent in the sense used here. Viktor Frankl (1963, p. 175) suggests that "self-actualization is not a possible aim at all, for the simple reason that the more a man would strive for it, the more he would miss it." It is best found in yielding a part of the self.

Transcendence, in Fromm's deeper meaning, is transpersonal, and intervention which plans and provides for it should end with the individual using the highest development of his personal gifts for social, that is, shared, achievements. Perceived from the center of health, the need for self-actualization should be a binding commitment to responsibility, not a boundary-defining mechanism

[5] Jessor (1956) believes that therapy should also encourage the client to eliminate the societal conditions which have created or exacerbated his problems and that the learning of the social value of working for change should be coterminous with education as a whole.

for the separation of an egocentric elite. "In the long run the satisfaction of the needs of individuals is best facilitated by furthering the need satisfactions of others. . . . Our needs are so intertwined with those of others that the best safeguard for an individual's satisfactions is the satisfaction of the needs of all people involved in a situation" (Handy, 1969, p. 162). Independence, as Buber (1947) has written, is a footbridge, not a dwelling place—a footbridge to communion.

The opportunity of environment, we may summarize, would be incomplete without, first, the activation of responsiveness by means of the therapeutic community and, second, the gaining of substantive knowledge and the establishment of strategies for information-processing which will serve later cognitive and affective functions. Third, and deeply vital in this survival crisis, is the transfer of capability from the self to the social context.

CHAPTER XIII

Democratic Socialization

The variables in the social scientist's equation must include not only the given set of structured institutions but also what the human carriers of those institutions are groping to become.

Robert S. Lynd
Knowledge for What?

B̲ehavior within a situation depends on the historical events which have made it a possibility or ruled it out. A life history, as Benedict (1934) and Mead (1935) have stressed, is an accompaniment to culture, for in each cultural group the possible personality types are limited. The goals of socialization fall naturally in that range and so it is that each generation is shaped to the dominant trends. Not even Rousseau's noble savage could escape learning a system of values. Its application is an essential element in any dynamic cultural pattern, and a configurational interpretation of education must include the historical process of acceptance or rejection of particular sets of traits, attitudes, beliefs, and values within a given society.

How, then, is any particular continuum of social and political behavior and values transmitted? There are as many theories to account for value-learning as there are theories of other types of learning. Behaviorists or associationists such as H. S. Eysenck (1960) and B. F. Skinner (1953) perceive the process as one of rewarded avoidance, a conditioned anxiety response, with value differences explained as differences in conditionability. Under these conditions, as Martin (1954) has written, the fact that the values of the child are identical with those of the parents is not a matter of identification and internalization. It is a consequence of imitative behavior which was learned because it was reinforced.[1] Robert Sears and his associates (1957) and John Whiting (1961) view the process of value-learning as the internalization of social rules in which the child forms an ego-ideal or standard which consists of the parents' standard. In psychoanalytic theory, the superego or conscience is acquired through identification and maintained through either external or internal sanctions. The parents, in this case, are society's representatives, and the interiorization process is a mechanism for making the adjustments required for enculturation.[2]

[1] "To explain the development of given values in children, we need only seek the behavioral models that are available, the patterns of behavior imitated, and the rewards and punishments ensuing" (Martin, 1954, p. 217).

[2] According to Titiev (1949), individuals never act for themselves alone; interiorization and enculturation are inseparable processes. See Hallowell (1955, p. 76): "The individual's self-image and his interpretation of

177

Cognitive-maturational theories of value acquisition, such as those of Piaget (1955), Kohlberg (1966, 1963), and Elliot Turiel (1968) imply structural change bases for judgment which are rooted both in developmental sequence and in experience which shapes the organization, adaptation, and equilibration of cognitive functioning. For these theorists, the emphasis is on the description of how judgments are made rather than on their etiology. In a cognitive-maturational school, too, played out against a backdrop of epigenetic development, we must place the experiential source of superordinate values described by Maslow. The quality of occurrences related to the self shapes the biological unfolding of the child; events and causes connect him with his conative functioning.

Except in the rare case of genetic defect, no child is born into a state of negative values, as man in Christian dogma was born into Original Sin. No child is born hating and hateful, distrustful and rejecting. He learns to be that way just as he learns more positive values. With his most fundamental needs satisfied, the purely ignorant may learn where learning is substantive and the opportunity of environment is provided; under the same conditions, the psychologically deprived child may not learn unless his state of need is in some way modified. Where the range of values taught by his society represents and reinforces those of the individual rooted in his personality, his personal values will be difficult to modify. Where they are socially acquired without this correspondence, as we have seen above, they may be manipulated or act in the temporary service of some situationally presenting need. In this view, values have a socially transactional genesis rooted in biological development, a genesis which is funded by experience representing an idiosyncratic and cultural unification. Values are learned when the organism is capable of learning them and the environment presents the opportunity.

Political values, like others, are acquired in the course of the socialization process, both formal and informal, by which the individual adds to his world view the expectations of a particular group, its orientations, and its tendencies to act. Just as social systems need among other requisites shared cognitive orientations and shared ar-

_____

his own experience cannot be divorced from the concept of the self that is characteristic of his society."

ticulate goals, adequate personal systems need attitudes, opinions, belief systems, and values. The process of their acquisition, which may occur at all stages of life as role, location, and membership changes are encountered, has more often been described in terms of its outcome than of its dynamics. However, in looking for cause and relationship, the one cannot be considered without the other.

Robert Hess and Judith Torney (1967) suggest that four models may be used to explain aspects of the acquisition, change, and stabilization of political attitudes and the way in which the child utilizes experience in the development of political roles. These models follow closely the theories of general value learning which we have just discussed briefly. They are all supposed to be applicable to political socialization, as Hess and Torney see it, although at various stages. In the first, the Accumulation Model, information is acquired by direct teaching. Both the capabilities of the student and the nature of the materials taught are assumed to be irrelevant. The properties of the child, his cognitive equipment and emotional orientations, are supposed neither to limit nor to facilitate the socialization process. The second, the Interpersonal Transfer Model assumes that attitudes developed toward one person are transferred to others. A fund of interpersonal experience and gratification is built up which is then drawn upon to develop emotional orientations toward political personages. Unlike this model, the third, the Identification Model, assumes that attitudes toward a given object are imitated directly from another significant person who has not deliberately attempted to transmit his viewpoint. The child adopts the behavior he sees.

Like other cognitive-maturational theories of learning, the fourth, the Cognitive-developmental Model, relates socialization to the phase of intellectual development of the child and assumes that the maturing learner develops more complex and abstract ways of manipulating his perceptions and reactions as he grows. A given concept may be taught only to the child who has reached the appropriate level of cognitive development. In illustration of this model, Hess and Torney postulate a maturational element to the form which content takes: from three to eleven years of age children develop a rather complete set of basic political orientations. By the end of eighth grade, political socialization is well advanced.

During the early stages of cognitive development, feelings about the authority of the parents are displaced to that of the government. Rules at home are not differentiated from laws in the nation as a whole. The first points of political contact—the Interpersonal Model—are through the embodiment of government in specific persons, especially the president; institutional knowledge comes later through the Accumulation and Identification Models.

Sociological factors, such as sex, level of intelligence, and socioeconomic status, as well as psychodynamic and maturational factors, appear to affect the content of political socialization. Girls, for example, see politics in more narrow, immediate, and personal terms than do boys (Greenstein, 1965a). Children of high intelligence are more interested in current events and more likely to discuss them. They also are more aware of the value of citizen participation and of the obligation to vote, and they are likely to have some sense of efficacy regarding the effect of their efforts. Richard Dawson and Kenneth Prewitt (1969) suggest that political learning experiences in the upper and lower social classes may be as different as between two nations.

But whatever the content actually received by the child being socialized, it comes to him from a variety of channels of influence whose bias is generally conservative. Alterations in political values which are dependent on the informal socialization process tend to be incremental rather than galloping. Social institutions are geared to their own replication. Primary groups, particularly the family, serve in central ways to supply the information which the child accepts, but sometimes cataclysmic social change—depression, revolution, invasion—alters this transmission. Sometimes, for either political or social reasons, the government may act to curtail this influence. The Communists in the Soviet Union, for example, limited parental power to transmit conventional values at the same time that they made parents responsible for rearing their children to further revolutionary aims. The school system was reshaped and a Communist system of guidance for parents was established (Mead and Calas, 1955). In Israel, the socialization functions of the family were sharply limited by the establishment of agricultural communes whose formal educational system assumed many of these responsibilities (Diamond, 1957). Political learning was based in the kibbutzim as social units and was reinforced by the family as well as by other members of each commune.

Let us look now at the effects of these channels of influence. In societies generally, parents have three courses of action: to actively provide information, to prepare the child to receive it elsewhere (and support the "elsewhere" agents), or to abdicate responsibility for the child's socialization in the hope that he will get along somehow. Where the latter occurs, strong social pressures are likely to be put on some other agent to supply the lack. Although the relationship between each of these choices and the outcome of political socialization of the child is not known, many researchers in the United States have closely related parental values and attitudes to those of their children. In a study in Appalachia, for example, children whose parents had a high degree of negative images toward regime figures displayed a considerable contrast to other Americans of low socioeconomic status who have a propensity to idolize political authorities (Jaros, Hirsch, and Fleron, 1968). As A. Campbell and his associates (1960) have pointed out, three out of four children grow up to support the political party of their parents, although during the high school years agreement between parents and children regarding specific political issues tends to decrease.

Parent-child transmission of political values, however, is not to be taken for granted. The twelfth grade students whom M. Kent Jennings and Richard Niemi (1968) studied were much less cynical than their parents and less likely to be suspicious of motives and actions. These investigators conclude that attitude objects in the "concrete, salient reinforced terrain of party identification lend support to the model of parent-child transmission, but this is the exception. . . . Change factors can work their will on the rising generation" (pp. 183–184). Where the family unit is disrupted, not only is the overall orientation of the child affected, but so are the direct input of information and the extent of its effect (Dawson, 1966).

In less immediate ways, peers operate as sources of politization for the individual. In most cases, they act largely as reinforcement agents in groups which have been formed as a result of similar interests, life-styles, and orientations. Where conflict occurs between primary and secondary sources of information, the beliefs of the face-to-face group are most likely to be accepted, with the emotionally distant groups serving as subsidiary reference points (Dawson, 1966). As agents of socialization, the media, particularly television, act through the provision of models as well as other forms of direct, descriptive input. Although to the layman this influence seems considerable, it appears to be reduced substantially by selective perception, the mechanism by which individuals choose to hear, see, and retain material from those messages which agree with beliefs and attitudes which are already held.[3]

Family, school, and work are all involved in patterns of nonpolitical activity which influence political attitudes. In each case, the roles played by the individual may be considered training for later performance of political roles. Almond and Verba (1963) believe that the impact of these three elements of participation training and decision-making is cumulative, with family, school, and work in rank order of importance. (They also state, however, that other elements—particularly education on the secondary level or above—may substitute for their effects. See Lipset [1959a, b] who described education as the single most important variable for the determination of democratic character.) Occupational socialization, however important, cannot concern us directly here, since we are dealing with children. Family and school are another matter.[4] According to Hess and Torney (1967), the effectiveness of the elementary school as an agent of politization has been underestimated. In the school today conscious emphasis is on cognitive acquisition of information about the operation of the political system, together with positive valuing elements. It is not on the affective and conative stances which comprise the underlying systems supporting a total view of political involvement. Nor has the intimate connection between social and political democracy been recognized and implemented. The school, as we have tried to show, has a wider mission than the direct teaching of political values. Its mission is the devel-

[3] If this is the case, then equal-time presentations are probably of limited value. See Klapper (1960, especially Chaps. 1–6) for the effects of the mass media on political socialization, and Sears and Freedom (1960) for the phenomenon of selective exposure.

[4] McDonald (1965, p. 378) suggests, with empirical support, that the possibility of school influence on values is limited to reinforcement through correspondence with parental values already learned by identification.

opment of democratic personality and the provision of specific opportunity for the practice of democratic skills—discussion, the ability to challenge authority intelligently and appropriately, and the art of creative and accommodating compromise—which will carry over into adult life (Dawson, 1966).

Part of the school's importance as a socialization agent lies in the fact that it is a microcosm of the larger social system and, as such, stands as an effective model for the success or failure of democracy. If the child is to learn to behave democratically, he must see the process in action and be part of it. Propaganda cannot replace tangible social experience. Those requisites which Lipset (1959c) describes as necessary for political democracy in the larger culture apply here too: the legitimacy of authority—that is, acceptance and belief in it—and a participating and effective opposition which adheres to decisions once they are made. Although they are society's representatives in the multi-value American culture, parents may still be expected to emphasize their personal versions of societal values, both implicitly and explicitly. It is the school whose function is the official implementation of socially preferred ends.

The schools, then, have a social imperative—but which one? Children learn there, as well as elsewhere, the expected behavior patterns which typical status incumbents exhibit.[5] They learn also the confusing and conflicting assignments which are attached to overlapping roles and memberships. American society, for example, does not demand tolerance as a part of its expected behavior, either as an expressed value or otherwise, except under particular conditions defined by location, role, and other situational factors. Prejudice and intolerance also are a part of the normative expectations of American society (Martin and Westie, 1959), and young people are most likely to encounter both patterns of expectations. The school which demands tolerance for the physically handicapped or

[5] They learn the negative value assigned to certain types of knowledge, such as evolution and communism, and the confusion evident in a society which gives formal instruction in cooking and driving but cannot agree to teach humans about their own sexuality, despite the fact that unmarried girls who become pregnant are much more likely to be those with less adequate information about sex than those who have it (Butman and Kamm, 1965).

the rich may not expect it for the psychologically deprived, the poor, or the culturally different.

Besides tradition and custom regarding specific values and their situational application, distrust of indoctrination and a strong folk belief that one man's opinion is as good as another's have often led to diffuseness and double messages in American culture. This lack of clarity may itself result in failures in socialization and lasting ambiguity about values. Perhaps most needed in an educational institution is a clear-cut, unambiguous message to the child regarding the social values his culture holds most fundamental, a message conveyed simultaneously through social structure which permits their enactment and through all the silent nuances of communication not spoken, as well as through direct teaching. At the least, such unitary counsel should include a value model, rules of conduct and expectation, the rationale or ideology to support them, and sanctions to preserve the model and its application.

Within the range of actual socialization, research into modes of conflict resolution between opposing values which are taught by different agents would be useful. We need a theory of social dissonance to explain the distribution of effects of absent reference groups on cognitive incongruence: which opposing values, taught by whom, are activated, and under what conditions? But who, or what group, is then to bell the cat? Who is to thrust consonance and consistency upon us, to insist that our forms and our rituals match our words, if not those who are aware of the interrelationships between structure and function? And where, if not in the school—that social microcosm of definable yet open boundaries, that containable unit where process and content may be functionally integrated?

Wilhelm Wundt has written of the "psychic inequivalence of social facts." Democratic values and behavior are dependent on the development of a personality which makes important and salient these values when they are taught. For the child to be a democrat, he must be capable of becoming one—able to utilize what he learns. Clearly, no conflict exists between substantive or skill-learning aims and goals of personality growth or mental health in the child. Neither can be achieved without the other. Cognitive and affective processes, as we have seen, interact intimately with personality variables, and intellectual development and the epigenesis of democratic values are functions of the nature of school, as well as other, life environments.

Three conditions, in summary, must be met for the emergence of democratic attitudes and behavior: the gratification of basic needs which represent antecedents, or preconditions; the opportunity of an immediate environment in which to learn and to practice these values; and a democratic social structure which not only permits but encourages their situational expression. We believe (and we have shown some evidence to support this belief) that the latter is a natural outcome of the former two. Children are insecure because their environment has made them so; they bear an overriding longing for membership and affection because they have not had the opportunity to discover what they, whatever their abilities, can master and that they, regardless of their idiosyncratic or group traits, are valued. Which of these needs cannot be alleviated if a democratic society, as it must, finds it necessary for its own preservation?

In the year 2500 there will still be those who doubt the theory of evolution. Will there also be those who believe that teaching words alone will affect behavior? Given a commitment not merely to the transmission of culture but to the building and maintenance of a democratic society, the school, like Luther, can do no other; it must take its stand for reform. The processes of political socialization may be, as Dawson and Prewitt (1969) have written, essentially conserving forces, but continuing to isolate the emotional, intellectual, and valuing components of institutional education will cost us freedom. These are critical times, and failure to adapt comes high in crises; its price is extinction, if not literally of man, then of man with a given set of values—those which have been most honored since man beheld his brother and found him both equal and good.

In this work I have tried to accomplish three tasks: a synthesis of the literature describing democratic values, basic biosocial needs, and the theoretical association of these two sets of variables; the presentation of a body of empirical evidence supporting the relationship; and a report of the further development of a simple instrument to measure psychological deprivation.

Although I have found tentative answers for the questions which plagued me at the start, I am now very much aware of the limitations of this research and the many bricks, both applied and pure, which remain to be added to the wall of evidence to which I have contributed. In the hope that others will follow after, a few of these are mentioned here:

Do levels of need gratification affect the cognitive-developmental process of moral judgment in the child?

Is creativity in the arts related to need level? Is success in the natural sciences related to the need for security?

Can teacher attitudes or orientation toward students, as well as toward tasks, be affected by creating cognitive dissonance? Given the documented interaction of cognitive and affective modes of functioning, would affective changes widen perceptual apertures to admit new substantive knowledge about students, subject matter, and tasks?

Would manipulation of teacher need gratification on the higher levels decrease dogmatism, inflexibility, and intolerance? (This manipulation might be accomplished through increased communication and changes in local social systems to revamp role definition and permit a greater diversity of teacher roles which are equally ego-satisfying.) Do variations in district status and pay affect the needs and cognitive styles of teachers?

Can the student referencing of undesirable groups be limited through the provision of other easily acceptable means of gratifying belongingness and esteem needs? Can belongingness and self-esteem satisfactions be served by creating, as Coleman has suggested, an academic whole-school rivalry with other schools?

Are dropouts being selected out of the schools because of psychological deprivation? Can need gratification affect the dropout rate? What needs do highly successful dropouts have and how have their lower needs been met in the past?

At what level, and under what conditions, is anxiety debilitating rather than facilitating? What is the relationship between quantity and quality of needs and academic achievement?

Is attitude change more easily effected, as Phares' results (1965) suggest, if it is attempted by individuals and groups who are internally oriented, that is, by those who believe that they can affect the environment and the reinforcements which it provides?

We need to know more about types of leadership in school groups of varying sizes and about the degree of group achievement and satisfaction associated with each. We need to experimentally manipulate need gratifications and observe the outcome.

Could public boarding schools, under community control and on a completely noncompulsory basis, providing all the basic needs for preschoolers and an enriched cognitive-affective environment, produce more democratic and open-minded students?

What is the relationship between school structure and the needs of administrators and teachers?

And last, does the structure of a social system, or certain varieties of social systems, change when its members are less needful or have needs of particular types and strength? This is a question which might be explored longitudinally or in a series of panel studies, utilizing Aronoff's (1968) model of reciprocal exchange.

Not only may social structure alter when fundamental needs are gratified; it seems highly possible that the deliberate revision of organization and function—authority and administration, the definition of roles and their interrelationship—may itself serve to provide these satisfactions and, thus, to recycle the interchange on an increasing scale through changes in motivation and values, restructuring, plan, and design. The individual shapes his environment as he is shaped by it, a cliche which, like most, contains much truth. In their present form, our organizations and institutions, corporate, military, educational, or religious, cannot survive if the questions here raised are taken seriously, for their answers are potentially far more destructive of our present Establishment than the burning or bombing of the buildings which contain it.

$\mathcal{A}$ PPENDIX $\mathcal{A}$

Description of Measures

$\mathbb{B}$ ecause all the measures (except the Index of Psychological Deprivation) used in this study are readily available in the literature (see bibliography), only that Index will be reproduced here.

Index of Psychological Deprivation

A pool of fifty-five items, incorporating sixteen items from Jeanne Knutson's index (1968) was judged to determine whether

188

each item indicated psychological deprivation and, if so, the level of deprivation it tapped. Clinical psychologists Joel Aronoff, Harrison Gough, C. Marshall Lowe, Jean Macfarlane, and Anne Roe, as well as Jeanne Knutson, a political scientist, and the investigator, were the judges. The criterion for the selection of items was agreement of five out of seven judges. Thirty-two items were retained from the pool. Of these, five represent physiological need, eight the need for security, eight the need for belongingness, and eleven the need for esteem in one of its two forms—esteem from others (other-worthiness) or self-esteem (self-worthiness). Subsequent to the initial judging, the last need level was divided into two distinct categories—the judgment of self about itself (based on mastery) and the perceived judgment of others about the self.

Kuder-Richardson reliability for the Tramontane sample (n = 232) was .61; test-retest (two weeks) reliability was .80. For the Bayamo sample (n = 114), Kuder-Richardson reliability was .75.

Physiological needs (The use of the term *physiological* for the first level of needs is misleading in its implication that the other needs are not also organismically based. Fundamental to this theory of personality is the assumption that all needs are based in the physiology of the organism.)

1. I think about food a great deal.
2. When I was a child, I was often sick.
3. I've usually had enough food so that I haven't felt hungry.
4. When I was growing up, we sometimes didn't have the things we really needed.
5. As a child, I had plenty of good warm clothes.

Security needs

1. One of the nice things about marriage is having someone to take care of you.
2. I like to work for someone who can really tell me what to do.
3. You can't tell what will happen to you just walking down the street.

4. It's really important to know what you're going to be doing next month, next year, and in the future.
5. Sometimes I've worried about not having a roof over our heads.
6. I want to be able to count on having enough money for food, shelter, and clothing—all the things I really need.
7. A person who leads an even, regular life in which few surprises happen really has a lot to be grateful for.
8. I've lost at least one person who looked after me.

Belongingness needs

1. I am lonely.
2. One nice thing about a family is feeling that you are all part of the group.
3. It's more important to have good friends than money in the bank.
4. I wish I had more friends than I do.
5. The most important thing about a job is working with people you really like.
6. I like the idea of belonging to groups where everybody knows each other really well.
7. Basically, the world we live in is a pretty lonesome place.
8. I feel as if I'm left out of a lot of fun that friends have together.

Esteem needs

Esteem-from-others

1. Nobody pays any attention to my opinions.
2. I want a nice home and nice things that other people will admire.
3. The most important satisfaction in life is being able to do something so well that everyone looks up to you.
4. The most important thing about a job is having people look up to you.
5. It really makes you mad how you never get any appreciation for a job well done.
6. Somewhere in the world there must be someone who will love me.

Self-esteem

1. I'm proud of a lot of the things I do.
2. I'm not as nice-looking as most people.
3. I'm ashamed of myself very often.
4. I get about as much praise as I want.
5. Usually I am quite sure of myself.

Faith-in-Human-Nature Scale

This scale was designed by Morris Rosenberg as a measure of social trust and the belief that human beings are fundamentally good and trustworthy. When used with a sample of almost three thousand college students (Goldsen, Rosenberg, Williams, and Suchman, 1960), it correlated with political cynicism, willingness to restrict freedom of speech, the view that political deviants should be suppressed, and measures of generalized intolerance.

Sample items: (Agree, Uncertain, Disagree)

a) *Human nature is basically cooperative;*
b) *If you don't watch yourself, people will take advantage of you.*

Socialization Scale (So)

Part of the California Psychological Inventory,[1] this scale is described by its author as a measure of the "degree of social maturity, integrity, and rectitude which the individual has attained" (Gough, 1960). It has been translated into eight languages and widely used in ten countries on a variety of samples which include high school students and prison inmates, and it has been found to discriminate between the delinquent and the nondelinquent and between those who cheat on exams and those who do not, and to identify the "more or less responsible high school student" (Gough,

[1] Items from the California Psychological Inventory reproduced by special permission from the California Psychological Inventory by Harrison Gough, Ph.D. Copyright 1956. Published by Consulting Psychologists Press, Inc.

1968, 1966a, b, 1965). The psychological continuum it represents corresponds to a sociological one.

Sample items: (True or false)

 a) *I always act on the spur of the moment without stopping to think;*
 b) *I would do almost anything on a dare.*

Dogmatism Scale

Milton Rokeach (1960) developed this scale to measure structural authoritarianism and intolerance which is neither of the right nor the left. Implicit in dogmatism are rigidity and intolerance of ambiguity, a belief system which is closed to the extent that the person cannot "receive, evaluate, and act on relevant information received from the outside on its own intrinsic merits, unencumbered by irrelevant factors in the situation arising from within the person or from the outside" (p. 57).

Sample items: (seven-point scale: agree strongly through disagree strongly)

 a) *Most people just don't know what's good for them;*
 b) *Even though freedom of speech for all groups is a good idea, it is unfortunately necessary to limit or shut off the speech of certain political groups.*

Tolerance Scale (To)

Like the Socialization Scale, this measure is part of the California Psychological Inventory. According to the manual, it was designed to detect "permissive, accepting, and nonjudgmental social beliefs and attitudes" and has been validated both by known groups (career military officers) and negative correlation with the Fascism Scale (Adorno, Frenkel-Brunswik, Levinson, and Sanford, 1950) which measures authoritarianism of the right.

Sample items: (True or false)

 a) *It makes me feel like a failure when I hear of the success of someone I know;*

b) *Most people will use somewhat unfair means to gain profit or an advantage.*

Survey of Ethical Attitudes (SEA)

The SEA consists of a number of items which appraise "the sorts of considerations a person uses to justify moral judgments made under conditions of normlessness, that is, moral dilemmas" (Hogan, 1969). It is designed to assess a habit of mind whose locus of authority lies in either natural law (the rules or laws which are inherent in man's nature and discoverable by reasoning) or positive law (the man-made, agreed-upon laws of groups and societies)' (Hogan, 1967). The validity of the SEA was established with known groups (policemen and activists)'.

Sample items: (True or false)'

a) *Capital punishment can be justified in most cases;*
b) *A family should eat dinner at regular hours every night.*

Rotter's I-E (Internality-Externality) Scale

Rotter's scale was developed to measure "generalized expectancy," that is, beliefs about the nature of the world and its controllability by the individual. It assesses the individual's feelings of efficacy and the degree of this belief that "his own behavior, skills, or internal dispositions determine what reinforcements he receives" (Rotter, 1966, p. 4). Subjects with a high I score on Rotter's scale were individuals (Peace Corps volunteers) who, in real life, made the attempt to better their environment or (inmates in a tuberculosis sanatorium) to keep themselves aware of their own condition and surroundings.

Sample item: (Choose [1] or [2])'

a. (1) *Becoming a success is mostly a matter of hard work: luck has little or nothing to do with it;*
(2) *Getting a good job depends on being in the right place at the right time.*

Shortened Manifest Anxiety Scale (MAS)

The original Manifest Anxiety Scale was designed by Janet Taylor (1953). Using thirty items validated on the basis of internal consistency in a study by Donald Hoyt and Thomas Magoon (1954), A. W. Bendig (1956) developed this twenty-item shortened revision. Items of low internal consistency were eliminated; the scores of the shortened form are about as reliable as those of the original fifty-item form and highly related (.93) to standard form scores. Bendig also suggests that the shortened form is probably more reliable than the longer Manifest Anxiety Scale.

Sample items: (True or false)

> *a) I frequently find myself worrying about something;*
> *b) I am happy most of the time.*

Communality Scale (Cm)

Each of the items of this California Psychological Inventory Scale has been verified in many different samples to insure a high frequency of endorsement (95 per cent or more of all respondents answering in one direction). Yet, in spite of their modality, the items do not sound like platitudes with little differentiating power. In its entirety of twenty-eight items, the scale is characterized by an extremely skewed distribution of responses. The modal score in a test sample is usually twenty-five or twenty-six. Because values below twenty are almost never observed, the test may be used as a measure of fakery.

Sample items: (True or false)

> *a) I could be perfectly happy without a single friend;*
> *b) I never seem to get hungry.*

Samples from Projective Protocols

1. Everybody worries sometimes. What are the things you worry about most?

   Physiological Needs

   > Food, money, shelter, and what others think about you. Old age and dying.[2]
   >
   > What would happen to me if my parents were to die right now.[2]

   [1] = Bayamo;　[2] = Tramontane;　[3] = Debouchement

Security Needs

> What I'm going to do out in the world on my own. When
> will people start paying attention to what's forthcoming ac-
> cording to Bible prophecy?[3]

> My future destiny; the destiny of the world; pollution, wars,
> cars, overpopulation, whether I should have children to con-
> tribute to overpopulation and whether my children will sur-
> vive the future. I am afraid of criminals and of being at-
> tacked.[2]

> I worry about my relationship with my family and friends.
> And the shape that this country is in. And about all the strange
> things that have been going on in this country lately, and
> about me.[1]

> The security of knowing that someone will take care of you,
> no matter what.[2]

Belongingness Needs

> I worry about the significance of the past and the future. It
> seems so very frightening. I want to have a baby and I am
> afraid that I can't. I want to make life [make love]. Not to
> have sex but make love. I want to meet somebody who I feel
> I can build a time line with.[2]

Esteem-from-Others Needs

> Being used by other people—not being accepted for who I
> am, not having any true friends.[2]

Self-Esteem Needs

> There is no friend that I am really close to and that under-
> stands me and I am not the type of person I would like to be.[1]

> Not being able to marry and achieve true married happiness;
> not being able to have children; not being able to support them
> and send them to college; not being able to offer them the
> benefits of life I didn't receive; my lack of social participa-
> tion; *my overriding feeling of inferiority and uselessness, my
> continuing doubt of my abilities.*[2] (Italics added.)

   [1] = Bayamo;   [2] = Tramontane;   [3] = Debouchement

2. What do you think you need in order to have a really good life?

No Needs

> To feel I am productive to life, to love, to feel that I am loved, and to share with all mankind.[2]

> I need to know myself. I do to a certain point. I do not struggle to survive. I have to be me. That is the most one can do to live to the extreme. I need learning, loving, hating. I need everything and nothing. I help myself to all I can get out of life—and death.[1]

> I need a free mind to think and act independently. To be able to express my ideas, to learn; to love everyone no matter how awful they appear on the outside because inwardly every person is beautiful. You just need to look for it. To have a really good life I don't need to worry about success or living in a big house with two cars, I just want to be happy and free![1]

[1] = Bayamo; [2] = Tramontane; [3] = Debouchement

APPENDIX C

Summary Tables

Table 1. RACE: VALUES AND NEEDS (F-TEST)

	Race			
	Nonblack (n = 302) $\overline{X}$	Black (n = 96) $\overline{X}$	f-ratio	p
Values				
Faith-in-human-nature	5.58	3.09	59.76	.0001
I-E	10.30	12.39	15.15	.0002
SEA	16.89	22.10	50.94	.0001
Dogmatism	128.40	175.60	75.95	.0001
Tolerance	19.99	12.72	113.13	.0001
Socialization	30.47	27.59	14.04	.0003
Needs				
Physiological	1.76	2.72	81.91	.0001
Security	4.23	5.24	38.99	.0001
Belongingness	5.36	5.37	.06	.8101
Esteem from others	2.40	3.66	65.13	.0001
Self-esteem	2.31	2.07	3.99	.0464
Manifest anxiety scale (Bendig)	8.17	8.79	.86	.3549

199

Table 2. SES AND RACE: PSYCHOLOGICAL NEEDS

SES and race	Physiological		Security		Belongingness		Esteem from others		Self-esteem		MAS		n
	$\overline{X}$	s.d.	$\overline{X}$	s.d.	$\overline{X}$	s.d.	$\overline{X}$	s.d.	$\overline{X}$	s.d.	$\overline{X}$	s.d.	
Low SES—Nonblack	1.83	1.67	4.17	.98	5.17	2.14	2.33	1.21	3.00	1.09	8.83	5.08	6
Low SES—Black	2.83	.95	5.33	1.36	5.47	1.28	3.80	1.08	2.01	1.22	9.23	3.52	75
Middle SES—Nonblack	1.80	.92	5.40	1.65	5.80	1.47	3.20	1.32	2.50	1.27	8.00	5.50	10
Middle SES—Black	1.83	.75	4.83	1.33	4.67	1.37	2.83	1.47	2.17	.98	6.83	4.49	6
High SES—Nonblack	1.76	.83	4.19	1.53	5.34	1.66	2.37	1.43	2.29	1.11	8.16	4.56	259
High SES—Black	2.37	1.19	4.62	1.30	5.00	1.07	3.00	.92	2.50	.53	6.12	4.36	8

Table 3. SES AND RACE: DEMOCRATIC VALUES

SES and race	Faith-in-human-nature		I-E		SEA		Dogmatism		Tolerance		Socialization		n
	X̄	s.d.	X̄	s.d.	X̄	s.d.	X̄	s.d.	X̄	s.d.	X̄	s.d.	
Low SES—Nonblack	6.17	2.48	11.17	3.19	14.33	7.03	138.67	21.25	18.50	3.21	29.50	3.62	6
Low SES—Black	2.96	1.74	12.52	3.18	22.99	4.49	179.49	17.72	11.97	3.92	27.64	5.25	75
Middle SES—Nonblack	5.10	4.01	13.00	3.65	19.80	6.99	160.70	27.18	18.30	6.15	30.50	7.00	10
Middle SES—Black	2.00	1.90	11.67	3.67	18.17	4.62	153.00	34.40	16.00	4.05	27.83	5.45	6
High SES—Nonblack	5.59	2.93	10.18	4.61	16.83	6.21	126.95	48.70	20.09	5.99	30.49	7.12	259
High SES—Black	5.12	2.29	11.75	4.56	16.75	7.17	155.50	28.03	17.25	5.15	27.00	4.60	8

Table 4. Comparison of Need–No Need Groups on Values Scales: t-test

Values scales	Need			No need			
	X̄	s.d.	n	X̄	s.d.	n	p
Physiological needs							
Faith-in-human-nature	4.00	2.76	31	5.52	2.71	347	.01
I-E	12.16	3.12	31	11.24	3.82	355	ns
SEA	20.03	7.07	31	18.44	5.63	367	ns
Dogmatism	169.94	28.52	31	149.14	23.79	343	.01
Tolerance	13.06	5.30	32	19.20	5.44	366	.01
Socialization	25.70	4.74	33	30.57	5.31	368	.01
Security needs							
Faith-in-human-nature	4.60	2.60	90	5.63	2.74	289	.01
I-E	11.90	3.33	98	11.12	3.89	290	.10
SEA	20.73	5.46	100	17.82	5.68	300	.01
Dogmatism	164.74	24.84	97	146.04	22.95	278	.01
Tolerance	15.70	5.43	100	19.74	5.39	301	.01
Socialization	29.39	5.34	101	30.47	5.42	302	.10

Table 4. Comparison of Need–No Need Groups on Values Scales: T-test (cont.)

Values scales	Need			No need			p
	X̄	s.d.	n	X̄	s.d.	n	
Belongingness needs							
Faith-in-human-nature	5.14	2.63	179	5.61	2.82	200	.10
I-E	11.98	4.00	182	10.73	3.45	206	.01
SEA	18.44	5.70	190	18.65	5.83	210	ns
Dogmatism	156.46	24.52	171	146.25	24.19	203	.01
Tolerance	17.86	5.61	187	19.51	5.63	213	.01
Socialization	29.28	5.59	188	31.00	5.14	214	.01
Esteem from others							
Faith-in-human-nature	4.08	2.51	123	6.02	2.62	256	.01
I-E	12.16	3.45	127	10.90	3.85	261	.01
SEA	21.12	4.78	131	17.29	5.79	269	.01
Dogmatism	167.18	22.46	124	142.82	21.82	251	.01
Tolerance	14.96	5.13	128	20.50	5.01	273	.01
Socialization	28.53	5.51	130	30.99	5.19	273	.01

Table 4. COMPARISON OF NEED–NO NEED GROUPS ON VALUES SCALES: T-TEST (cont.)

Values scales	Need			No need			p
	X̄	s.d.	n	X̄	s.d.	n	
			Self-esteem				
Faith-in-human-nature	4.81	2.75	54	5.49	2.73	326	.10
I-E	12.23	3.34	53	11.17	3.81	336	.10
SEA	16.65	5.96	57	18.85	5.67	344	.01
Dogmatism	152.56	20.43	52	150.58	25.43	324	ns
Tolerance	17.55	5.25	56	18.94	5.71	346	.10
Socialization	27.87	6.71	56	30.58	5.09	349	.01
			Combined need for esteem				
Faith-in-human-nature	4.32	2.58	81	5.67	2.71	298	.01
I-E	12.35	3.31	80	11.04	3.84	308	.01
SEA	19.45	5.60	84	18.31	5.79	316	ns
Dogmatism	159.49	23.72	80	148.54	24.63	295	.01
Tolerance	16.23	5.14	82	19.38	5.62	319	.01
Socialization	28.11	6.02	84	30.75	5.11	319	.01

204

Table 5. NEED-VALUE CORRELATIONS (r)

Needs	Tramontane (n = 232)	Bayamo (n = 114)	Debouchement (n = 66)	Total sample (n = 412)
	Faith-in-human-nature scale			
Physiological	−.099	−.144	.152	−.239***
Security	−.049	−.037	−.110	−.172***
Belongingness	−.126	−.173	.108	−.097
Esteem from others	−.202**	−.292**	.101	−.330***
Self-esteem	−.243***	−.061	.197	−.081
Combined esteem	−.280***	−.277**	.215	−.300***
Combined needs	−.223**	−.253*	.146	−.301***
Anxiety (MAS)	−.231***	−.169	.087	−.188***
	Internality-externality scale			
Physiological	.171*	.033	.003	.155**
Security	.178**	−.046	.058	.145**
Belongingness	.253***	.097	.116	.186***
Esteem from others	.182**	.107	.129	.204***
Self-esteem	.208**	.061	−.072	.113*
Combined esteem	.246***	−.277**	.033	.223***
Combined needs	.317***	.086	.087	.265***
Anxiety (MAS)	.241***	.263**	.195	.245***

* p < .05; ** p < .01; *** p < .001.

205

Table 5. Need-Value Correlations (r) (cont.)

Needs	Tramontane (n = 232)	Bayamo (n = 114)	Debouchement (n = 66)	Total sample (n = 412)
	Survey of ethical attitudes (SEA)			
Physiological	−.041	.127	.032	.163**
Security	.201**	.351***	.080	.287***
Belongingness	−.030	−.020	.085	−.013
Esteem from others	.355***	.381***	−.046	.404***
Self-esteem	−.018	−.214*	−.206	−.169***
Combined esteem	.244***	.203*	−.123	.214***
Combined needs	.176**	.256**	.019	.244***
Anxiety (MAS)	−.044	−.124	.118	−.010
	Dogmatism scale			
Physiological	.107	.311***	.265*	.384***
Security	.314***	.377***	.239	.413***
Belongingness	.322***	.307**	.336**	.264***
Esteem from others	.407***	.513***	.433***	.553***
Self-esteem	.234***	−.078	−.131	−.022
Combined esteem	.420***	.395***	−.194	.415***
Combined needs	.465***	.536***	.406***	.538***
Anxiety (MAS)	.278***	.235*	.375**	.264***

* p < .05; ** p < .01; *** p < .001.

206

Table 5. NEED-VALUE CORRELATIONS (r)˙ (cont.)˙

Needs	Tramontane (n = 232)	Bayamo (n = 114)	Debouchement (n = 66)	Total sample (n = 412)
		Tolerance scale		
Physiological	−.192**	−.392***	−.119	−.426***
Security	−.227***	−.319***	−.039	−.360***
Belongingness	−.198**	−.283**	−.081	−.165***
Esteem from others	−.337***	−.427***	−.132	−.485***
Self-esteem	−.324***	.031	.113	−.076
Combined esteem	−.428***	−.345***	−.004	−.423***
Combined needs	−.416***	−.504***	−.087	−.501***
Anxiety (MAS)	−.508***	−.496***	−.610***	−.445***
		Socialization scale		
Physiological	−.160*	−.287**	−.378**	−.303***
Security	−.038	−.103	−.130	−.133**
Belongingness	−.060	−.170	−.194	−.106*
Esteem from others	−.135*	−.203*	−.210	−.232***
Self-esteem	−.235***	−.099	−.151	−.162**
Combined esteem	−.231***	−.229*	−.254*	−.275***
Combined needs	−.183**	−.287**	−.368**	−.291***
Anxiety (MAS)	−.241***	−.264**	−.476***	−.277***

* p < .05; ** p < .01; *** p < .001.

207

Table 6. SES:[a] VALUES (F-TEST)

Values	SES			f-ratio	p
	Low (n = 81) $\overline{X}$	Middle (n = 16) $\overline{X}$	High (n = 279) $\overline{X}$		
Faith-in-human-nature	3.20	3.94	5.58	2.77	.064
I-E	12.42	12.50	10.22	.21	.812
SEA	22.35	19.19	16.83	5.40	.005
Dogmatism	176.50	157.80	127.80	2.03	.133
Tolerance	12.46	17.44	20.00	4.38	.013
Socialization	27.78	29.50	30.39	.04	.963

[a] Low SES = Manual workers: laborers, non-officers in Armed Services, craftsmen not self-employed, etc. Middle SES = Lower white collar: office workers, non-commissioned officers, foremen, service workers, entertainers, etc. High SES = Upper white collar: teachers, salesmen, technicians, social welfare, pilots, commissioned officers, etc.; self-employed; professionals; executives.

208

Table 7. SES: Needs (F-Test),

Needs	SES			f-ratio	p
	Low (n = 81) $\overline{X}$	Middle (n = 16) $\overline{X}$	High (n = 279) $\overline{X}$		
Physiological ·················	2.75	1.81	1.78	4.27	.015
Security ·················	5.27	5.19	4.20	1.06	.347
Belongingness ·················	5.44	5.37	5.33	.95	.387
Esteem from others ·················	3.69	3.06	2.39	2.47	.086
Self-esteem ·················	2.09	2.37	2.29	.70	.498
Manifest anxiety scale ·················	9.20	7.56	8.10	2.44	.089

Bibliography

ADORNO, T. W., FRENKEL-BRUNSWIK, E., LEVINSON, D. J., AND SANFORD, R. N. *The Authoritarian Personality*. New York: Wiley, 1950.

ALLPORT, G. *The Nature of Prejudice*. Garden City: Doubleday Anchor, 1958. (Originally published 1954.)

ALLPORT, G. *The Person in Psychology*. Boston: Beacon, 1968.

ALMOND, G. AND VERBA, S. *The Civic Culture*. Princeton: Princeton University Press, 1963.

ANGYAL, A. *Neurosis and Treatment: A Holistic Theory*. Edited by E. Hanfmann and R. M. Jones. New York: Wiley, 1965.

ARENDT, H. *The Origins of Totalitarianism*. 2d enlarged ed. Cleveland: World, 1958.

ARENDT, H. *On Revolution*. New York: Viking, 1963.

ARONOFF, J. *Manual for Scoring Abraham Maslow's Theory of the Hierarchy of Needs*. First draft, n.d.

ARONOFF, J. *Psychological Needs and Cultural Systems*. Princeton: Van Nostrand, 1967.

211

ARONOFF, J. "Psychological Needs as a Determinant in the Formation of Social Structure." Unpublished manuscript, 1968.

ASCH, S. E. "Effects of Group Pressure upon the Modification and Distortion of Judgments" in H. Guetzkow (ed.). *Groups, Leadership, and Men*. Pittsburgh: Carnegie Press, 1951.

AUSUBEL, D. *Educational Psychology: A Cognitive View*. New York: Holt, Rinehart, and Winston, 1969.

AUSUBEL, O. *Maori Youth: A Psychoethnological Study of Cultural Deprivation*. New York: Holt, Rinehart, and Winston, 1961.

BANDURA, A. AND MC DONALD, F. "Influence of Social Reinforcements and the Behavior of Models in Shaping Children's Moral Judgments," *Journal of Abnormal and Social Psychology*, 1963, *67* (3), 274–281.

BANDURA, A. AND WALTERS, R. *Adolescent Aggression*. New York: Ronald Press, 1959.

BARBU, Z. *Democracy and Dictatorship*. New York: Grove, 1956.

BARKER, E. N. "Authoritarianism of the Political Right, Center, and Left," *Journal of Social Issues*, 1963, *19*, 63–74.

BARRON, F. *Creativity and Psychological Health*. Princeton, N. J.: Van Nostrand, 1963.

BATESON, G. AND MEAD, M. *Balinese Character: A Photo-graphic Analysis*. New York: N. Y. Academy of Sciences, 1942.

BAY, C. *The Structure of Freedom*. Stanford: Stanford University Press, 1958.

BENDIG, A. W. "The Development of a Short Form of the Manifest Anxiety Scale," *Journal of Consulting Psychology*, 1956, *20*, 384.

BENDIX, R. AND LIPSET, S. M. (eds.). *Class, Status, and Power: A Reader in Social Stratification*. New York: Free Press, 1966.

BENEDICT, R. *Patterns of Culture*. Boston: Houghton Mifflin, 1934.

BENNIS, W. G. AND SLATER, P. E. *The Temporary Society*. New York: Harper and Row, 1968.

BERELSON, B. "Democratic Theory and Public Opinion," *Public Opinion Quarterly*, 1952, *16*, 315–330.

BERELSON, B. AND STEINER, G. A. *Human Behavior: An Inventory of Scientific Findings*. New York: Harcourt, Brace, and World, 1964.

BERGER, E. M. "The Relation between Expressed Acceptance of Self and Expressed Acceptance of Others," *Journal of Abnormal Psychology*, 1952, *47*, 279–284.

BETTELHEIM, B. *Children of the Dream*. London: Macmillan, 1969.

BETTELHEIM, B. *The Empty Fortress*. New York: The Free Press, 1967.

BETTELHEIM, B. *The Informed Heart*. New York: The Free Press, 1960.

BETTELHEIM, B. *Love Is Not Enough*. Glencoe, Ill.: The Free Press, 1950.

BIBER, B. "A Learning-Teaching Paradigm Integrating Intellectual and Affective Processes," in Bower and Hollister, *Behavioral Science Frontiers in Education*, 1967.

BIDDLE, B. J. AND THOMAS, E. J. (eds.). *Role Theory: Concepts and Research*. New York: Wiley, 1966.

BIDDLE, B., ROSENCRANZ, H. A., TEMICH, E., AND TWYMAN, J. P. "Shared Inaccuracies in the Role of the Teacher," in Biddle and Thomas, *Role Theory: Concepts and Research*, 1966.

BILLS, R. E. "Index of Adjustment and Values." Mimeographed. Auburn: Alabama Polytechnic Institute, n.d.

BLANKSTEN, G. I. "The Politics of Latin America," in G. A. Almond and J. S. Coleman (eds.). *The Politics of the Developing Areas*. Princeton: Princeton University Press, 1960.

BOSSOM, J. AND MASLOW, A. H. "Security of Judges as a Factor in Impressions of Warmth in Others," *Journal of Abnormal Psychology*, 1957, *55*, 147–148.

BOWER, E. M. AND HOLLISTER, W. G. (eds.). *Behavioral Science Frontiers in Education*. New York: Wiley, 1967.

BRAMELD, T. *Cultural Foundations of Education*. New York: Harper, 1957.

BROCK, J. F. AND AUTRET, M. *Kwashiorkor in Africa*. Monograph Series, No. 8. Geneva: World Health Organization, 1952.

BRONOWSKI, J. *The Face of Violence*. New York: Braziller, 1955.

BROWN, G. I. *Now: The Human Dimension*. A report of the Ford-Esalen Project for Innovation in Humanistic Education. Esalen Monograph No. 1. Big Sur: Esalen Institute, 1968.

BROWN, R. *Social Psychology*. New York: The Free Press, 1965.

BRUNER, J. "The Cognitive Consequences of Early Sensory Deprivation," *Psychosomatic Medicine*, 1959, *21*, 89–95.

BRUNER, J. AND GOODMAN, C. "Value and Need as Organizing Factors in Perception," *Journal of Abnormal and Social Psychology*, 1947, *42* (1), 33–44.

BRUNER, J. AND POSTMAN, L. "An Approach to Social Perception," in Wayne Dennis and others (eds.). *Current Trends in Social Psychology*. Pittsburgh: University of Pittsburgh Press, 1948.

BUBER, M. *Between Man and Man*. New York: Macmillan, 1965. (First published 1947.)

BUHLER, C. "Theoretical Observations about Life's Basic Tendencies," *American Journal of Psychotherapy*, 1959, *15*, 561–581.

BURLINGHAM, D. T. AND FREUD, A. *Infants without Families*. New York: International University Press, 1962.

BUTMAN, J. W. AND KAMM, J. A. "The Social, Psychological, and Behavioral World of the Teen-age Girl." Ann Arbor: Institute for

Social Research, University of Michigan, 1965. Cited in Clausen. *Socialization and Society,* 1968.

CAMPBELL, A., CONVERSE, P. E., MILLER, W. E., AND STOKES, D. E. *The American Voter.* New York: Wiley, 1960.

CAMPBELL, A., GURIN, G., AND MILLER, W. E. "Sense of Political Efficacy and Political Participation," in H. Eulau and others (eds.). *Political Behavior.* Glencoe, Ill.: The Free Press, 1956.

CASWELL, H. L. AND FOSHAY, A. W. *Education in the Elementary School.* 3rd ed. New York: American Book Co., 1957.

CENTERS, R. "Motivational Aspects of Occupational Stratification," *Journal of Social Psychology,* 1948, *28,* 187–217.

CERVANTES, L. F. *The Dropout: Causes and Cures.* Ann Arbor: University of Michigan Press, 1965.

CHAPANIS, N. P. AND CHAPANIS, A. "Cognitive Dissonance: Five Years Later," *Psychology Bulletin,* 1964, *61,* 1–22.

Children and Their Primary Schools: A report of the Central Advisory Council for Education (England). (Plowden Report) London: H. M. S. O., 1967.

CHRISTIE, R. AND JAHODA, M. (eds.). *Studies in the Scope and Method of "The Authoritarian Personality."* Glencoe, Ill.: The Free Press, 1954.

CLAUSEN, J. A., ed. *Socialization and Society.* Boston: Little, Brown, 1968.

CNUDDE, C. F. AND NEUBAUER, D. E. (eds.). *Empirical Democratic Theory.* Chicago: Markham, 1969.

COCH, L. AND FRENCH, J. R. P., JR. "Overcoming Resistance to Change." in G. E. Swanson, T. M. Newcomb, and E. L. Hartley (eds.). *Readings in Social Psychology.* New York: Holt, 1952.

COHEN, A. *Deviance and Control.* Englewood Cliffs: Prentice-Hall, 1966.

COHEN, A. R. *Attitude Change and Social Influence.* New York: Basic Books, 1964.

COLEMAN, J. *The Adolescent Society.* Glencoe, Ill.: The Free Press, 1961.

COMBS, A. W. (ed.). *Perceiving, Behaving, Becoming.* Washington, D. C.: Association for Supervision and Curriculum Development, National Education Association, 1962.

COMBS, A. W. AND SNYGG, D. *Individual Behavior: A Perceptual Approach to Behavior.* Rev. ed. New York: Harper and Row, 1959.

COOLEY, C. H. *Human Nature and the Social Order.* New York: Schocken, 1964. (First published 1902.)

COOPERSMITH, S. *The Antecedents of Self-Esteem.* San Francisco: W. H. Freeman, 1967.

COOPERSMITH, S. Lecture at the University of California, Berkeley, March, 1969.

COTTRELL, L. S., JR. "The Analysis of Situational Fields in Social Psychology," *American Sociology Review,* 1942, *7,* 370–387.

CRANDALL, V. J. AND BELLUGI, U. "Some Relationships of Interpersonal and Intrapersonal Conceptualizations to Personal-Social Adjustment," *Journal of Personality,* 1954, *23,* 224–232.

CRANSTON, M. *What Are Human Rights?* New York: Basic Books, 1962.

CRONBACH, L. J. *Educational Psychology.* 2nd ed. New York: Harcourt, Brace, and World, 1963.

DAHL, R. *A Preface to Democratic Theory.* Chicago: University of Chicago Press, 1956.

DAVIDS, A., HENRY, A. F., MCARTHUR, C. C., AND MCNAMARA, L. F. "Projection, Self-evaluation, and Clinical Evaluation of Aggression," *Journal of Consulting Psychology,* 1955, *19,* 437–440.

DAVIES, J. C. "The Family's Role in Political Socialization," *Annals of the American Academy of Political and Social Science,* 1965, *361,* 10–19.

DAVIES, J. C. *Human Nature in Politics.* New York: Wiley, 1963.

DAWSON, R. E. "Political Socialization." *Political Science Annual, 1966.* Edited by J. A. Robinson. Indianapolis: Bobbs-Merrill, 1966.

DAWSON, R. E. AND PREWITT, K. *Political Socialization.* Boston: Little, Brown, 1969.

DERBER, C. AND FLACKS, R. "An Exploration of the Value System of Radical Student Activists and Their Parents." Youth and Social Change Project, University of Chicago, Dept. of Sociology, August, 1967.

DEUTSCH, M. AND GERARD, H. B. "A Study of Normative and Informational Social Influences upon Individual Judgment," *Journal of Abnormal and Social Psychology,* 1955, *51,* 629–636.

DEUTSCH, M. AND OTHERS. *The Disadvantaged Child: Selected Papers of Martin Deutsch and His Associates.* New York: Basic Books, 1967.

DEWEY, J. *Democracy and Education.* New York: Macmillan, 1916.

DEWEY, J. *Experience and Education.* New York: Collier, 1938.

DIAMOND, S. "Kibbutz and Shtetle: The History of an Idea," *Social Problems,* 1957, *5,* 71–99.

DICKS, H. V. "Personality Traits and National Socialist Ideology," *Human Relations,* 1950, *3* (2), 111–154.

DUKES, W. F. "Psychological Study of Values," *Psychology Bulletin,* 1955, *52* (1), 24–50.

DURKHEIM, E. De la division du travail social, 1902, xxxii. Quoted in *The Human Group.* Written by George Homans. New York: Harcourt, Brace, and World, 1950.

DURKHEIM, E. *Education and Sociology*. New York: The Free Press, 1956. (First published as articles between 1903 and 1911.)

EASTON, D. AND DENNIS, J. "The Child's Acquisition of Regime Norms: Political-Efficacy," in Cnudde and Neubauer. *Empirical Democratic Theory*. 1969.

EASTON, D. AND HESS, R. "The Child's Political World," *Midwest Journal of Political Science*. 1962, *6*, 229–246.

ECKHARDT, W. "The Values of Fascism," *Journal of Social Issues*, 1968, *24* (1), 89–104.

EDWARDS, A. L. *The Social Desirability Variable in Personality Assessment*. New York: Dryden Press, 1957.

EKSTEIN, R. AND MOTTO, R. L. *From Learning for Love to Love of Learning*. New York: Brunner-Mazel, 1969.

ELLIS, A. "A Weekend of Rational Encounter," in A. Burton (ed.). *Encounter*. San Francisco: Jossey-Bass, 1970.

ERIKSON, E. *Childhood and Society*. 2d ed. New York: Norton, 1963.

ERIKSON, E. *Identity: Youth and Crisis*. New York: Norton, 1968.

ETZIONI, A. *Modern Organizations*. Englewood Cliffs: Prentice-Hall, 1964.

EYSENCK, H. J. *Structure of Human Personality*. 2d ed. New York: Wiley, 1960.

FALLDING, H. "A Proposal for the Empirical Study of Values," *American Sociological Review*, 1965, *30* (1), 223–233.

FEATHER, N. T. "Acceptance and Rejection of Arguments in Relation to Attitude Strength, Critical Ability, and Intolerance of Inconsistency," *Journal of Abnormal Psychology*, 1964, *59*, 127–136.

FESTINGER, L. *A Theory of Cognitive Dissonance*. Stanford: Stanford University Press, 1957.

FEY, W. F. "Acceptance by Others and Its Relation to Acceptance of Self and Others: A Reevaluation," *Journal of Abnormal and Social Psychology*, 1955, *50* (2), 274–276.

FEY, W. F. "Acceptance of Self and Others, and Its Relation to Therapy Readiness," *Journal of Clinical Psychology*, 1954, *10*, 269–271.

FISHBEIN, M. (ed.). *Readings in Attitude Theory and Measurement*. New York: Wiley, 1967.

FLAVELL, J. H. *The Developmental Psychology of Jean Piaget*. Princeton: Van Nostrand, 1963.

FRANKL, V. *Man's Search for Meaning: An Introduction to Logotherapy*. New York: Washington Square Press, 1963.

FRAZIER, A. (ed.). *New Insights and the Curriculum*. ASCD Yearbook, 1963. Washington, D. C.: National Education Association, 1963.

FREUD, S. "Analysis Terminable and Interminable," *International Journal of Psychoanalysis*, 1937.

FREUD, S. *The Basic Writings of Sigmund Freud*. Edited by A. A. Brill. New York: Modern Library, 1938.

FREUD, S. *Civilization and Its Discontents*. New York: Norton, 1962. (First published 1930.)

FROMM, E. *Escape from Freedom*. New York: Holt, Rinehart, and Winston, 1941.

FROMM, E. *Man for Himself*. New York: Holt, Rinehart, and Winston, 1947.

FROMM, E. *The Sane Society*. New York: Holt, Rinehart, and Winston, 1955.

FROMM, E. "Selfishness and self-love." *Psychiatry*, 1939, *2*, 507–523.

GAGNÉ, R. *The Conditions of Learning*. New York: Holt, Rinehart, and Winston, 1965.

GLIDEWELL, J. C. AND STRINGER, L. A. "The Educational Institution and the Health Institution," in Bower and Hollister. *Behavioral Science Frontiers in Education*. 1967.

GLOCK, C. Y. AND NICOSIA, F. M. "The Consumer," in Lazarsfeld, Sewell, and Wilensky. *The Uses of Sociology*. 1967.

GLUECK, S. AND GLUECK, E. *Predicting Juvenile Delinquency and Crime*. Cambridge, Mass.: Harvard University Press, 1959.

GOLDFARB, W. "Effects of Early Institutional Care on Adolescent Personality: Rorschach Data," *American Journal of Orthopsychiatry*, 1944, *14*, 441–447.

GOLDFRIED, M. R. "Feelings of Inferiority and the Depreciation of Others: A Research Review and Theoretical Reformulation," *Journal of Individual Psychology*, 1963, *19* (1), 27–48.

GOLDMAN, S. "Profiles of an Adolescent," *Journal of Psychology*, 1962, *54*, 229–240.

GOLDSEN, R. K., ROSENBERG, M., WILLIAMS, R. M., JR., AND SUCHMAN, E. A. *What College Students Think*. New York: Van Nostrand, 1960.

GOODE, W. J. "A Theory of Role Strain," *American Sociological Review*, 1960, *25*, 483–496.

GOODENOUGH, W. H. *Cooperation in Change*. New York: Russell Sage, 1963.

GOODLAD, J. AND ANDERSON, R. rev. ed. *The Nongraded Elementary School*. New York: Harcourt, Brace, and World, 1963.

GORER, G. *The Danger of Equality*. New York: Weybright and Talley, 1966.

GORER, G. "National Character: Theory and Practice," in Mead and Metraux. *The Study of Culture at a Distance*.

GOUGH, H. "Appraisal of Social Maturity by Means of the CPI," *Journal of Abnormal Psychology*, 1966a, *71* (3), 189–195.

GOUGH, H. "Cross-Cultural Validation of a Measure of Asocial Behavior," *Psychology Reports*, 1965, *17* (2), 379–387.

GOUGH, H. "Graduation from High School as Predicted from the CPI," *Psychology in the Schools,* 1966b, *3* (3), 208–216.

GOUGH, H. "An Interpreter's Syllabus for the California Psychological Inventory," in McReynolds. *Advances in Psychological Assessment.* 1968.

GOUGH, H. "Theory and Measurement of Socialization," *Journal of Consulting Psychology,* 1960, *24,* 23–30.

GREENBERG, J. W., GERVER, J. M., CHALL, J., AND DAVIDSON, H. H. "Attitudes of Children from a Deprived Environment Toward Achievement Related Concepts," *Journal of Educational Research,* 1965, *59,* 57–62.

GREENSTEIN, F. *Children and Politics.* New Haven: Yale University Press, 1965a.

GREENSTEIN, F. *"Personality and Political Socialization:* The Theories of Authoritarian and Democratic Character," *Annals of the American Academy of Political and Social Science,* 1965b, *361,* 81–95.

GRIER, W. AND COBBS, P. *Black Rage.* New York: Basic Books, 1968.

GRINKER, R. M. (ed.). *Toward a Unified Theory of Human Behavior.* New York: Basic Books, 1956.

GUTTENTAG, M. "The Relationship of Unemployment to Crime and Delinquency," *Journal of Social Issues,* 1968, *24* (1), 105–114.

HAAN, N., SMITH, M. B., AND BLOCK, J. "The Moral Reasoning of Young Adults: Political-Social Behavior, Family Background and Personality Correlates." Unpublished manuscript, Institute of Human Development, University of California, 1969.

HALLOWELL, A. I. *Culture and Experience.* New York: Schocken Books, 1967. (First published 1955.)

HANDY, R. *Value Theory and the Behavorial Sciences.* Springfield, Ill.: Thomas, 1969.

HANNA, L. A. "An Educational Imperative: Commitment to a Humane and Open Society." In M. M. Scobey and G. Graham (eds.). *To Nurture Humaneness: Commitment for the '70's.* ASCD 1970 Yearbook. Washington, D. C.: Association for Supervision and Curriculum Development, NEA, 1970.

HARLOW, H. F. "The Nature of Love," *The American Psychologist,* 1958, *13* (12), 673–685.

HARLOW, H. F. AND HARLOW, M. K. "Social Deprivation in Monkeys," *Scientific American,* 1965, *207,* 136–146.

HARLOW, H. F., HARLOW, M. K., DODSWORTH, R. O., AND ARLING, G. L. "Maternal Behavior of Rhesus Monkeys Deprived of Mothering and Peer Associations in Infancy," *Proceedings of the American Philosophical Society,* 1966, *110* (1), 58–66.

HART, H. L. A. *The Concept of Law.* Oxford: Oxford University Press, 1961.

HARTSHORNE, H. AND MAY, M. "A Summary of the Work of the Character Education Inquiry," *Religious Education*, 1930, *25*, 607–619.

HARVEY, O. J., PRATHER, M., WHITE, B. J., AND HOFFMEISTER, J. K. "Teachers' Beliefs, Classroom Atmosphere, and Student Behavior," *American Educational Research Journal*, 1968, *5*, 151–166.

HARVEY, O. J., WHITE, B. J., PRATHER, M., ALTER, R. D., AND HOFFMEISTER, J. K. "Teachers' Belief Systems and Preschool Atmosphere," *Journal of Educational Psychology*, 1966, *57*, 373–381.

HEIDER, F. *The Psychology of Interpersonal Relations*. New York: Wiley, 1958.

HENRY, A. F. "Family Role Structure and Self Blame," *Social Forces*, 1956, *35*, 34–38.

HENRY, J. "A System of Socio-Psychiatric Invariants," in Grinker. *Toward a Unified Theory of Human Behavior*. 1956.

HESS, R. D. AND TORNEY, J. V. *The Development of Political Attitudes in Children*. Chicago: Aldine, 1967.

HOFFER, E. *The True Believer*. New York: Harper, 1951.

HOGAN, R. "Moral Development: An Assessment Approach," Ph.D. dissertation, University of California (Berkeley), 1967.

HOGAN, R. Private Communication, 1969.

HOLLINGSHEAD, A. B. AND REDLICH, F. C. *Social Class and Mental Illness: A Community Study*. New York: Wiley, 1958.

HOLMES, M. B. *A Cross-cultural Study of the Relationship between Values and Modal Conscience*. The Psychoanalytic Study of Society. Vol. I. New York: International Universities Press, 1960.

HOMANS, G. *The Human Group*. New York: Harcourt, Brace, and World, 1950.

HOOK, S. *Reason, Social Myths, and Democracy*. New York: Humanities Press, 1940.

HOOVER, K. H. AND SCHUTZ, R. E. "Development of a Measure of Conservation Attitudes," *Science Education*, 1963, *47* (1), 63–68.

HORNEY, K. *Neurotic Personality of Our Time*. New York: Norton, 1937.

HORNEY, K. *New Ways in Psychoanalysis*. New York: Norton, 1939.

HORTON, R. E. "American Freedom and the Values of Youth." Ph.D. dissertation, Purdue University, 1955.

HOVLAND, C. I. AND MANDELL, W. "An Experimental Comparison of Conclusion-Drawing by the Communicator and by the Audience," *Journal of Abnormal and Social Psychology*, 1952, *47*, 581–588.

HOYT, D. P. AND MAGOON, T. M. "A Validation Study of the Taylor Anxiety Scale," *Journal of Clinical Psychology*, 1954, *10*, 357–361.

HSU, F. L. K. *Psychological Anthropology: Approaches to Culture and Personality.* Homewood, Ill.: Dorsey Press, 1961.

HUNT, J. M. "The Effects of Infant Feeding-Frustration upon Adult Hoarding in the Albino Rat," *Journal of Abnormal Psychology,* 1941, *36,* 338–360.

HUNT, J. M. *Intelligence and Experience.* New York: Ronald Press, 1961.

HYMAN, H. *Political Socialization.* New York: Free Press, 1959.

HYMAN, H. AND SHEATSLEY, P. B. " 'The Authoritarian Personality': A Methodological Critique," in Christie and Jahoda. *Studies in the Scope and Method of "The Authoritarian Personality."* 1954.

INKELES, A. "National Character and Modern Political Systems," in Hsu. *Psychological Anthropology: Approaches to Culture and Personality.* 1961.

INKELES, A. "Society, Social Structure, and Child Socialization," in Clausen. *Socialization and Society.* 1968.

INKELES, A. AND BAUER, R. H. *The Soviet Citizen.* Cambridge, Mass.: Harvard University Press, 1961.

INKELES, A. AND LEVINSON, D. J. "National Character: The Study of Modal Personality and Sociocultural Systems," in Gardner Lindzey (ed.). *Handbook of Social Psychology.* Cambridge, Mass.: Addison-Wesley, 1954.

JAMES, W. *The Principles of Psychology.* Vols. I and II. New York: Dover, 1950. (First published 1890.)

JAROS, D., HIRSCH, H. AND FLERON, F. J., JR. "The Malevolent Leader: Political Socialization in an American Subculture," *American Political Science Review,* 1968, *62,* 564–575.

JENNINGS, M. K. AND NIEMI, R. "The Transmissions of Political Values from Parent to Child," *American Political Science Review,* 1968, *62,* 169–184.

JENSEN, A. R. "Authoritarian Attitudes and Personality Maladjustment," *Journal of Abnormal and Social Psychology,* 1957, *54,* 303–311.

JESSOR, R. "Social Values and Psychotherapy," *Journal of Consulting Psychology,* 1956, *20* (4), 264–266.

JESSOR, R. AND FESHBACH, SEYMOUR, (eds.). *Cognition, Personality, and Clinical Psychology.* San Francisco: Jossey-Bass, 1968.

JONES, R. M. *An Application of Psychoanalysis to Education.* Springfield, Ill.: Thomas, 1960.

JONES, R. M. *Fantasy and Feeling in Education.* New York: New York University Press, 1968.

KALHORN, J. "Values and Sources of Authority among Rural Children." In K. Lewin and others (eds.), *Authority and Frustration.*

Studies in Topological and Vector Psychology, No. 3. University of Iowa Studies in Child Welfare, Vol. XX. Iowa City: University of Iowa Press, 1944.

KEYS, A. "Experimental Induction of Neuropsychoses by Starvation." *Biology of Mental Health and Disease.* Milbank Memorial Fund. New York: Harper and Row, 1952.

KIRSCHT, J. P. AND DILLEHAY, R. C. *Dimensions of Authoritarianism: A Review of Research and Theory.* Lexington: University of Kentucky Press, 1967.

KLAPPER, J. T. *The Effects of Mass Communication.* New York: Free Press, 1960.

KLUCKHOHN, F. R. "Dominant and Variant Value Orientations," in C. Kluckhohn, M. Murray, and D. Schneider (eds.). *Personality in Nature, Society, and Culture.* New York: Knopf, 1956a.

KLUCKHOHN, F. R. "Value Orientations," in Grinker. *Toward a Unified Theory of Human Behavior.* 1956b.

KLUCKHOHN, F. R. "Variations in Value Orientation as a Factor in Educational Planning," in Bower and Hollister. *Behavioral Science Frontiers in Education.* 1967.

KLUCKHOHN, F. R. AND STRODTBECK, F. L. *Variations in Value Orientations.* Evanston, Ill.: Row, Peterson, 1961.

KNUTSON, J. *The Human Basis of the Polity: A Study of Political Man.* Chicago: Aldine, forthcoming.

KOHLBERG, L. "The Child as a Moral Philosopher," *Psychology Today,* September 1968, 25–30.

KOHLBERG, L. "The Development of Children's Orientations Toward a Moral Order," *Vita Humana,* 1963, *6,* 11–33.

KOHLBERG, L. "Moral Education in the Schools: *A Developmental View,*" *School Review,* 1966, *74,* 1–30.

KOHLBERG, L. "Relationships between the Development of Moral Judgment and Moral Conduct." Paper presented at Symposium on Behavioral and Cognitive Concepts in the Study of Internalization at the Society for Research in Child Development, Minneapolis, Minnesota, March 26, 1965.

KRUGMAN, H. "The Appeal of Communism to American Middle Class Intellectuals and Trade Unionists," *Public Opinion Quarterly,* 1952, *16,* 331–355.

KUBIE, L. "Are We Educating for Maturity?" *NEA Journal,* 1959, *48,* 58–63.

LABOV, W. *The Social Stratification of English in New York City.* Washington Center for Applied Linguistics, 1966.

LAING, R. D. *The Politics of Experience.* New York: Random House, 1967.

LAMBERT, N. "Predicting and Evaluating the Effectiveness of Children in School." In Bower and Hollister. *Behavioral Science Frontiers in Education.* 1967.

LANE, R. E. "Fathers and Sons: Foundations of Political Belief," *American Sociology Review,* 1959, *24,* 502–511.

LANE, R. E. "The Fear of Equality," in Ulmer. *Introductory Readings in Political Behavior.* 1961.

LANE, R. E. *Political Ideology.* New York: Free Press, 1962.

LANGER, S. *Mind: An Essay on Human Feeling.* Vol. I. Baltimore: The Johns Hopkins Press, 1967.

LASSWELL, H. D. *The Political Writings of Harold D. Lasswell.* New York: The Free Press, 1951.

LASSWELL, H. D. "Psychology Looks at Morals and Politics," in Ulmer *Introductory Readings in Political Behavior.* 1961.

LASSWELL, H. D. *Psychopathology and Politics.* Chicago: University of Chicago Press, 1930.

LASSWELL, H. D. *World Politics and Personal Insecurity.* New York: Free Press, 1965. (Originally published 1935.)

LASSWELL, H. D. AND KAPLAN, A. *Power and Society.* New Haven: Yale University Press, 1950.

LAZARSFELD, P., SEWELL, W. H., AND WILENSKY, H. L. *The Uses of Sociology.* New York: Basic Books, 1967.

LERNER, D. *The Passing of Traditional Society.* New York: The Free Press, 1958.

LEVY, D. M. "Primary Affect Hunger," *American Journal of Psychiatry,* 1937, *94,* 643–652.

LEWIN, K. "Group Decision and Social Change." In G. E. Swanson, T. M. Newcomb, and E. L. Hartley (eds.). *Readings in Social Psychology.* New York: Holt, 1952.

LIFTON, R. J. *Death in Life: Survivors of Hiroshima.* New York: Random House, 1967.

LIFTON, R. J. *Thought Reform and the Psychology of Totalism.* New York: Norton, 1961.

LINTON, R. *The Cultural Background of Personality.* New York: Appleton-Century, 1945.

LIPPITT, R. AND WHITE, R. K. "An Experimental Study of Leadership and Group Life," in G. E. Swanson, T. M. Newcomb, and E. L. Hartley (eds.). *Readings in Social Psychology.* New York: Holt, 1952.

LIPPITT, R., FOX, R. AND SCHMUCK, RICHARD. "Innovating Classroom Practices to Support Achievement Motivation and Ego Development," in Bower and Hollister. *Behavioral Science Frontiers in Education.* 1967.

LIPPMANN, W. *A Preface to Morals.* New York: Macmillan, 1929.

LIPSET, S. M. "Democracy and Working-Class Authoritarianism," *American Sociology Review,* 1959a, *24,* 481–501.

LIPSET, S. M. *Political Man,* Garden City, N. Y.: Doubleday, 1959b.

LIPSET, S. M. "Some Social Requisites of Democracy: Economic Development and Political Legitimacy," *American Political Science Review,* 1959c, *53,* 69–105.

LIPSITZ, L. "Working-Class Authoritarianism; a Re-evaluation," *American Sociology Review,* 1965, *30* (1), 103–109.

LOEVINGER, J. AND OSSORIO, A. "Evaluation of Therapy of Self-Report: A Paradox," *Journal of Abnormal and Social Psychology,* 1959, *58,* 392–394.

LONG, B. "Critique of Soares and Soares' 'Self-perception of Culturally Disadvantaged Children,'" *American Educational Research Journal,* 1969, *6* (4), 710–711.

LONG, B. AND HENDERSON, E. H. "Self-Social Concepts of Disadvantaged School Beginners," *Journal of General Psychology,* 1968, *123,* 41–51.

LYND, R. S. *Knowledge for What?* Princeton: Princeton University Press, 1946.

MC CARTHY, C. "The Bishops' Business," *The New Republic,* 1968, *21,* 21–24.

MC CLELLAND, D. C. AND ATKINSON, J. W. "The Projective Expression of Needs: I. The Effect of Different Intensities of the Hunger Drive on Perception," *Journal of Psychology,* 1948, *25,* 205–222.

MC CLOSKEY, H. "Consensus and Ideology in American Politics," *American Political Science Review,* 1964, *58,* 361–382.

MC CLOSKEY, H. "Conservatism and Personality," in Ulmer. *Introductory Readings in Political Behavior.* 1961.

MC CLOSKEY, H. "Reply to Srole and Nettler," *American Sociology Review,* 1965, *30* (5), 763–767.

MC CLOSKEY, H. AND SCHAAR, J. H. "Psychological Dimensions of Anomy," *American Sociological Review,* 1965, *30* (1), 14–40.

MC CONAUGHY, J. B. "Certain Personality Factors of State Legislators in South Carolina," in Ulmer. *Introductory Readings in Political Behavior.* 1961.

MC DILL, E. L. "Anomie, Authoritarianism, Prejudice, and Socioeconomic Status: an Attempt at Clarification," *Social Forces,* 1961, *39,* 239–245.

MC DONALD, F. J. *Educational Psychology.* 2d ed. Belmont, Calif.: Wadsworth, 1965.

MC GUIRE, C., HINDSMAN, E., KING, F. J., AND JENNINGS, E. "Dimensions of Talented Behavior," *Educational and Psychological Measurement,* 1961, *21,* 3–38.

MC GUIRE, W. J. "Cognitive Consistency and Attitude Change," *Journal of Abnormal and Social Psychology,* 1960, *60,* 345–353.

MC NEIL, E. B. "Analysis of an Ailing Monster: School Organization," in Bower and Hollister. *Behavioral Science Frontiers in Education*. 1967.

MC REYNOLDS, P. (ed.). *Advances in Psychological Assessment*. Vol. I. Palo Alto: Science and Behavior Books, 1968.

MAIER, H. W. *Three Theories of Child Development*. New York: Harper and Row, 1965.

MALLER, J. "The Effect of Signing One's Name," *School and Society,* 1930, *31,* 882–884.

MANNHEIM, K. *Freedom, Power, and Democratic Planning*. New York: Oxford University Press, 1950.

MARTIN, J. G. AND WESTIE, F. R. "The Tolerant Personality," *American Sociology Review,* 1959, *24,* 521– 529.

MARTIN, W. E. "Learning Theory and Identification: III. The Development of Values in Children," *Journal of Genetic Psychology,* 1954, *84,* 211–217.

MASLOW, A. "Criteria for Judging Needs to be Instinctoid," in A. M. Jones (ed.). *International Motivation Symposium*. Lincoln: University of Nebraska Press, 1964.

MASLOW, A. " 'Higher' and 'Lower' Needs." *Journal of Psychology,* 1948a, *25,* 433–436.

MASLOW, A. *Motivation and Personality*. New York: Harper and Row, 1954.

MASLOW, A. *New Knowledge in Human Values*. New York: Harper and Row, 1959.

MASLOW, A. "Some Educational Implications of the Humanistic Psychologies," *Harvard Educational Review,* 1968, *38* (4), 685–696.

MASLOW, A. "Some Frontier Problems in Psychological Health." In A. Combs (ed.). *Personality Theory and Counseling Practice*. Gainesville: University of Florida, College of Education, 1961.

MASLOW, A. "Some Theoretical Consequences of Basic Need Gratifications." *Journal of Personality,* 1948b, *16,* 402–416.

MASLOW, A. "A Theory of Human Motivation." *Psychology Review,* 1943, *50,* 370–396.

MASLOW, A. *Toward a Psychology of Being*. Princeton: Van Nostrand Co., 1962.

MATHEWS, W. M. "Social Values and Research in Child Development," *Journal of Social Issues,* 1949, *4,* 47–49.

MEAD, G. H. *Mind, Self, and Society* Chicago: University of Chicago Press, 1934.

MEAD, M. *Continuities in Cultural Evolution*. New Haven: Yale University Press, 1964.

MEAD, M. *Sex and Temperament in Three Primitive Societies*. New York: Morrow, 1935.

MEAD, M. AND CALAS, E. "Child-Training Ideals in a Post-Revolutionary Context: Soviet Russia," in M. Mead and M. Wolfenstein (eds.). *Childhood in Contemporary Cultures.* Chicago: University of Chicago Press, 1955.

MEAD, M. AND METRAUX, R. *The Study of Culture at a Distance.* Chicago: University of Chicago Press, 1953.

MEEHL, P. E. AND HATHAWAY, S. R. "The K-Factor Variable in the Minnesota Multiphasic Personality Inventory," *Journal of Applied Psychology,* 1946, *30,* 525–564.

MENZEL, H. AND KATZ, E. "Social Relations and Innovation in the Medical Profession: The Epidemiology of a New Drug," *Public Opinion Quarterly,* 1955, *19,* 337–352.

MERTON, R. K. *Social Theory and Social Structure.* Rev. ed. Glencoe, Ill.: The Free Press, 1957.

MILLER, D. R. AND HUTT, M. "Value Interiorization and Democratic Education," *Journal of Social Issues,* 1949a, 5 (4), 31–43.

MILLER, D. R. AND HUTT, M. "Value Interiorization and Personality Development," *Journal of Social Issues,* 1949b, 5 (4), 2–30.

MILLER, S. M. AND RIESSMAN, F. " 'Working-Class Authoritarianism': A Critique of Lipset," *British Journal of Sociology,* 1961, *12,* 263–276.

MILLER, W. B. "Lower Class Culture as a Generating Milieu of Gang Delinquency," *Journal of Social Issues,* 1958, *14,* 5–19.

MONTAGU, M. F. A. *The Direction of Human Development.* New York: Harper, 1955.

MORRIS, C. W. *Varieties of Human Value.* Chicago: University of Chicago Press, 1956.

MURRAY, H. A. *Explorations in Personality.* New York: Oxford University Press, 1938.

NEUGARTEN, B. "Social Class and Friendship among School Children," *American Journal of Sociology,* 1946, *51,* 305–313.

NIYEKAWA, A. M. "Factors Associated with Authoritarianism in Japan," Ph.D. dissertation, New York University, 1960.

OLSON, W. C. "The Waiver of Signature in Personal Reports," *Journal of Applied Psychology,* 1936, *20* (20), 442–450.

OMWAKE, K. "The Relationship between Acceptance of Self and Acceptance of Others Shown by Three Personality Inventories," *Journal of Consulting Psychology,* 1954, *18,* 443–446.

ORTEGA Y GASSET, J. *Historia Como Sistema.* Madrid: Revista de Occidente (Cuarta Edición en Castellano), 1962.

OSGOOD, C. E. "Cognitive Dynamics in the Conduct of Human Affairs," *Public Opinion Quarterly,* 1960, *24,* 341–365.

OSGOOD, C. E., SUCI, G. J., AND TANNENBAUM, P. H. *The Measurement of Meaning.* Urbana: University of Illinois Press, 1957.

PADOVER, S. K. *Thomas Jefferson on Democracy*. New York: Appleton-Century, 1939.

PANNES, E. D. "The Relationship between Self-Acceptance and Dogmatism in Junior-Senior High School Students," *Journal of Educational Sociology*, 1963, *36* (9), 419–426.

PARSONS, T. AND SHILS, E. (eds.). *Toward a General Theory of Action*. Cambridge, Mass.: Harvard University Press, 1951.

PASLEY, V. *21 Stayed*. New York: Farrar, Straus, 1955.

PATRICK, J. H. *Political Socialization of American Youth: Implications for Secondary School Social Studies*. Research Bulletin No. 3. Washington, D. C.: National Council for the Social Studies, 1967.

PERLIN, L. I. "The Appeals of Anonymity in Questionnaire Response," *Public Opinion Quarterly*, 1961, *25* (4), 640–647.

PFLIEGER, E. AND WESTON, G. *Emotional Adjustment: A Key to Good Citizenship*. Detroit: Wayne University Press, 1953.

PHARES, E. J. "Internal-External Control as a Determinant of Amount of Social Control Exerted," *Journal of Personality and Social Psychology*, 1965, *2* (5), 642–647.

PIAGET, J. *The Moral Judgment of the Child*. New York: Macmillan, 1955.

PIOTROWSKI, Z. A. "Basic Human Motives According to Kurt Goldstein," *American Journal of Psychotherapy*, 1959, *15*, 553–560.

POLANYI, M. *Personal Knowledge: Toward a Post-Critical Philosophy*. Chicago: University of Chicago, 1958.

POSTMAN, L., BRUNER, J. S., AND MC GINNIES, E. "Personal Values as Selective Factors in Perception," *Journal of Abnormal and Social Psychology*, 1948, *43*, 142–154.

PROTHRO, J. W. AND GRIGG, C. M. "Fundamental Principles of Democracy: Bases of Agreement and Disagreement," in Cnudde and Neubauer. *Empirical Democratic Theory*. 1969.

PROVENCE, S. AND LIPTON, R. C. *Infants in Institutions*. New York: International University Press, 1962.

RATHS, L. E. "Let Us Keep Seeking to Clarify Values," in N. Bell, R. Burkhardt, and V. Lawhead (eds.). *Introduction to College Life: A Book of Readings*. Boston: Houghton Mifflin, 1962.

RATHS, L. E., HARMIN, M., AND SIMON, S. *Values and Teaching*. Columbus, Ohio: Merrill, 1966.

REJAI, M. *Democracy: The Contemporary Theories*. New York: Atherton Press, 1967.

RIBBLE, M. *The Rights of Infants*. New York: Columbia University Press, 1943.

ROBERTS, A. H. AND ROKEACH, M. "Anomie, Authoritarianism, and Prejudice: a Replication," *American Journal of Sociology*, 1956, *61*, 355–358.

ROE, A. *The Psychology of Occupations.* New York: Wiley, 1956.

ROGERS, C. "Toward a Modern Approach to Values," *Journal of Abnormal and Social Psychology,* 1964, *68* (2), 160–167.

ROGOW, A. "Some Relations between Psychiatry and Political Science," in Sherif and Sherif. *Interdisciplinary Relationships in the Social Sciences.* 1969.

ROKEACH, M. *Beliefs, Attitudes, and Values.* San Francisco: Jossey-Bass, 1968.

ROKEACH, M. *The Open and Closed Mind.* New York: Basic Books, 1960.

ROKEACH, M. "On the Unity of Thought and Belief," *Journal of Personality,* 1966, *25,* 244–250.

ROKEACH, M. AND FRUCHTER, B. "A Factorial Study of Dogmatism and Related Concepts," *Journal of Abnormal and Social Psychology,* 1956, *53,* 356–360.

ROSENBERG, M. J. "Cognitive Structure and Attitudinal Affect," *Journal of Abnormal and Social Psychology,* 1956, *53* (3), 367–372.

ROSENBERG, M. J. "Cognitive Structure and Attitudinal Affect," in Fishbein, *Readings in Attitude Theory and Measurement.* 1967.

ROSENBERG, M. J. *Attitude Organization and Change.* New Haven: Yale University Press, 1960a.

ROSENBERG, M. J. "A Structural Theory of Attitude Dynamics," *Public Opinion Quarterly,* 1960b, *24,* 319–340.

ROSENBERG, M. *Society and the Adolescent Self-Image.* Princeton: Princeton University Press, 1965.

ROSENBERG, M. "Self-Esteem and Concern with Public Affairs," *Public Opinion Quarterly,* 1962, *26,* 201–211.

ROSENTHAL, R. AND JACOBSON, L. *Pygmalion in the Classroom.* New York: Holt, Rinehart, and Winston, 1969.

ROTTER, J. B. "Beliefs, Social Attitudes, and Behavior: A Social Learning Analysis," in Jessor and Feshbach. *Cognition, Personality, and Clinical Psychology.* 1968.

ROTTER, J. B. "Generalized Expectancies for Internal vs. External Control of Reinforcement." *Psychological Monographs: General and Applied,* 1966, *80* (1).

RUBIN, I. "The Reduction of Prejudice Through Laboratory Training," *Journal of Applied Behavioral Science,* 1967, *3* (1), 28–48.

SAENGER, G. H. "Social Status and Political Behavior," in Bendix and Lipset. *Class, Status, and Power.* 1953.

SANFORD, N. "The Approach of the Authoritarian Personality." In J. L. McCary (ed.). *Psychology of Personality: Six Modern Approaches.* New York: Logos Press, 1956.

SANFORD, N. "The Development of Cognitive-Affective Processes Through Education," in Bower and Hollister. *Behavioral Science Frontiers in Education.* 1967.

228 Democracy's Stepchildren

SARNOFF, I. "Identification with the Aggressor: Some Personality Correlates of Anti-Semitism among Jews," *Journal of Personality,* 1951, *20,* 199–218.

SCHAAR, J. H. *Escape from Authority.* New York: Harper and Row, 1961.

SCHMUCK, R. AND VAN EGMOND, E. "Sex Differences in the Relationship of Interpersonal Perceptions to Academic Performance," *Psychology in the Schools,* 1965, *2,* 32–40.

SCHREIBER, D. (ed.). *Profile of the School Dropout.* New York: Random House, 1967.

SCHUTZ, W. C. *Joy: Expanding Human Awareness.* New York: Grove, 1967.

SCOTT, W. A. "Empirical Assessment of Values and Ideologies," *American Sociological Review,* 1959, *24* (3), 299–310.

SCOTT, W. A. "International Ideology and Interpersonal Ideology," *Public Opinion Quarterly,* 1960, *24,* 419–435.

SEARS, D. O. AND FREEDMAN, J. L. "Selective Exposure to Information: A Critical Review," *Public Opinion Quarterly,* 1960, *31,* 194–213.

SEARS, R. R., MACCOBY, E. E., AND LEVIN, H. *Patterns of Child Rearing.* Evanston, Ill.: Row, Peterson, 1957.

SEEMAN, M. "On the Meaning of Alienation," *American Sociology Review,* 1959, *24,* 782–791.

SEXTON, P. *Education and Income.* New York: Viking, 1961.

SHERIF, M. *The Psychology of Social Norms.* New York: Harper and Row, 1936.

SHERIF, M. AND SHERIF, C. (eds.). *Interdisciplinary Relationships in the Social Sciences.* Chicago: Aldine, 1969.

SHERIF, M. "A Study of Some Social Factors in Perception," *Archives of Psychology,* 1935, *27* (187).

SHERIF, M. AND SHERIF, C. *Reference Groups.* New York: Harper and Row, 1964.

SHILS, E. "Authoritarianism: Right and Left," in Christie and Jahoda. *Studies in the Scope and Method of "The Authoritarian Personality."* 1954.

SHOSTROM, E. L. *Personal Orientation Inventory (POI).* San Diego: Educational and Industrial Testing Service, 1963.

SIGEL, R. "Assumptions about the Learning of Political Values," *Annals of the American Academy of Political and Social Science,* 1965, 361.

SILBERMAN, C. *Crisis in the Classroom.* New York: Random House, 1970.

SKINNER, B. F. *Science and Human Behavior.* New York: Macmillan, 1953.

SMITH, G. H. "The Relation of 'Enlightenment' to Liberal-Conservative Opinions," *Journal of Social Psychology*, 1948, *28*, 3–17.

SMITH, M. B. "An Analysis of Two Measures of 'Authoritarianism' among Peace Corps Teachers," *Journal of Personality*, 1965, *33*, 513–535.

SMITH, M. B. "Foreword" to Kirscht and Dillehay. *Dimensions of Authoritarianism*. 1967.

SMITH, M. B. "Personal Values as Determinants of a Political Attitude," *Journal of Psychology*, 1949, *28*, 477–486.

SMITH, M. B., BRUNER, J., AND WHITE, R. W. *Opinions and Personality*. New York: Wiley, 1956.

SOARES, A. T. AND SOARES, L. M. "Self-Perceptions of Culturally Disadvantaged Children." *American Educational Research Journal*, 1969, *6*, 31–45.

SPITZ, R. A. "The Role of Ecological Factors in Emotional Development in Infancy," *Child Development*, 1949, *20*, 145–155.

SROLE, L. "Social Integration and Certain Corollaries: An Exploratory Study," *American Sociological Review*, 1956, *21*, 709–716.

STAATS, A. "An Outline of an Integrated Learning Theory of Attitude Formation and Function," in Fishbein. *Readings in Attitude Theory and Measurement*. 1967.

STAHL, W. *Education for Democracy in West Germany*. New York: Praeger, 1961.

STEMBER, C. H. *Education and Attitude Change*. New York: Institute of Human Relations Press, 1961.

STEWART, D. AND HOULT, T. "A Social-Psychological Theory of 'The Authoritarian Personality,'" *American Journal of Sociology*, 1959, *65*, 274–279.

STOUFFER, S. A. *Communism, Conformity, and Civil Liberties*. Garden City: Doubleday, 1955.

STRAUSS, A. (ed.). *The Social Psychology of George Herbert Mead*. Chicago: University of Chicago Press, 1956.

SULLIVAN, H. S. *The Interpersonal Theory of Psychiatry*. New York: Norton, 1953.

SUTTIE, I. *The Origins of Love and Hate*. London: Kegan Paul Ltd., 1935.

TAYLOR, J. A. "A Personality Scale for Manifest Anxiety," *Journal of Abnormal and Social Psychology*, 1953, *48*, 285–290.

TAYLOR, R. G. "Personality Traits and Discrepant Achievement: A Review," *Journal of Counseling Psychology*, 1964, *11*, 76–82.

THOMAS, E. J., AND BIDDLE, B. J. "Basic Concepts for the Variables of Role Phenomena," in E. J. Thomas and B. J. Biddle (eds.). *Role Theory: Concepts and Research*. New York: Wiley, 1966.

THOULESS, R. H. "Effects of Prejudice on Reasoning," *British Journal of Psychology*, 1959, *50*, 289–293.

TISDALE, J. R. "Psychological Value Theory and Research: 1930–1960." Ph.D. dissertation, Boston University, 1961.

TITIEV, M. "Cultural Adjustment and the Interiorization of Social Values," *Journal of Social Values*, 1949, *4*, 44–46.

TROW, M. "Value Concepts in Educational Psychology," *Journal of Educational Psychology*, 1953, *46*, 449–462.

TURIEL, E. "Developmental Processes in the Child's Moral Thinking," in P. Hussen, J. Langer, and M. Covington (eds.). *New Directions in Developmental Psychology*. New York: Holt, Rinehart, and Winston, 1968.

ULMER, S. S. (ed.). *Introductory Readings in Political Behavior.* Chicago: Rand, McNally, 1961.

WAGMAN, M. "Attitude Change and Authoritarian Personality," *Journal of Psychology*, 1955, *40*, 3–24.

WALLACE, A. F. C. "Identity Processes in Personality and Culture," in Jessor and Feshbach. *Cognition, Personality, and Clinical Psychology.* 1967.

WALLACE, A. F. C. "The Psychic Unity of Human Groups," in R. A. Manners and D. Kaplan (eds.). *Theory in Anthropology: A Sourcebook.* Chicago: Aldine, 1968.

WALLAS, G. *Human Nature in Politics.* Lincoln: University of Nebraska Press, 1921.

WEBSTER, N. "Eating Is Part of Class War, Peking Warns," *San Francisco Chronicle*, March 5, 1970.

WEISS, A. P. "Value as an Objective Problem for Psychology," *Journal of Abnormal and Social Psychology*, 1936, *27*, 111–129.

WHEELER, S. "Socialization in Correctional Communities," *American Sociological Review*, 1961, *26*, 697–712.

WHITE, R. K. "Value Analysis: A Quantitative Method for Describing Qualitative Data," *Journal of Social Psychology*, 1944, *19*, 351–358.

WHITE, R. W. "Ego and Reality in Psychoanalytic Theory," *Psychological Issues*, 1963, *3* (3).

WHITING, J. W. M. "Socialization Process and Personality," in F. L. K. Hsu. *Psychological Anthropology.* 1961.

WILDER, R. M. "Experimental Induction of Psychoneuroses through Restriction of Intake of Thiamine." *Biology of Mental Health and Disease.* Milbank Memorial Fund. New York: Harper and Row, 1952.

WILLIAMS, B. "Democracy and Ideology," *The Political Quarterly*, 1961, *32*, 374–384.

WILSON, A. B. *Educational Consequences of Segregation in a California Community.* Berkeley: University of California Survey Research Center, 1966.

WOODRUFF, A. D. "An Approach to the Cultural Personality Type," *Journal of Educational Sociology,* 1944, *18,* 45–50.

WOODRUFF, A. D. "Personal Values and Direction of Behavior," *School Review,* 1942, *50,* 32–42.

WOODRUFF, A. D. "The Roles of Value in Human Behavior," *Journal of Social Psychology,* 1952, *36,* 97–107.

WOODRUFF, A. D. AND DI VESTA, F. J. "The Relationship between Values, Concepts, and Attitudes," *Educational and Psychological Measurement,* 1948, *8,* 645–660.

WORCHEL, P. "Adaptability Screening of Flying Personnel, Development of a Self-Concept Inventory for Predicting Maladjustment." School of Aviation Medicine, U. S. A. F. Report No. 56–62, 1957.

WRIGHT, Q. "The Nature of Conflict," *Western Political Quarterly,* 1951, *(4),* 193–209.

WYLIE, R. C. *The Self-Concept: A Critical Survey of Pertinent Research Literature.* Lincoln: University of Nebraska Press, 1961.

WYLIE, R. C. "Some Relationships between Defensiveness and Self-Concept Discrepancies," *Journal of Personality,* 1957, *25,* 600–616.

YINGER, J. M. "Research Implications of a Field View of Personality," *American Journal of Sociology,* 1963, *68* (5), 580–592.

YINGER, J. M. *Toward a Field Theory of Behavior: Personality and Social Structure.* New York: McGraw-Hill, 1965.

ZAGONA, S. AND ZURCHER, L. "Participation, Interaction, and Role Behavior in Groups Selected from the Extreme of the Open-Closed Cognitive Continuum," *Journal of Psychology,* 1964, *58,* 255–264.

ZEIGLER, H. *The Political Life of American Teachers.* Englewood Cliffs: Prentice-Hall, 1967.

ZELEN, S. L. "Acceptance and Acceptability: An Examination of Social Reciprocity," *Journal of Consulting Psychology,* 1954a, *18,* 316.

ZELEN, S. L. "The Relationship of Peer Acceptance, Acceptance of Others, and Self Acceptance," *Proceedings of the Iowa Academy of Sciences,* 1954b, *61,* 70–72.

ZIBLATT, D. "High School Extracurricular Activities and Political Socialization," *Political Socialization: Its Role in the Political Process.* The Annals of the American Academy of Political and Social Science, Philadelphia, 1965.

ZILLER, R. C., HAGEY, J., SMITH, M. D. C., AND LONG, B. H. "Self-Esteem: A Self-Social Construct," *Journal of Consulting and Clinical Psychology,* 1969, *33* (1), 84–95.

ZIMMER, H. "Motivational Factors in Dyadic Interaction," *Journal of Personality*, 1956, *24*, 251–261.

ZUCKERMAN, M., BAER, M., AND MONASHKIN, I. "Acceptance of Self, Parents, and People in Patients and Normals," *Journal of Clinical Psychology*, 1956, *12*, 327–332.

Index

Acceptance, 61–62
Accumulation Model, 179
Achievement, conditions for, 69
Actuality practice, 172–173
ADORNO, T. W., 16, 84, 87, 89
Affective arousal, 33
Alienation, 44, 44n, 45, 160
ALLPORT, G., 54, 58, 73, 160
ALMOND, G., 13, 14, 15, 17, 82, 93, 94, 182
American culture, 183–184
American society, 183–184
ANGYAL, A., 43–44
Anomie, 16–17, 20
Anti-Semitism, 65–66
Anxiety: basic, 24; and cognitive closure, 106–108; definitions of, 106–108; as emotional response to danger, 156. *See also* Manifest Anxiety Scale
ARENDT, H., 45, 46, 46n
ARONOFF, J., 14, 105, 112, 139–140, 141, 187

ASCH, S. E., 157–158
ATKINSON, J. W., 33
Attitude change: components of, 159–160; within education, 156; and group influence, 155, 157–158; and Internality-Externality (I-E), 158; and leadership, 158; principal cognitive models of, 147–148; self-relational aspect of, 160; in teachers, 152–153, 152–153n, 153–154, 155
Attitudes, 147
AUSUBEL, D., 64, 75, 136n
Authoritarian, 92; behavioral channels for, 91; character of, 85–86, 85–91; defining the, 88
Authoritarian personality: character sketch of, 84–85; description of, 85; and mental health, 87–88; origins and development of, 89–90
Authoritarianism, 18, 77, 84–85, 86–87, 90; dynamics of, 90–91; fascist beliefs and, 88–89; of leaders in

233